MAMPARA

MAMPARA

Rhodesia Regiment Moments of Mayhem
by a Moronic, Maybe Militant, Madman

Toc Walsh

Published in 2014 by:
30° South Publishers (Pty) Ltd
16 Ivy Road
Pinetown 3610
South Africa
info@30degreessouth.co.za
www. 30degreessouth.co.za

ISBN 978-1-928211-30-3
ebook 978-1-928211-36-5

Designed & typeset by Blair Couper
Cover design by Kerrin Cocks
Printed by Pinetown Printers, Durban, South Africa

I would like to dedicate this book to my father.
He is a man of his word and a very good friend.

RHODESIA: 1976 –1980

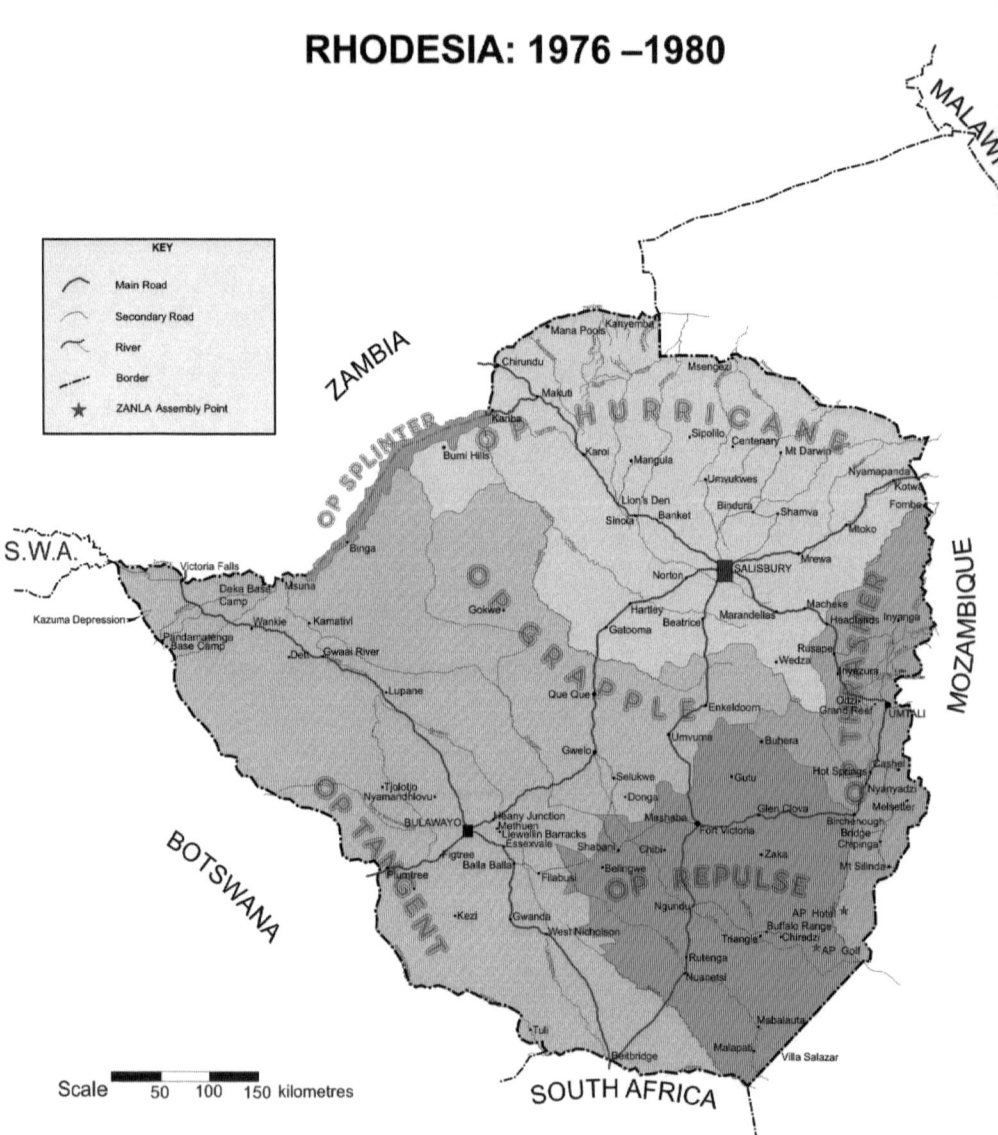

KEY

⌒ Main Road

⌒ Secondary Road

⌒ River

– Border

★ ZANLA Assembly Point

Scale 50 100 150 kilometres

Contents

Preface

My mother was waiting for me at the entrance to my parents' business when I arrived after school. This was unusual, as she was normally in the back office preparing lunch for our family of five. As she opened the door, I could see that she had been crying, and when her eyes met mine, more tears flushed down her cheeks.

"What's wrong, Ma?" I asked, as I let my bicycle and school satchel drop to the ground.

"Come in," she whispered, "and sit down."

She had never spoken like this before and I realized that there was something terribly wrong. Between stifled sobs, mother informed me that her brother had been killed in action on the north-eastern border of Rhodesia.

My uncle Del, then owner of the tobacco farm Trossacks in the Centenary area and a member of the Police Reserve, had taken a round through the head while tracking a group of communist terrorists.

Mum and I talked for a while and then I excused myself and retired to a vacant office in the front of the building. As I sat down, grief welled up inside me and I mourned for the lost family member whom I had greatly admired and also considered a friend.

I remembered how much our families had enjoyed spending time together whenever we gathered to celebrate Christmas at the farm in Centenary. Diving into the pool in which I had learned to swim on scorching December afternoons, I would shout for Dad to watch as my bony body plummeted through the air, stinging as it hit the surface of the water. My two younger sisters and I floated walnut shells down the stream that gurgled through the bottom of the garden, shot using real rifles instead of air guns, and went bundu-bashing in Del's Toyota land cruiser.

Aunt Nancy had natural musical talent and could play the piano beautifully without having to read from sheet music. Our families would sit and sing songs until the witching hour and then we children would be ushered off to bed, protesting violently. By that time, the adults would be drinking expensive liqueurs and single malt whiskeys, and the children would have consumed litres of fizzy soft drinks. And the food!

Uncle Del would sit tranquilly through all the entertainment, smiling as he sang. He always seemed to have a grin on his face. On the odd occasion, I would catch his eye and nod, and then we would sneak off into the main bedroom where the rifle safe had been installed. I would carefully lay all his firearms out on the bed so that I could admire them and he would tell me stories while I sat and glowed, dreaming of one day doing great things like he had.

Through bitter tears, I childishly vowed to avenge his needless death.

The next week, my parents left my two sisters and me in the care of neighbours and travelled to Salisbury to attend Del's funeral and console Aunt Nancy, and help her to plan for her bleak future.

Del was buried with full honours.

I rewrote my final examinations on 19 June 1973, my 17th birthday, and left school without any farewells or regrets. My parents counselled me not to enlist but rather to wait until I was called up for national service so that I could see whether or not a military career would be suitable. My mother organized an apprenticeship for me in Salisbury. I endured the torture of this apprenticeship for six months and then left without resigning, to volunteer for the next national service intake.

I endured a year of military mayhem after being conscripted into intake 138, Depot Rhodesia Regiment on 18 April 1974. This was followed by a year at the Bulawayo Technical College as I had, at the end of my national service, signed on as an apprentice at my father's business. On completion of my studies at college, I was called up and suffered military madness with 10th Battalion, Rhodesia Regiment. The country was in a state of national emergency and all available servicemen were called up for six weeks active service with ten days off, indefinitely. These continual call-ups lasted until early 1978. Under the call-up system then, territorial soldiers were required to alternate six weeks of call-up with six weeks of normal civilian work. In July 1979, I completed my apprenticeship and was employed by the Electricity Supply Commission of Zimbabwe-Rhodesia where I was exempt from military call-up as I was considered essential services. In July 1981 I immigrated to South Africa, a move that I have not regretted considering the intolerable state of affairs in Zimbabwe, a country now under the dictatorship of one Robert Gabriel Mugabe, proponent of murder and the ultimate terrorist.

The following is an account of my experiences between leaving school and immigrating to South Africa in July 1980.

I have decided not to bore my readers with the full step-by-step account of this period. Instead, I have concentrated on individual incidents that are burned into my memory. My recollection of some of these events is vague, but I have tried to give accurate accounts of what happened, and to build suitable stories to fill in the blanks wherever my grey matter has failed to retain aspects of any occurrence.

It is not my intention to humiliate or offend anyone, least of all friends or relatives of the characters in this book, which is merely a collection of events and my interpretation of actions taken at the time. Thus, I have changed some of the names.

I have taken great efforts to recreate the emotions I experienced back then so that I could record events as I perceived them. Thus any record in this book may not necessarily reflect my current point of view on any subject.

Glossary of terms

Ag: An Afrikaans term expressing exasperation or indifference

Bomb-shell: Scatter in all directions

CSM: Abbreviation for Company Sergeant-Major

Dagga: Marijuana, cannabis, joint, *zol*, grass, *boom*

DB: Detention barracks, commonly known as the box

Defaulter: A soldier charged with an offence

Dogleg: A method of circling around to arrive at a specific point, with the objective of fooling the enemy apropos your actual position

Double-march: Marching at a run

Dumpy: Small bottles of beer that originate in a six-pack

Ek sê: Afrikaans for 'I say'. A slang phrase that possibly originated either in the RLI or in Rhodesia's Coloured community.

FAF: (Forward Air Force base) Air force base located in an operational area

Fireforce: Helicopter borne reaction team

Fire-bucket: A kidney shaped steel or aluminium vessel designed to hold a plastic water bottle. This assembly in turn fitted into a soldier's webbing to maximize limited carrying space. The fire-bucket had a steel handle which could clip under the base when not required.

FN: A light semi-automatic rifle

Fudd: Female pubic area

G-car: An armed Alouette helicopter capable of transporting four fully equipped soldiers

Gook: A word for a terrorist used in the Korean War. Also referred to as an insurgent, communist terrorist, rebel, unfriendly, terr, freedom fighter, dissident and *gandanga*, which is a Shona word meaning wild savage.

High-density operation: An action, usually at company strength, in which an identified area is surrounded to prevent enemy soldiers from escaping

High port: A military drill movement in which a soldier positions his rifle diagonally across his chest

Howzhit: 'How's it' is a traditional Rhodesian greeting. After a few beers it becomes 'howzhit'.

Jungle juice: Orange-flavoured cool drink powder supplied in our ration packs. I quite liked it, especially as a mix for cane spirits!

K-car: An Alouette helicopter armed with a 20mm cannon which was used as a gun platform. The fireforce commander normally conducted operations from within the K-car.

Kopjie: A granite hill

Kraal: A collection of mud and pole huts or a fenced off area for containing livestock

Long-drop: Slang for a toilet positioned above a hole in the ground

Leapfrog: A method of uplifting troops by vehicle or helicopter and transporting them to a location to intercept fleeing enemy troops

MAG: A general purpose machine gun

Makonya: Shona word for an experienced and wise man

Mampara: Shona word meaning idiot, halfwit or numbskull

Mr Willy: The author's male member. Don't laugh. He's quite sensitive y' know.

Nag aapies: Night apes

NCO: Non-commissioned officer

Okes: Slang for men who originated in the RLI (*Ou* is singular)

Porra: Portuguese (derogatory slang)

Propon: Quite an effective pain killer mainly used for recreational purposes

R & R: Rest and recreation

RAR: Rhodesian African Rifles

RLI: Rhodesian Light Infantry

Sadza: A stiff porridge made by steaming ground maize meal

SAS: Special Air Service

Scope magazine: A South African publication which challenged South African morality laws from the 1960s until closure in 1996

Stop group: Soldiers placed in an ambush position to intercept fleeing terrorists

Takkie: A canvas shoe with a rubber sole

Thunder-box: A toilet seat mounted around a hole in a wooden structure placed over a hole in the ground to form a long-drop

ZANLA: Zimbabwe African National Liberation Army

ZIPRA: Zimbabwe People's Revolutionary Army

Chapter 1
School leaver

Those lazy days

My future did not occupy my juvenile mind at all. Why, life was good. Living with my parents, the comfortable roof over my head came with three wholesome meals a day and a serviced room. Cash could easily be squeezed from my mother whenever required. This happened quite frequently as I had now become a full time smoker and was partial to drinking on weekends.

My mates all wore branded togs. My skinny frame therefore required more opulent clothing than what I had worn as a wasteful scholar. I alleviated this peer pressure by persuading mum to purchase some Levis and a few cool T-shirts for her doting son whenever we went down to Durban on holiday. Thus, I was a contented youngster with no need to plan for the future.

I obsessed over unfruitful schemes to bed various girls, and hid this with an extremely immature approach and a good plastering every Friday and Saturday night. Actually I was dead scared of girls but would not admit this to anyone–not even my Catholic God as I prayed at night. Of course this excluded weekend nights as I usually had no recollection of God or anything else by bedtime. Ah well, getting roaring drunk and having a good laugh with my mates was a good outlet for my frustrations.

My life had not always been so depraved. Everything changed when I met Kevin Thomas one weekend soon after having left school. He had started dating my sister and she had persuaded my parents to allow a house party.

I was to supervise.

"Just make sure the house is still in one piece when I get home," said my concerned father, "and make sure your sisters are safe, or else!"

He then escorted my anxious mother to an uneasy night on the town.

Kevin roared up to the house in his ancient Vauxhall and skidded to a halt, burying the bonnet of his car in my father's well-manicured hedge.

"You'd better hope that hedge hasn't been damaged," I said, "or my father will have a few words with you."

"Piss off Walsh," he said, and inferred that I should be hoping my father would come home soon to save his son from a good whipping.

Half a dozen inebriated hippies fell out of the Vauxhall's doors as Kevin walked unsteadily towards the boot. Puppy Dog rolled over to the lawn and let his bulky body flop down onto the grass. Dark liquid spilled from the glass clutched in his ham fist as he pointed a thick finger at his grinning face and started singing in a course tenor:

'She said wig wham bam gonna make you my man, wham bam bam gonna get you if I can.' This was a popular song on the hit parade at the time.

I stood there feeling a little bewildered.

Kevin opened the boot, hauled out some packs of beer, and handed them to his friends.

"Don't drop any," he said.

Ron Williams snarled a grin at me as he sauntered past with four six-packs cuddled in his long arms. My sister ran out of the house and kissed Kevin on the lips. She was dressed in a wet bikini and clung to him like a podgy limpet. He squeezed her bum.

My blood started boiling.

Who was this philistine invading my house and assailing my sister? I decided to become the most obstreperous person he had ever met just to needle him, and berated my sister at every opportunity.

Finally I exploded and swore at her when she came into the kitchen, soaking wet after a swim. In an instant, I found myself pushed up against the fridge with Kevin's fingers encircling my scrawny neck. He squeezed slowly and said, quite casually, that he would thump me in my own kitchen if I didn't apologize to my sister. Phillip Nel said, "Go for it, Kev," and Ron chuckled in the corner, a cigarette hanging from his mouth. I vaguely contemplated fighting back as this was the straw on top of the cake...or the cherry that bit the camel's back or... something. Instead I heard my own voice squeaking, "Ok I'm sorry."

Kevin released me and looked at me intently for a second.

"Ron, give him a beer. It might give him a sense of humour," he said.

Ron pushed a cold dumpy into my hand.

"Drink!" he ordered.

Phillip pushed his nose against mine and asked what I was waiting for (and I had thought clothing represented heavy peer pressure)!

I lifted the bottle to my lips. Bitter liquid gurgled down my oesophagus and I swallowed and swallowed and swallowed, this to a chorus of 'down, down, down, all the way down,' sung by the scoundrels in my mother's kitchen. Burping violently into the bottle, I lunged for the kitchen sink with fluid gushing from my nose, and coughed up a torrent of cold, fizzy beer which splattered into the stainless-steel basin. The kitchen resounded with uncouth laughter. I wiped my nose and turned to giggle with them.

"Give him another one," somebody cried.

A fresh beer was proffered, which I accepted, gingerly. Kevin came over, placed his arm around my shoulders, and said that I would be quite a nice bloke if I made some effort.

"Don't worry about unnecessary stuff," he coached, "life is more important than that! You should concentrate on chicks and beer," he advised.

I experienced his first proposal as confusing and scary...but beer. Now that could be a success story to write home about (thus, I am encouraged to write to you now).

I sipped the beer and it tasted sort of nice. The next slug tasted better and so I spent the next few hours becoming acquainted with my new friends, both men and beer. My sister and her friends ran riot through the house but I worried not. Kevin's sound advice had impressed me no end. I stumbled around, falling in love with everyone, and groped and kissed all the girls, confident with new-found prowess. The house, which appeared to be spinning around a phantom axis while people floated up the walls, fascinated me. I undoubtedly became a tad tiresome later in the evening and my new friends laughingly escorted me to bed, where I floated into a spinning dream pursued by pretty girls who were spewing cold beer all over me.

I woke up early with a dry throat and a head full of down. There was still a gaggle of geese attached to the feathers and they pecked incessantly at the bread rolls floating around inside my skull. I slid out of bed cautiously, visited the bathroom, and then walked through the house apprehensively. I needed to fabricate a story for my father before he got up. As I stepped into the lounge, I marvelled at the neat and orderly furniture, arranged as it had always been. The kitchen was sparkling with cleanliness and military order. There was no evidence of a boisterous party anywhere to be seen.

My father greeted me and gratefully complimented me on the fine job I had done of ensuring that his property, including his daughters, had been maintained in their original state.

My sister winked at me.

I glowed modestly but felt massively proud of my new friends who had understood my concern for my parents' property. They had cleaned the place beautifully before leaving, sometime prior to my parents' return.

My family and I dressed in our glad rags (Levis and a cool T-shirt for me) and father drove us all to church. Our smallholding was about ten kilometres away from town. Halfway there, we drove past a huge pile of beer bottles and six-pack packaging that had been dumped on the side of the road.

My new friends were experimenting with a prototype bottle farm!

I was so proud of them.

A new set of wheels

My mother had organized employment with Hawker Siddeley Electric in Salisbury where I was due to start in October 1973. I told my parents that it was very negligent of them to send their only son off to the big city without appropriate transport. My father offered to buy me a car and agreed to let me pay him back on very reasonable terms.

After searching the smalls, my parents and I found a Renault R8 for sale in Gwelo and drove through one fine Saturday morning to inspect it. It was beautiful to behold and pleasurable to drive. I fell in love with the machine and my father parted with $150.

We left the previous owners 'heartbroken' but smirking and hugging each other triumphantly.

My parents drove on to Bulawayo to visit my grandparents and I raced back to Fort Victoria with a joyous heart. After about half-an-hour's travelling, a strange noise sounded from the engine compartment. I stopped the vehicle and opened the bonnet. A pressure valve located on the cooling system was spouting steam and sounding like a ram's horn being blown. It later became apparent that the engine was overheating because the head gasket had blown. So much for the heartbreak I had affected by relieving the previous owners of their charge. I chugged on slowly until I came to a stream where I laboriously topped up the radiator using an empty cool drink bottle and then continued my journey. After two similar stops, I raced into my hometown with the radiator valve blasting off steam and thunder.

I hurtled through town like a triumphant rally driver, half hoping that my friends would see me in my new car. Reciprocally, I half hoped that my drive through town would not be observed by anyone who knew me as I would be mercilessly mocked about the strange, noisy vehicle I was driving.

That evening was dance night at the Flamboyant Motel and I arrived in my new car with much pomp. My mates immediately all insisted on being given a turn to drive. I felt like a fellow whose new girlfriend was being hit on by a gang of lustful rogues. I offered to drive so that they could suss out the car's performance and so avoided giving the keys to any uncaring drivers. Thus, I passed the evening without losing face or letting my car lose her virtue. My popularity immediately went up a notch with the girls in our crowd, who hardly ever went out with a boy who did not own a set of wheels. What a grand evening!

Long weekend at Hot Springs

The annual Rhodes and Founders weekend was upon us. My parents roped me in to join them camping at Hot Springs. I agreed and convinced them to allow Kevin and Ron to join us.. We checked equipment and packed it into the back of my father's Peugeot van along with boxes of food and supplies. Mum went in her car with my two sisters and their friends. I followed with Kevin and Ron in another of my father's vans, also loaded with supplies. We further increased our load by stopping at the local bottle store for more essential provisions.

I drove and Ron sat on the vehicle's bench seat between Kevin and me. Ron was the proud owner of a battery-powered portable record player with detachable twin speakers. He skilfully balanced the turntable on his knees, propped the speakers on the back of the seat and played my only record, *Slade Alive*.

We sang as I drove at breakneck speed with the volume turned up to maximum. Kevin had his feet propped up on a case of six-packs positioned on the floor and he pulled out a refill whenever needed. Drained beer bottles flew out of the windows every so often and the box containing beer emptied rapidly.

Kevin and Ron had both left school the previous November, and I in June just a month before. Their hair had grown long over the previous nine months or so. The wind buffeted in through the open windows making Ron's hair riffle over my face but I cared not and swore at him, calling him a long haired hippy. He teased back, saying that I was just a schoolboy and should not tangle with rough types like him. Every now and then he jabbed me in the ribs. This movement made the needle bounce all over the record causing a terrible sound. I started caring, but after a few beers, trying to save my music didn't seem worth the trouble.

We arrived later that afternoon and helped my parents to put up the tents and sort out the campsite, this after having set up our music which we were still playing at full volume. My mother thought I had heatstroke as I was a mite incoherent and stumbling all over the place, and demanded that I swallow some salt tablets and lie down in the shade.

I complied.

Naturally, my friends teased me and called me a mama's boy.

Idiots.

Friends of my parents' arrived with their daughter, Jude, and her boyfriend.

That evening, we joined the vast crowd that had congregated to participate in an open-air dance. The dance floor was a great expanse of smooth cement. I sat on a low stone wall with Kevin and Ron. Mogg the Dogg, a mutual friend from our school days, joined us. It was a beautiful evening. We drank and danced the night away, until I happened to trip and crash into Tony (another acquaintance from school) as I stumbled forward to greet him. He took exception and punched me in the face. A melee broke out as my friends jumped in to help me and Tony's friends to help him. The fight seemed to last for hours with antagonists vying for superiority. There was a lot of talking accompanied by accusations, followed by a flurry of punches and then more arguing. All the while, music played and couples danced around the two angry groups.

I woke up very early the next morning, still dressed in my clothes. The front of my shirt was thick with congealed blood. A throbbing nose indicated the source of this mess. Rising from my camp-bed I woke my friends who muttered ugly words and told me to leave them alone. I showered and brushed in the ablutions where the mirror reflected a deep gash on the bridge of my nose. I soaked my shirt to remove the blood stains. This was to no avail so I tossed the garment into a dustbin. Rather lose a cool T-shirt than have to explain the details to my mother, I thought.

My friends were still fast asleep when I got back to the tent so I placed a speaker next to each of their heads, switched on the record player, and left. I heard meaningful threats interspersing Slade's blaring music as I ran away laughing riotously.

I joined Mogg the Dogg who was wandering around aimlessly and we walked down to the Sabi River. It was dry season and only a shallow trickle of water flowed down the centre of the riverbed leaving a wide expanse of bleached sand. The Dogg was still ticking from the night before (I don't think he had slept at all). He decided the sand would make an excellent practice-ground for rugby and started to run and tackle anybody who happened to be walking along the river. I was the first to be crunched by his giant body. As I nursed my crushed bones, I watched him tackling anyone he could reach–girls too! Fortunately no one took too much offence and magically, a tennis ball appeared. Teams were formed and a test match ensued. The only difference between a normal game of rugby and this was that Mogg the Dogg found himself the sole member of his team. The opposing team ran circles round him all the while passing the ball. Then someone passed the ball to the Dogg and a huge scrum of men all tackled him at the same time.

Poor Mogg the Dogg.

When the game was over he was as crushed as I was, except I was recovering fast and laughing at him as he lay on the sand. He turned his head towards me, grinned slyly, and charged me again. Thus I lay winded on the pure white sand a second time. The winning team walked past the Dogg and me. One of them pointed at me and said, "Isn't he sweet when he's sober?"

"Morning gents," I greeted, "nice day."

"Let's keep it that way. Don't drink anymore," another replied.

"Fat chance," shouted the Dogg, throwing himself down on his back on the sand, "its party time."

Suddenly sober, Mogg the Dogg stood up and reached down to pull me up, saying that he was hungry and we should see to breakfast. What he actually meant was that I should see to breakfast since he had arrived the previous day with nothing but the clothes he was wearing. We strolled back to the resort and found my family awake, washed and refreshed.

Mum enquired about the deep gash on my nose. I hedged the question and asked if the Dogg would be welcome for breakfast. My mother had a soft spot for the huge Dogg and was quite happy for him to join us.

Kevin and Ron scragged me as payback for their rude awakening, this with uncalled for assistance from a howling Dogg. Then we knuckled down to bacon, eggs, and toast.

Mother mentioned that they had all heard a disturbance during the dance the night before. "Plenty of shouting and foul language," she mentioned, "really disgusting."

Kevin, Ron and I grew quite still, feigning ignorance of the previous evening's proceedings. Mogg the Dogg cunningly announced that he knew what had happened, and said he would tell all if my mother refilled his plate with more eggs and bacon. However, my older sister interjected and spilled the beans, stating that it was I who had started the fight. My three friends threw back their heads and roared with laughter. I became the subject of merciless teasing from everyone sitting around the breakfast table.

Mother scowled at me.

Girls!

I suppose I deserved to be snitched on as I was a bit of a bully when it came to my sisters. My older sister had delivered payback and sat smugly, revelling in my discomfort.

Slade's rowdy music boomed all the while, but my parents seemed to be ignoring it.

When breakfast was over, we helped with some camp chores and then went swimming. A natural spring fed the hot pool which thronged with excited people, all enjoying the holidays. Jude spent most of her time in the water with her arms and legs tightly clamped around her boyfriend.

Then we returned to the campsite for lunch, followed by some relaxation time in our tent. My sisters and their friends joined us, followed by Jude and her beau. We took it easy while Slade continued to entertain us at full volume. Jude and her admirer slunk to the back of the tent and fiddled with each other happily.

Suddenly the tent-flap was pulled open and Jude's mother stepped in, saying that she had something important to tell us. Her gaze fell on her daughter who was lying on the groundsheet with her boyfriend snuggled contentedly between her wide-spread legs. His hands were roaming her bikini-clad body like a pair of hungry Jack Russells snaffling scraps from a kitchen floor. There was a conspicuous bump in the front of his swimming trunks.

Jude's mother fled, aghast.

A minute later, Jude's irate father called her out from the tent and admonished her for her promiscuity in a muffled baritone. She called her boyfriend and they left for a solemn family powwow.

I am not sure what happened in that meeting but after that, Jude confined herself to holding her boyfriend's hand demurely and we didn't witness any more wanton pawing. Truth be told, had we been living in darker ages she would have been clamped into a chastity belt and he would have been hung, but not by the neck!

I wondered what Jude's mother had wanted to say that was so important.

We carried on lazing around listening to music when again, the flap was thrown open and a large ogress stormed into the tent. She boomed horrible threats as she rolled meaningfully up to the record player and roughly lifted the needle from the vinyl with a meaty hand. Then she removed the record which she dropped onto the camp table. Ignoring our protests, she unplugged the speakers, tucked the record player under her sweaty armpit, and turned to face us.

"I will keep this until I leave on Monday," she wheezed venomously, "and if there is so much as a peep out of any of you till then, I will kill you."

Then she stomped out of the tent like a matriarch who had just disciplined a herd of disobedient juveniles, and locked the record player in her car. Her husband, who was having lunch at their tent, grinned at us.

My parents sat in the shade next to their tent and seemed not to notice what had happened. They did appear more content though.

I wonder?

Naw!

They would never have conspired with such a trashy woman, would they?

That evening the resort management arranged a pick-a-box show. I am not sure whether this had been scheduled, or if it was a contingency plan to avoid another dance fight.

Pick-a-box goes like this:

Members of the audience purchase tickets. There are a number of locked boxes containing prizes. When your ticket number is called you participate by negotiating with the host, who offers you money for the box, but you opt for the box because the monetary offer is initially low.

The host increases his offer until he feels that the value of the prize could be equal to his cash offer. He then relents and lets you have the contents of the box. You can change your decision and accept the host's bribe at any time.

It's a silly game, but the Dogg participated fervently. When a pretty girl's number was called, he came into his own and roared, "The box, take the box!" at the top of his voice as she swung her hips up onto the stage.

Of course we knew he was teasing and implying that the box was actually the fudd. The girl blushed and giggled and this inspired the Dogg to fits of rowdy shouting as he sucked down great gulps of beer. Kevin, Ron and I were helpless with mirth in response to the Dogg's irreverent sense of humour. Our ruckus did not go unnoticed by those were still suffering from humour failure due to the previous evening's fight. Some words were directed at the Dogg to shut up so Kevin, Ron and I joined him and shouted even louder for the girl to "TAKE THE BOX!"

The host became concerned that a repeat of the previous night's fight was about to rear its ugly head, and pleaded with the crowd to remain calm lest he cancel the show. We quietened down until the next pretty girl walked down for her turn.

"THE BOX, TAKE THE BOX," we all shouted.

The host smiled nervously and bartered with the girl who was laughing and enjoying the attention.

"THE BOX, THE BOX," we howled.

The host placed the cash in her hand and announced that the show was over. The Dogg called him a box as he walked out. Workers moved onto the stage and started packing all the equipment away. The Dogg quickly became sensible and suggested we leave before the murderous crowd killed us.

We slunk away into outer darkness and retired to our tent.

We slept and in the morning, told my parents that we were going home a day early because we were bored. We packed our gear into the van and Ron went to beg for his record player. The old tart refused, announcing that she would only give it back on Monday.

"So what if you are leaving. Monday morning and that's that. I will give it to your mother. And good riddance!"

We left feeling like fugitives.

Vengeful payback felt good to her I am sure!

Woories

Woories was a middle aged man who worked somewhere in town. I did not know his history or whether he was married with kids or not, but he seemed to pop up every now and then.

One day while fishing with a friend, Woories blundered to the front of the boat to answer a call of nature. There he stood in the bows, urinating over the side.

Woories' friend was ignoring him as this was a regular call performed by fishermen. The man swept his fishing rod back over his right shoulder to cast his line. The bass lure, tied neatly onto the line, swung into Woories' horizon and curled down to pierce his ample foreskin. The barbed hooks dug deep and Woories screamed at his partner, telling him to hold his cast. Fortunately the fisherman heeded Woories' desperate cry and turned to see him vaulting around in the bows with a plastic fish biting the end of his penis.

Woories calmed down and instructed his friend to cut the barbs off the lure so that the hooks could be extracted from his painful appendage. This meant that the friend would have to hold Woories' willy in one hand and cut the barbs off with his other, using a side cutter.

"No way am I gonna touch that thing," exclaimed Woories' partner.

So Woories was escorted to a waiting car to be driven off to a doctor, much to the amusement of all the weekenders who had gathered around the jetty to assist or observe. Woories gingerly stepped off the boat onto the jetty with an old overall wrapped around his waist. Both his hands were occupied supporting his ripped member. The crowd clapped enthusiastically as a red-faced Woories climbed into the car and was driven off.

Woories returned some hours later after a doctor had removed the offending hook and stitched his penis back together. He called some of us aside and proudly dropped his shorts so that we could have a look at his wound. His flange hung down with a fresh white bandage wrapped neatly around the end.

It looked like a turbaned orang-utan hanging upside down from a thick clump of bamboo.

Digs

One Sunday afternoon I coasted into the grounds of the YMCA in Salisbury where my mother had organized accommodation for me. The droning from my car engine resounded through the building, interrupting a congregation of Christians who were gathered in the reception area, praising God. Their singing and handclapping drifted off into uneasy silence as I struggled to remove my bag which had snagged on some protrusion under the seat. The small group of young people gaped at me as I felt around under the seat trying to release the strap, all the while swearing to cover my embarrassment. The radiator moaned its incessant song.

Red faced, I plucked out the bag and slammed the car door.

Embarrassment stopped my brain from instructing my right knee to move out of the car door's path. With a distinctive thwack, the door clobbered my knee causing further expletives to tumble from my mouth.

My mortification was now total.

Some mocking words from school friend, Craig, floated down from the second story landing. He warned me that my grand entrance would ensure that everyone in reception would be driving demons from my soul for the duration of my stay.

"You be watching yourself, young Craig," admonished a stern voice from the reception area.

I limped to the entrance and sheepishly entered the reception area, all the while cursing the intrinsic worthlessness of my useless life. A lanky, middle aged man with a scraggly beard balanced his guitar against a coffee table and stood up as I entered. The remainder of the group, which included a few pretty girls, sat looking at me with expressions ranging from awe to absolute disgust. They remained seated. "That is no way to speak of our Lord," the lanky fellow stated.

"So what," stated I, "he helped me bugger all just now?"

Muffled hisses and 'Oh No's' from the seated members.

"This is a Christian establishment and we will not tolerate that type of language here, so you can change your ways or take your bag and leave."

"*Ag*, sorry man," I said, "didn't mean to ruffle yer feathers."

A relieved sigh filtered around the room and I was allowed to book in. I leaned against the reception counter which was next to the coffee table. The establishment's rules were thoroughly drummed into my head by the lanky fellow who turned out to be the manager. When he was finished I stepped back and my heel accidently bumped his guitar which slid down the side of the coffee table and smacked down onto the floor with a musical twang. Icy stares froze the blood circulating through my evil heart.

I was frostily escorted to my room. As I walked past the reception window, I heard fervent prayers being offered up for my dark soul.

My new job

I started work the next day and was incorporated into a team of artisans whose job it was to assemble electrical switchgear. We were controlled by a jovial foreman who introduced me to my new team-mates, a coloured man, Aaron Renders, and an Indian, Rafark Qidisi.

After work, I suggested we get together for a quick drink. Neither had transport but both agreed on condition I drive them home afterwards. We sat at a table at a pavement restaurant somewhere in town and drank a few beers, that is Aaron and I did. Rafark was Muslim and his religion forbade the consumption of alcohol.

After drinks, I dropped Aaron off at his digs and then drove Rafark to his home on Rotten Row. He was a polite man and invited me in to meet his family. The alcohol kicked in as I walked up the stairs. I tripped over the threshold and bumped into his corpulent mother, who was dressed in long black robes. She wheeled backwards and sat on the floor with a plump plop. As I moved forward to assist her, I stepped on Rafark's foot and we both crashed down on top of his distressed mother. Rafark's father was not impressed with the disgraceful way in which I had treated his wife and he berated me, calling me a stupid infidel. When he smelled my beery breath, he cast me out of the house with an Islamic curse. I looked back at Rafark who shrugged and gave me a compassionate grimace. Behind him, I saw the giggling faces of his six or seven younger sisters.

Two days in the city and I'd had about enough of religion, for sure!

After two weeks it was deemed necessary for me to gain experience in building installation work, and in early November, I was transferred to the new Andrew Fleming hospital construction site. There was a different crew here and a rough collection of characters they were. The foreman was a surly man who disdainfully refused to shake my proffered hand and instead, turned on his heel, giving me a curt order to follow him. We weaved through a twisted maze of scaffolding and scurrying construction workers, up unfinished stairs where the stale smell of curing concrete entered my nose. I was introduced to a swarthy Portuguese artisan who was to be my journeyman. He also refused to shake my extended hand. A grinning black labourer pulled me aside and explained how things worked around here.

His name was Gift and we became good friends.

Often, Gift and I would connive to frustrate our brusque journeyman by pulling the wrong wires through the steel conduits. We would lean against the unfinished walls for support as we giggled, all the while ignoring his rude pidgin English when he shouted at us to pull wires, as was his wont.

"*Poolla, bastaaaards, pool, filho da puta!*' he would swear.

When he walked around to admonish us, we would sneak to where he had been working by a different route as though to ask him what he had wanted us to do. We could hear him swearing great oaths with vindictive intent as he approached. He became a very frustrated foreigner.

Christmas loomed and most of the workers became lethargic at the onset of the holiday season. This frustrated our churlish foreman, who was rapidly falling behind schedule. He would disturb us with chilling tales of who he was going to fire if we did not pull up our socks.

Everyday my journeyman would suggest he make an example of me.

When the foreman glared at me, I would just state that I did not understand Portuguese and he would warn me to be careful or he would send me back to the switchgear assembly line.

This sounded like an excellent idea to me and I pleaded with him to do so but was further rudely ignored.

Akkie was a middle-aged hippy who often skived off to smoke marijuana during teatime. He had eyes that looked as though they were about to pop out of their sockets. This became more pronounced when the marijuana made them bloodshot and misty.

When he entered the tearoom after his smoke, he would recite an extremely rude joke from the large library of funny stories shelved in his mind, so we heard a different yarn every day. Actually his facial expressions and Greek accent enhanced the humour of what he was saying and we would all laugh along with Akkie as his belly wobbled happily.

Sometime in mid December, we were due to knock off early for the annual builders' holidays and I sneaked off with Blond Johnny before morning tea. He owned a Matchless 500 and we backfired our way to a nearby supermarket and purchased a dozen Cola-Canes. These were a potent drink distilled from sugar cane. Quickly downing one each, we placed the remainder in Blond Johnny's carry-bag which I slung over my shoulder. The Matchless weaved through congested traffic at breakneck speed. I think the fervent prayers of the Christian group from the YMCA helped stay my martyrdom that morning.

We got back to the construction site and melted into the piles of material and containers that surrounded the building area. Blond Johnny and I sat sucking blissfully on our little green bottles, all the while puffing cigarettes. He then pulled a well fingered envelope from his shirt pocket, extracted some pills, and swigged them down with a generous mouthful of Cola-Cane. When I asked what they were, he uneasily replied that I was too young to know.

We drank the last of our drinks and then Johnny collapsed. His head hit a brick and some blood dripped to the ground. Alarmed, I pulled his body straight and checked to ensure an open airway. He was gasping raggedly and his breath was sour. I left him lying on his side and rushed off to the tearoom where Akkie was finishing one of his jokes. I burst in unceremoniously and pulled Akkie by his arm. My journeyman started shouting excitedly and demanded to know where I had been. I ignored him. Akkie followed me out of the door and I lurched over to where Blond Johnny was lying. Akkie asked me what had happened as he reached down to Blond Johnny. When I explained about the booze and the pills, he cursed and ordered me to get rid of all the empty Cola-Cane bottles. Then he reached into Blond Johnny's pocket, pulled out the paper packet, and tipped the contents into the palm of his hand.

"How many did he take?" he asked.

I slurred that I did not know. Akkie swore again and ordered me to call an ambulance. Staring back at him cross-eyed I reeled backwards over the rocky ground, sputtering that I did not know how. He took one hard look at me and told me to go home and sleep it off before the foreman caught me drinking on the job. He then ran to the foreman's office to call an ambulance. I hovered in the background as the ambulance arrived. Blond Johnny had an oxygen mask placed over his nose and a bandage wrapped around his head. He was then stretchered into the ambulance and driven away.

When I returned to work after the holidays, I learned that Blond Johnny had been discharged from his duties. Man, I really felt terrible as I had been a part of his Christmas party. Akkie took me aside and explained that it was not good policy to imbibe at work but it was OK if you did not get caught. I thought Akkie probably had a lot of experience not getting caught! This was a principle that would be explained to me more than once in my life.

An Orca in Kyle Dam?

Kyle Boat Club was a beautiful venue where we spent many a sunny weekend. The scenic msasa trees changed colour throughout the year, morphing from green through shades of red and orange, to yellows and hues of brown. We would swim in the dam or fish, perched on the solid granite domes at the water's edge.

A wooden jetty with used car tyres tied along its sides poked out into the dam. Water skiers launched from this position and then swished back to the lakeshore on their skis after having been pulled around the bay.

The clubhouse provided us with plenty of beer and invariably, intoxication took its toll. One fine afternoon after a few beers, Pales decided that it was his turn to ski. He tottered over to the jetty, bummed a pull from one of the boat owners, struggled into a pair of borrowed skis, and stood waiting. The skipper was concerned as Pales was slightly inebriated.

"No way," slurred Pales, "thish ish a piesh of pish!"

"Ok," said the skipper, shaking his head.

He faced forward and played the ski-rope out. Pales, who was determined to give us a heroic display of his water skiing talents, gripped the handle tightly and watched the rope uncoiling with ever widening eyes. The rope flicked tight and the skipper opened the throttle. Pales burst forth from the jetty, shot up into the air and flew parallel to the horizon for an instant. The skis fell onto the jetty with a clatter.

"Yeeeeee!" he screeched, just before plunging into the water. Still clutching the ski-rope's handle tightly, Pales submerged as the boat engine thundered, and flitted silently underwater, completely unaware that his swimming trunks were now floundering in the wash.

When the force of the dive had dissipated, the rope pulled Pales to the surface. He breached like a killer whale attacking a seal, turned onto his back and waved his pelvic fin at us. Pales thus continued being trolled on his back with his manhood flapping in the breeze like Free Willy's fin.

The skipper turned to assist the now exhausted Pales. The boat padded over its wake and wallowed in the water as a spluttering Pales climbed aboard. Still unaware that his shorts were not where they should have been, he unwittingly mooned us all.

By this time we were all clasping desperately at our aching ribs and hanging on each others' shoulders for support, such was our amusement at Pales' escapade.

Paddy's budgie

One Friday evening, Kevin and I gave our friend Paddy a lift to Fort Victoria to visit his girlfriend, Heather. He brought a gift for her, a budgie contained in a shoebox.

Paddy forbade us to curse en route lest the bird develop a taste for strong language and offend his girlfriend. He rebuked us every time we cussed and whispered to the bird, telling it not to pay any attention to our expletives.

We arrived later than planned due to an impromptu stop at the Enkeldoorn Pub. Heather had already gone out. Paddy let us into her parents' house and tossed the contents of the shoebox into her bedroom cupboard. Thus assured that the budgie would be safe, we left to meet Heather in town.

Heather and Paddy returned home much later that evening.

The next morning, we all met for pie and chips at one of the local cafés. Kevin and I squeezed onto a bench among the crowd of young people and asked Heather whether she liked her budgie. She frowned. Paddy grinned wryly and recounted the last event of the previous evening.

When they arrived home, Paddy had ushered Heather into her bedroom excitedly. He had insisted that she keep her eyes closed until he told her to open them, and opened the cupboard with a flourish.

There lay Heather's purring cat, surrounded by a pile of budgie feathers.

The R8 says goodbye

One Friday morning in late March of 1974, I packed my bags, signed out of the YMCA and drove to a used car lot. A salesman with whom I had been negotiating paid me a pittance for the car and I pocketed the cash. I'd had enough of being followed by the thundering boom of the pressure valve wherever I drove. I had also decided that nothing would force me to return to work at the hospital construction site.

The delighted salesman drove me to the main road to Fort Victoria and I hitched a lift home. My parents were not amused to learn that I had left work, and even less so to hear that I had sold my car.

They descended into utter despondency when I mentioned having arranged to be drafted the following month.

Call-up preparation

I was aware of what was going to happen when we arrived at Llewellin Barracks. The first attack on our persons would be a crew cut, after which we would be subjected to hours of physical training out in the blazing sun. The first item on my agenda was to cut my hair and sit in the sun for long enough to brown my ears and neck to prevent sunburn. I also spent a few weeks running each day to build up a vestige of physical fitness.

My friends mocked me mercilessly, implying that the army stores would not have a uniform small enough for my bony body.

"The quartermaster will have to go to the OK Bazaars and buy a kiddie's camouflage suit for you," teased Ron.

"And a toy gun," quipped Kevin.

"The nurse is gonna want to cup yer balls and make you cough," cracked Phillip, "but she won't be able to find them 'cos they haven't dropped yet."

Then the jesters would roar with laughter, especially if they were making these silly remarks among a crowd of friends.

I just grinned and endured the mockery.

Chapter 2
Llewellin Barracks

Mama's suitcase

"Aw, Ma! Don't you have anything smaller?" I asked, as she set a huge old leather suitcase down on my bed. She glanced at me through her horn-rimmed spectacles and then stated, quite clearly, that this was the only one she was prepared to lend me for my sojourn into the world of the national serviceman.

"You could go and buy a new one," she said. This psychology was well applied as I had, at the tender age of 17, newly absconded my first ever job as an unsuccessful apprentice and had limited personal funds available.

Grudgingly, I opened the heavy brown coffer. It had reinforcing ribs and clasps that would have secured a cell in any high security prison. A small crane was required to lift it, even when it was empty.

Mum left me on the side of the road to Bulawayo with less than 24 hours to report to the city hall for roll call. I made it by taking a succession of lifts from those fortunate enough to have vehicles.

Massed in the car park behind the city hall were small groups of family and friends waiting to see their unfortunate conscripts off. Nick Toughey stood off to one side guarding a small duffle bag at his feet. I greeted him and he smiled with obvious relief at not having to endure the imminent future on his own.

A number of army trucks ground down the street and juddered to a halt next to the pavement. A very starched corporal climbed out of each cab. These men marched towards the crowd, took roll call, and ordered the enlisted men to board the vehicles. Toughey and I joined the throng at the tailgate of one of the vehicles and assisted each other into the open bin.

"Jeez Toc, what the hell have you got here?" he asked, as he reached down from the back of the truck and pulled the monstrous suitcase from my raised hands.

"You gonna shit bricks with this," he stated.

I acknowledged being well aware of the torments that the suitcase was bound to make me endure.

The aged trucks vibrated their way through Bulawayo, past Heaney

Junction, and then rolled through the gates to Llewellin Barracks, where they coughed to a stop in front of an old aircraft hangar.

"You are to form a straight line facing me when I tell you to debus, and not before," explained a stocky sergeant.

Then he screamed, "Get off!" and we all scrambled for the rears of our vehicles and jumped, baggage in hand, onto the tarmac below.

"I did not tell you to debus, you bladdy wankers," he shrieked. "Get back on and do as you're told."

As we hastily scrambled back up the tailgates, he screamed the order to debus. We hesitated in confusion. As we jumped down, he shouted an instruction to get back up again saying that we had been far too slow. When we were halfway up, he again ordered us to debus, causing more confusion as the men who had climbed aboard turned around and crashed into those just managing to stand on the vehicle's bin.

My suitcase became a flying machine as I had started throwing it on and off the cursed vehicle. After half an hour of confusing orders interspersed with loud shouting and swearing, we were all lined up, breathless and trembling, in front of the hangar. My mother's suitcase was missing a corner piece, and some buffing from the tarmac had uncovered shredded cardboard. My mother's leather suitcase was a fraud.

When finally, we had been allocated a barrack room, I squeezed the case into a concrete locker where it lived for just over three months until we were relocated to Wankie. On this day, I was terribly hung over from our farewell party the night before, and paid two batmen an extorted dollar each to carry my kit to where we were to embus the vehicles. They balanced my baggage on their heads and marched behind me like porters following an explorer of old. The whole company roared with laughter at how resourceful I had been to hire them.

The suitcase was a blight. I packed all my civvies into my half-full issue kit bag and dumped the bastard on the station platform.

Sorry Mum!

First pass out

Finally the big day arrived and we walked out of Llewellin Barracks' gates, having earned our first pass. It was Friday morning and we were due back at 06h00 on Tuesday morning. Friends had organized a lift from Bulawayo to Chiredzi, and offered to drop me off at Fort Victoria, which was en route.

My parents and sisters welcomed me enthusiastically as I waltzed into my father's business premises on Friday afternoon. I spent an enjoyable evening with them, catching up on local gossip and entertaining them with stories about basic training.

My mates arrived on Saturday morning and we went to the Flamboyant Motel for the day. I found that the pressures of basic training had impeded my ability to communicate with my friends, especially the girls. The stress of being shouted at for six weeks had taken its toll on my confidence and I just sat and drank. Phillip had completed his national service and understood my dilemma, but he still mocked me mercilessly. After a couple of beers, the effects of alcohol on a super fit body were making my head reel.

Saturday and Sunday were a blur and I was grateful for Monday morning when everyone was back at work or school.

It was a cool morning and I stepped out of the front door and strolled onto the lawn. Some warm fluid sprayed onto my bare feet and I turned to face a huge cobra with its hood extended. The alarmed snake had spat poison defensively. I shouted for Edson the gardener, and told him to keep an eye on it.

Edson possessed a straw hat which he painted every week. On this day, it was decorated with vibrant blue and red lines on a white background. It looked as though he had tied a rigid Union Jack bandana around his head.

I hurried into the house to fetch my father's 12 bore shotgun. Removing it from the gun safe, I inserted buckshot into each barrel as I ran down the passage to the front door.

Rushing outside, I called for Edson and he answered, pointing to a sheet of zinc half buried in the ground, under which the snake had hidden. Looking under the sheet, I saw a shiny reptilian outline. I told Edson to move out of the way, raised the shotgun, and discharged one barrel at the snake. The recoil punched the barrel of the gun upward and the smell of cordite briefly filled the air. The snake bolted, unharmed, from the cloud of dust that erupted from under the now perforated zinc plate. I jumped back in fright and before

I could bring the gun to bear, the snake had slithered into long grass.

Edson was nowhere to be seen.

'There is no way I am following that snake through grass that dense,' I thought.

I was convinced that I had shot the snake and was amazed that it did not appear even slightly injured. My pride was going to suffer injury when my old man learned about the missed shot. I cleaned the shotgun and returned it to the safe.

At lunch, my mother collected me and left me on the road. I quickly secured a lift because I was in uniform, and arrived at Llewellin Barracks just after nightfall.

On my next pass, my father confronted me about my great shot and moaned about it having cost him some hard earned cash. I had shot the electric cable that supplied power to a cottage that my father rented to tenants. The zinc sheet had been placed over a hole in which two sections of cable had been joined together. The buckshot had ripped through the cable, making the neutral connect across one of the phases of the circuit. This had increased the voltage substantially and a number of appliances had burned out as a result.

My father was responsible as he supplied power to the tenants. It had set him back a few hundred dollars to replace the damaged equipment and repair the cable. He was not amused with his only son.

Sorry Dad!

Woorichie

We expected the worst from our instructors during morning inspections. They would cast their beady eyes about for the smallest fault and mete out vindictive discipline. They examined our uniforms for foreign particles and if any were found, they would launch a tirade of spiteful vocabulary into the face of the unfortunate rookie involved. Feathers were the worst, as they provoked accusations concerning intercourse with chickens. The defaulter would then be forced to perform lewd movements with his pillow squeezed between his thighs.

There were also times when humour would reign, even at the cost of bodily harm from our trainers. One such time involved Woorichie, who was not quite a retard, and bore the brunt of cruel sarcasm from most of our instructors.

Woorichie had a thick, dark beard and no amount of shaving could distract the instructors from noticing that Woorichie could do with more. When the saying 'four o'clock shadow' was applied to Woorichie, four o'clock referred to four minutes after he had clocked his last shave. Thus, most mornings, Woorichie was subject to physical torture on account of his mouldy chin.

One morning, the instructors were strutting by, busy with inspection. When my turn came, I slammed my right heel into the cement floor as I came to attention and shouted, "99910 Rifleman Walsh, SERGEANT!"

The sarge snorted as he walked past and looked at Toughey. Toughey performed the same action and shouted, "99919 Rifleman Toughey, SERGEANT!"

This continued up and down the barrack room until the instructors had gathered around to inspect the row of men standing opposite to and facing Toughey and me. Woorichie was one of these men. The instructors inspected Woorichie but found no fault with their pet hate and the sergeant grudgingly complimented him on his excellent turnout.

The instructors, all standing with their backs to Toughey, did not see Toughey pulling a face at Woorichie. Now Toughey could do a very good impression of Bugs Bunny because he was missing some teeth on either side of his middle top incisors, and had ears that stood at 90 degrees to his head.

Hey! What's up, Doc?

Woorichie was standing impassively in his moment of glory, blinking and casting his eyes warily from instructor to instructor, not knowing what to expect next. Then he saw Toughey, who was in the middle of doing his Bugs Bunny imitation, and burst out laughing. Shocked by this response to his compliment, the astonished Sergeant Ferreira stepped back. Then he swivelled his hips and punched Woorichie viciously in the solar plexus with his right fist. Woorichie collapsed onto the floor, wheezing. The other instructors proceeded to kick him in the ribs, all the while shouting at him to do 100 push-ups.

Poor Woorichie!

After punching Woorichie, Sergeant Ferreira immediately turned and saw Toughey and me sniggering at Woorichie's bad luck. It was the kind of uncontrollable giggling that is experienced in the quiet of church. You think of something extremely hilarious and you know that you are not allowed to make any noise, but you cannot suppress your laughter.

Realizing that Woorichie's misfortune had originated with Toughey and me, Sergeant Ferreira screamed, leaped across the barrack room and fastened a hand to each of our throats. His anger gave him enough strength to lift us off the floor and bang our heads together with stunning force. We crumpled to our knees, stunned, while the incensed instructor tried to force us to stand. Toughey and I understood the dire situation we were in. We each cast a whirlpool of blackness from our minds and tried to stand to attention. The screaming attracted all the other instructors in the barrack room and they assembled around us like a pack of Rottweilers. They hit and kicked and swore at us profusely. Woorichie struggled to his feet and grinned at us while clutching his injured stomach.

The imbecile certainly enjoyed his moment of inadvertent payback!

On account of us, everyone in the barrack room was ordered to go outside in full drill kit and double march to the assault course immediately. Toughey and I had to stand to attention at the beginning of the assault course and the platoon was ordered to complete the course. Each member of the platoon threatened horrible retribution as they ran past us on their way to tackle the first obstacle.

As a rule, anyone who was guilty of misconduct did not take part in the punishment meted out to the team. This was done to instil in us an ethos of governing each other, as no one likes to be punished for the sins of another. The platoon was expected to pressure defaulters to toe the line. This approach had the desired effect. For example, a man who did not care to shower every day was hauled off to the showers and scrubbed clean with yard brooms.

The assault course destroyed many a shiny toecap that morning. Payback is a bitch, especially when delivered instantly, and in full view of all.

Woorichie was selected to join the air force as an air-dispatch controller. I hope he did not fall out of his aircraft.

Italian heritage
My history lessons at school created a picture in my mind, of Roman soldiers

standing unbroken in their ranks as an invincible nation against the barbaric hoard. The Roman Empire stretched from ancient Persia right through Europe and across the channel into Britannica.

But the comic books that I paged through as a semi-literate youngster always illustrated the Italian army in full flight, chased by triumphant British troops. Then my interest in the Second World War revealed that Italy had capitulated twice. Thus I started perceiving Italians as a cowardly, duplicitous people, and my vision of a mighty Roman nation was supplanted.

They even hugged and kissed each other when playing soccer!

My grandfather, Charles James Vincent, honourable English gentleman, married my grandmother soon after the First World War. They immigrated to Zambia where he was killed in a rock fall in one of the copper mines.

My grandmother was left with three children. There was the eldest, Charles, and then Delville, followed by my mother, who had not yet learned to walk. In my grandfather's defence, I must clearly state here that Delville was so named to honour those killed in the Delville Wood massacre. My grandfather was one of the few who, though wounded in the battle, survived.

Some years later while my mother was in the process of trying to obtain a British passport, the South African Home Affairs department in East London told her that her father had not been of British descent. She discovered that the cad had changed his name and lied to her mother about his ancestry. He had actually been born in East London as Charles James Santagati of the Vincenz lineage from a small rustic village in downtown Italy.

Mama Mia!

Now when my mother revealed to me that a quarter of the blood flowing through my veins was tainted Italian I was mortified. How could this have happened? My motivation immediately changed and I sought, wherever possible, to find information which would change my attitude towards Italians. They made Ferraris and I certainly enjoyed spaghetti bolognaise.

And Sophia Loren, *amore a prima vista!*

Oh well, that was enough to start with.

I did not realize, until some years later, that the nation of Italy had defected in World War Two due, initially, to the dictator Mussolini having been overthrown and imprisoned by his own people. The nation then capitulated again after Hitler sent troops to free Mussolini from his mountaintop jail. Thus the Italian people were forced to fight a war against the armies they would have preferred to have as allies. My honour was restored. They actually are a cool, though excitable nation, who were led astray by a cruel dictator.

Viva Italia!

And we turn a blind eye to the football kissing.

Classical warfare training

During our conventional warfare exercise, I was seconded to the headquarter element as the mortar man. No amount of protesting could change the mind of my platoon commander and I ended up having to carry a prehistoric two-inch mortar and two smoke bombs in addition to my normal gear. It was June and our training ground was close to the small town of Essexvale, about 30 kilometres east of Bulawayo. On arrival, we were introduced to the officers in training, chosen from our intake by the officer selection board. My platoon sergeant was a certain Pevil, who treated me with scorn. I responded by disliking him.

Battle camp commenced and we advanced forward to where we had to halt for the night in company formation. We were ordered to dig in and prepare to face a frontal attack at any time. Pevil pointed out where our trench was to be excavated and ordered me to carry on. Pevil was as much a trainee as I, so I felt no fear in challenging him. I stated that I was not going to dig the trench by myself and that he should assist, but he left to join his mates at headquarters. I slowly removed tons of stony dirt from the trench. Afternoon became evening and salt dripped off my face as I sank deeper into the rank earth.

The trench was to be six feet deep with an adjoining sleeping area. I removed enough earth to create the sleeping area and half the trench, and left the rest for an unsuspecting Pevil. At around 19h00, he returned to find me lying in the sleeping area. He incorrectly surmised that the trench was complete and jumped in. Expecting to drop six feet, he encountered hard ground at three feet and fell over the trench parapet heavily as his rifle clattered on the trench floor.

"Walsh, why are you sleeping, the trench is not complete?" he hissed.

I stated, between spurts of suppressed chuckling, that I had left the rest for him. He was outraged and stated that he was an officer and that his duties required more from him than trench digging. I replied that he should continue digging the trench now that his other duties were over, as we were due for inspection at first light. He threatened to charge me with insubordination, but I declared that nothing was going to make me dig any further, and pointed out that it was not going to look good for him if he could not coordinate one trainee in performing as minor a task as sinking a trench.

"I wonder if they will keep you on at the School of Infantry," I punctuated.

My mother's applied psychology did the trick and he cursed and fumbled around in the trench. When I asked him what he was doing, he replied that he was looking for my trenching tool.

"It's packed away on my webbing," I replied, "use your own."

He had left his tool at HQ during his last vacation. I suggested he retrieve it before dawn. As he left, he tripped over my webbing and fell to the ground, cursing.

"You're gonna pay for this, Walsh," he spat.

Pevil completed the trench well before morning. He never spoke to me again and I heard, when our training was complete, that he had signed on with the RAR as a regular officer.

The inevitable training attack started during the course of the morning. Pevil had disappeared and I was sitting with my bum on the trench's parapet, observing all the action. There was a lot of firing from machine guns mounted in fixed positions. Piston driven aircraft throbbed overhead and explosions and smoke had been arranged to further enhance the effects of battle.

I was disturbed by someone shouting behind me as I sat enjoying the warm sun on my back. I turned and saw one of the instructors who screamed an order to get into my trench as I was not out sailing on my daddy's yacht. Then he pulled the fuse on a thunderflash and threw it at me. A rookie from intake 137 had been killed by one of these explosives the previous month so I was a little wary. The thunderflash burst on the parapet with a mighty bang just as I threw myself into the trench. Popping my head up, I saw the instructor running towards me with an expression of rage on his face. Flames licked at the grass bordering my trench and he ordered me out to help extinguish the fire. We stomped the fire out and he bellowed again, ordering me back into the trench. In, out, in, make up your mind. He told me to start acting like a bladdy soldier, not some spoiled kid waiting for his wet-nurse.

When the frontal attack was over and the enemy had retreated, we were ordered to close trenches and prepare to move out. Pevil was once again in short supply. I filled in the trench and was ready to move when the order came. Slinging the mortar over my shoulder, I moved out with headquarters and we continued our march into mock battle. The tracers that ripped the twilight sky close above our heads made me flinch and walk doubled over.

The next morning, we engaged in more battle drills. I was to use the mortar to provide smoke to cover my platoon. An instructor took control and ushered me onto the crest of a low rise. Below us in the valley, I could see our platoon, spread out in formation, advancing towards an old house where the enemy were entrenched. The officer told me where to lay smoke and ordered me to prepare to fire. I loosened the bombs from my webbing, armed one of them, slipped it down the mortar tube, and waited for his order to fire. The command did not transpire as the wind changed direction. The instructor directed me to another position.

Now what?

I did not feel comfortable sprinting with a loaded mortar. I tried to explain my predicament to the officer but he would not listen, and ordered me forward.

"C'mon, hurry up then, boy. No dawdling out here."

When we reached the new position, he again ordered me to load. His face turned pink when I told him that there was already an armed bomb in the tube.

"You're on a charge, boy," was all he said through a vibrating handlebar moustache.

Then he pointed to where he wanted the bombs to fall and ordered me to fire. I set the mortar base on the ground, aimed, and clicked the trigger down.

Poof.

The missile flew out of the tube and I watched it climbing to its apex and then falling down to target. I sent the second bomb skywards and leaned back to watch the result. No smoke plumed out of the two dud shells and I felt totally cheated, having carried this useless burden for days.

When battle camp was over, I was marched into Captain Drake's office on a charge of misconduct. I halted in front of my commanding officer's desk and the charge was recited. I had created the impression of having conducted the whole training exercise with a bomb in the mortar tube and I was ordered to give my explanation. This, I related. The charges were dropped and I was pardoned with a sound ear bending and fatigues.

Some years later, I saw Lieutenant Pevil in the operational theatre. He was being uplifted by helicopter. He scowled when he recognized me and I doffed my combat cap at him in mock respect.

The unfortunate engineer

After our classical war training, we were allowed to attend a party in one of the function halls at Llewellin Barracks. Toughey, Robbins, Salisbury and I found ourselves together at the bar. There was a whole crowd of Bulawayo girls there, surrounded by the Bulawayo members of our intake. We realized that our chances of scoring without complications were minimal and resigned ourselves to a night of drinking instead.

Eventually we grew bored and decided to leave. As we were walking out, a muscular engineer stepped into our path. Slurring a 'howzhit,' he demanded to know where we were going and was duly ignored. He continued to question us needlessly as we sauntered past him, carrying the last of our beers. Someone from a small group of people outside told us to ignore him as he was newly promoted and drunk. We did this and carried on walking away. Toughey and Robbins walked ahead deep in conversation while Salisbury and I dragged behind. The engineer persisted in questioning us until I turned around and threatened him.

Too slow to avoid the long armed punch that the engineer delivered, I found myself lying on the tarmac, staring up at the stars. I heard sounds of another scuffle and sat up to stare at the engineer who now lay groaning on his back with blood running from his forehead. Toughey and Robbins lifted me up and I shook my head and rubbed the bump that was growing above my left ear. We all walked off discussing how Salisbury had floored the huge lance-corporal by hitting him on the forehead with a beer bottle.

And did we laugh at his downfall!

With our evening over, we stripped, climbed into the squeaky beds in our respective barrack rooms, and drifted off to sleep, only to be rudely interrupted by the lights suddenly being switched on. Noisy, angry men surged into the barrack room and ordered us all to stand to attention at the foot of our beds.

An indignant voice piped up saying, "It was just two little guys. They beat me up."

In walked our harrowed engineer with a crisp white bandage wrapped neatly around his head. Everyone in the barrack room burst out laughing until a staff sergeant from the medical corp shouted, 'Shut up.' The engineer immediately pointed at three of us after being ordered to identify his assailants. The staff sergeant berated us viciously, called us cowards, and said that we would be going to jail for the rest of our army careers.

Robbins was hauled out of an adjacent barrack room. There were some regimental police in the crowd of persecutors and they immediately placed us under arrest. We were ordered to dress in our combat denims. Handcuffs were roughly snapped around our wrists and we were doubled off to the guardrooms, where we were thrown into cells to await interrogation. It is not easy to double-march when you have your hands cuffed behind your back and beer swilling around your eyeballs.

Lance-Corporal Dors, who I knew from my hometown, addressed me. *Dors* means thirsty, in Afrikaans. I often wondered what had been going through his mamma's mind when she christened the infant. I had actually seen his mama loading sacks of maize onto the back of a truck. She had not even built up a sweat, so it could not have been the exertion of birthing that caused her to be thirsty. Possibly she had just wanted a drink?

Dors ordered me out of my cell and double marched me to a pokey little office containing a desk and two chairs. It looked just like a movie set, except I was not part of the audience. I was an actor, and the villain at that.

I refused to give a statement, saying that I would speak to my platoon commander and no one else. The lance-jack threatened to call my commander and implied that he would not be too pleased as it was after midnight. I stuck to my decision and after an hour, I was returned to my cell.

At 05h00, we were woken up by the change of guard and left in our cells until orders at 08h00. We were double-marched through our company lines and straight into Captain Drake's office. Was this possibly a bad habit that Toughey and I were developing? We were fined ten dollars apiece (nearly half a month's pay) and ordered to perform fatigues that weekend. So much for the life sentence predicted by the angry medic.

Once we had fallen in to our respective company ranks, we were immediately accosted as our dress was not up to the required standard for inspection. This earned us more fatigues but we were unfazed, such was our relief at having avoided detention barracks.

Salisbury's life flashes past his eyes

We were required to charge through an enemy post during one of our counter-insurgency exercises. Our rifles were loaded with blanks and had blank firing attachments screwed into the flash hiders. This was done to maintain pressure in the gas system so that the rifles would eject spent cartridges effectively.

Salisbury was one of the enemy. As we assaulted the position, I discharged my rifle in his general direction. He yelped, dropped his rifle, and rolled over onto his back, clutching at his face. I fired a few more shots at him and his screeching rose to a high pitch, interspersed with magnificent swearing. My charge carried me past Salisbury and I laughed at him as I ran since he was obviously clowning around pretending to die a heroic death.

When our exercise was over, a red faced Salisbury approached me and called me more disgusting names. I thought he was flushed from exertion until he declared that my shots had injured him. The hot gas discharging through the aperture in the blank firing attachment had singed his face which was pock-marked with tiny black spots, each surrounded by a circle of puffy, burned skin–possibly particles of burned cordite. Salisbury seemed quite upset by this incident as his pretty face was stinging and possibly scarred for life. After I teased him about his new rugged look and told him the girls would love him now, he cheered up and asked if I really thought this was true.

He became rather upset when I told him that no known procedure would make him more attractive to the ladies.

Fight with Westergard

I was relaxing in the beer garden of the troopies' canteen with Tingaling,

Joey van der Horn, Keith Tamblyn and Steve Westergard. Tingaling's sister had come to visit him, and was sitting with us. I was aware that I was niggling Westergard and he was growing increasingly agitated but I ignored him. Evening drew close, and Tingaling's sister bade us farewell. After complimenting Tingaling on his sister's personality, I mentioned that she could well do with some surgery, as she was in every way as ugly as he was.

Tingaling agreed with me but Westergard howled with indignation and charged at me with tightened fists. Standing up, I indicated for him to halt with the palm of my outstretched hand and reprimanded him, stating that gentlemen did not fight in public. I added that I would be delighted to whip him behind a close by hedge. My silly schoolboy conformation to some vestige of Queensbury Rules halted an astonished Westergard. He indicated that I should lead the way and he would follow. Walking behind the hedge, I turned to explain to this ignoramus how things worked in the real world.

As I turned, he gave me a mighty kick between my slightly spread thighs. I fell, as an ox axed, no pun intended here! Whimpering in pain, I rolled into the foetal position and clutched at where my testicles had hung so happily. Westergard appeared to be astonished at this lack of resistance and sauntered back to our grinning friends. I lay in agony for many minutes and then pulled my painful body into a bowed upright position.

Bending double through a gap in the hedge, I scolded Westergard for being a coward and challenged him to return for the walloping due to him. He stared at me. I think my ignorant persistence in annoying him shook him a little that afternoon. He left his beer on the concrete table and exited the beer garden.

I am looking at the company photograph. I do not see Westergard's face on the portrait. He may have been selected for specialisation. He certainly taught me a lesson about how things work in the real world that afternoon!

I notice that the two men posing on either side of me were both killed in action after our national service had been completed. Joey van der Horn, who was with Second Battalion, was shot during a contact. Frank Wiggell, who was with Tenth Battalion, was killed when a mortar bomb exploded next to his head.

A strange feeling creeps down my back.

Chapter 3
1 Independent Company, Rhodesia Regiment

First days at 1 Independent Company

We passed the millennia of training at Llewellin Barracks and then travelled to 1 Independent Company in Wankie by train. On arrival, the company was fallen in by CSM Williams, who introduced Charlie Company to our new commanding officer, Captain Bruce Snelgar, and spelled out the rules and consequences of failure to comply. Our platoon was graced with the leadership of Second Lieutenant Doug Havanar from the School of Infantry, and Sergeant Sandy Wood from our Leader Training Unit at Llewellin Barracks.

First patrol

The sand was loose under a firm crust, baked by the unrelenting blaze of the African sun. Each step resulted in the foot breaking through and then sinking a few centimetres down. This exaggerated the effort required to walk and we described it as walking three steps forward and two steps back. Our calf muscles ached after a few kilometres of this torture.

Evening dawned and we holed up in the heart of an evil smelling swamp. Lieutenant Havanar stated that we would spend the night here as we had covered slightly more ground than originally planned. Protesting vehemently, I stated that come nightfall, we would be inundated with mosquitoes and sleep would not be easy. I suggested that we continue to a ridge some two kilometres ahead. My tenacious leader rebuked me, stating that he was in charge of this mission and that we would sleep where he bloody well told us to and that was that.

'OK, boss.'

I resigned myself to a miserable night and Toughey and I prepared our evening meal together. We set our gas cookers aflame to boil rice and fry some bully beef. Before the meal had been cooked, the sky darkened as a thick cloud of ravenous mosquitoes descended upon us. There was a mad scramble to switch gas cookers off prior to hastily rolling out and climbing into our sleeping bags.

The only way I could endure was to lie on one side, tuck the opening of the sleeping bag tightly around my head, and breathe through a small opening in front of my face. After a short while, the mosquitoes would enter with much whining. I would then turn over and recreate the same scenario until the new breathing hole had been discovered. This continued all night long and my discomfort was aggravated by the intense heat building up in the synthetic sleeping bag. Sweat poured off my skin and I was soaked through as though lying in a hot tub.

None of us experienced a wink of sleep that night. The attacking force withdrew just before sunrise and we all emerged from our sleeping bags. I took one look at my senior's puffy face and smiled.

I refrained from saying, 'I told you so,' as I suspected he might hit me, so angry was the scowl on his swollen features.

We threw out our half-cooked meals, kitted up, and moved out at a speed in case the mosquitoes sent a second attack wave. Breakfast was prepared and eaten on the ridge I had pointed out the previous day. We ate ravenously and rested for a few hours before advancing out of the depression to where a road bisected the Kazuma forest area. The map indicated that there was a pump, at which we would be able to replenish our water supplies, situated alongside this road.

Our commander was not sure of our exact position.

"Do we go east or west to find the pump?" he asked.

I said that the pump was positioned to the east, which was to our left (I have a good sense of direction).

"Off you go, Walsh," said my chief as he swung the pack off his back, "find the pump and return to fetch us."

When will I ever learn to shut up and let those in positions of authority make their own decisions?

He lay down next to the road in the shade of a huge thorn tree. I asked if I could fire a shot into the air when I had found the pump. He told me that I was far too arrogant and required some exercise to round me off.

"Return and show us the way," was his order.

Off I went while the others rested in the shade. Whatever happened to the buddy system they had drummed into us at Llewellin?

'Never go into the bush alone,' they had said...

I found the pump less than a kilometre down the road and filled my water bottles. Then I refreshed myself and lay down in the shade of a densely leaved fig tree. Watching a troop of monkeys playing in the branches, I dozed off for a while, and then decided to fetch my own troop of primates. I met them just down the road. My leader was furious about me having been gone so long with the pump just a kilometre away but his barking rolled off me like water off a baboon's back. I ignored him for the rest of the patrol, which was monotonous and without incident.

Keep your mouth shut, Walsh, for you know not what misery it will bring you in future.

Our first kill

An informant had made it known that a group of dissidents would be accessing a certain track in the Zambezi valley. We were going to conduct an ambush, just as we had been trained to do at Llewellin Barracks. Our platoon was split into two sections of eight men each, one in ambush and the other resting in a reserve position. Changeover would take place just before first light.

Cooking was restricted to the reserve detail only.

The section in the actual ambush position would have to remain as motionless as possible for the full shift. This also meant that they would not be allowed to move in order to relieve themselves. If this became unavoidable, the unfortunate soldiers would have to fill up their underpants.

Standard-issue sleeping bags were forbidden lest their rustling alert the enemy. This meant that we would all be sleeping in nothing but our combat denims unless we could acquire blankets to ward off the freezing night cold.

H-hour arrived and the platoon was uplifted by a single helicopter, five men at a time. Prior to emplaning, we were all inspected for any noisy or shiny equipment that might risk revealing our ambush position. Concealment was top priority.

I was in the first load to be uplifted and Captain Snelgar accompanied us. I sat in the centre of the machine on the wooden back seat and the captain sat facing me from where he sat next to the pilot.

When we were airborne he asked me why I was carrying a bayonet for my rifle on my webbing. He stated that we were not fighting a classical war and there would be no requirement for bayonet charges. I told him that I used it as a tin and bottle opener as well as a utensil with which to eat my food. His mouth hung open at my reply and he struggled to find words with which to express his amazement at my logic but found none.

What a flight! Hills and ravines undulated below as our machine soared over the scorched countryside. The rotor blades slapped the air in protest to their heavy load as thermals made the helicopter surge upwards and then drop. The alternating G-forces made my stomach churn and left me feeling elated.

Exhilarating!

We landed and spread out in a strong defensive position around the landing zone. The captain had a few words with our platoon commander and encouraged us as we waited for the helicopter to ferry the rest of the ambush detail. He then left for Wankie on the last return flight.

Our marching order was prepared and we headed for the canyon that we were to negotiate down to the Matetsi River. Towards the front of the procession I saw Rhodesian U-20 rugby player, Norman Mellet, pull on his backpack and then strap a heavy TR48 radio across his broad chest. He then placed his FN on top of the radio and hobbled on down the path. I felt for him. Even with his great strength, I knew that he would be exerting a great deal more effort than the rest of us.

We arrived at the point from which we were to descend into the valley. The silence of the scorching bush was disturbed only by the call of the emerald spotted dove....tooot tooo too tu-tu-tu-tu-tu. At the time, I did not know that the bird was a dove and I had named it the heat bird because it seemed to call in the dead-heat of midday when all else was resting or dead, except for us stupid soldiers.

The loose earth that comprised most of the trail downward made our descent into the canyon difficult. But for this, the decline was uneventful and we made it to the bottom in good time. Mellet slid a great deal of the way down on his backside with the TR48 bouncing up and down beneath his chin and an expression of resignation on his sweaty pink face.

The heat down in the river bed was intense and still. Disheartened leaves

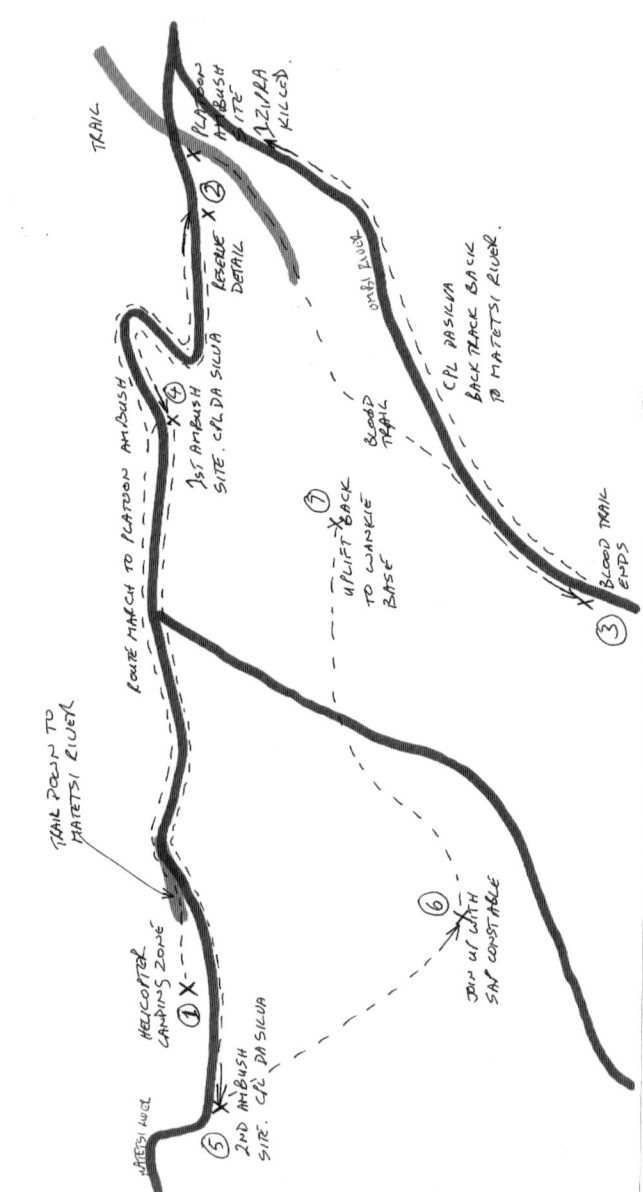

MAP 3

NORTH

TRAIL

TRAIL POINT TO MATETSI RIVER

HELICOPTER LANDING ZONE

ROUTE MARCH TO PLATOON AMBUSH

RESCUE DETAIL

PLATOON AMBUSH SITE AZUMA KILLED.

① X

② X

④ X 1st AMBUSH SITE. CPL DA SILVA

⑦ UPLIFT BACK TO WANKIE BASE

BLOOD TRAIL

ONE BLOCK

CPL DASILVA BACK TRACK BACK TO MATETSI RIVER.

③ X BLOOD TRAIL ENDS

⑥ JOIN UP WITH SAP CONSTABLE

⑤ X 2ND AMBUSH SITE. CPL DA SILVA

MATETSI RIVER

hung limply in the lifeless air and the short, dry grass snapped and crunched under our feet as though frosty. A trickle flowed through many small pools dotted down the length of the river. These pools were a welcome boon and we doused our hats and face-veils to cool our boiling heads. The grey cliffs rose majestically to the sky, streaked with yellow and rust from years of undisturbed exposure to sun and rain.

Later in the day, the canyon petered out and the terrain along the river course became more hilly than mountainous. Zambezi teak and torchwood trees grew lush and green at the re-entry points to all the tributaries. The late afternoon chorus of a million birds sang sweetly in our ears.

At 17h00 we stopped and a reconnaissance team went forward to survey the ambush site where Havanar calculated possible approaches and determined that his killer group should lie in wait under a thick canopy of trees.

We were cautioned to expect anything as we had received no information about the strength, dress, or modus operandi of the insurgents. There were no other security forces in the area and there were no local inhabitants, so anyone who moved was to be a suspect. Nevertheless, we were also ordered to challenge anyone prior to shooting as there was no curfew in effect.

That night at approximately 21h00, I lay with my head on my pack as part of the reserve detail, looking at the bright stars overhead. We had already seen some satellites and shooting stars, and Toughey and I were competing quietly to see who could spot the next cosmic wonder. A red light streaked across the horizon and I tried to work out what it was. Then rifle fire popped off from the direction of the ambush site and we all realized that the ambush had been sprung. The radio was switched on and we were immediately informed that the forward ambush had initiated contact with a small group traversing the site. They suspected that one terrorist had been dropped. We shivered throughout the cold night, waiting in trepidation for the morning when we would be able to go forward and see what had happened.

At first light, we advanced towards the ambush area and there I saw my first dead man. He lay on his back on the dirt track with the bottom of his shirt-front thrown open. He was dressed in a strange camouflage uniform and a pair of light-brown combat boots. Communist chest webbing was strapped across his chest and a brand new but dusty AK-47 lay at his side. He could not have been much older than twenty.

Dry tears streaked his grey cheeks and his dark eyes stared blindly at the verdant canopy above. A green fly crawled over his dry, protruding tongue. There was a small hole just above his navel which had leaked a bloodless substance, now dry and powdery.

"Native beer," explained a proud de Beer, and told us how he had challenged the insurgents and then opened fire when they had ignored his challenge. The man had moaned and cried for hours before becoming silent in the early hours of the morning.

The incident reminded me of one of Wrex Tarr's recordings, The Terrorist's Lament. Part of the song goes:

On a very hot day in the Zambezi vlei,
a terrorist ame a sliding.
Down a scorching track, with a heavy pack,
looking for a hiding.
The chorus goes: (C'mon, sing with me boys)
Oh the stinging tsetse flies and the crocodile eyes.
This is no place to dally, for there's no food here and I thirst for beer.
In the hot Zambezi valley.

There was also a strange black man sitting under one of the trees. When the shots started, he had intuitively dropped to the ground and lain very still. When he was certain that the ambushers were Rhodesian troops, he had called out, stating that he was a district assistant who had been abducted by ZIPRA. He was instructed to approach the ambush position with his hands up in the air, which he did, and was then tied to a tree. Ken Waghorn watched him shrewdly and saw him loosening his bonds slightly so that he could lie comfortably.

How innocent is a rookie troopie?

Follow-up

There was a blood trail leading away from the river and we were informed that a tracker was being flown in. The helicopter landed adjacent to the killing-ground and an exultant Captain Snelgar exited. With him, were a policeman from special branch who had come to process information on the dead terrorist, and a tracker by the name of Johnny Johnston. Snelgar beamed at his soldiers, offered congratulations for a job well done, and shook de Beer's hand fervently.

Johnston instructed us to prepare to move fast and abandon all unnecessary gear. This amounted to some tins, some blankets and the claymore mines, all of which we placed in a bag.

The reserve section deployed to follow-up immediately with Johnston taking the lead. We followed up in a standard Y-formation: two riflemen flanking the tracker and the rest of the section in single file behind him. The tracker, whose eyes would be dropped to the ground searching for signs, would not be able to see ahead. Thus, the flanking riflemen would be his eyes searching forward.

The blood trail led us over a rocky outcrop and up along one of the Matetsi River's tributaries. We tracked until midday the following day when we reached a high waterfall. The fine mist was most refreshing.

Here we found the feathery remains of a rock pigeon which the fleeing terrorist had shot and used to lay a false blood trail. Our quarry had succeeded in eluding us as we found no further signs of the man. We spent the night in the ravine close to the waterfall. We had no blankets so we all shivered and rubbed ourselves as we fought to keep warm.

Our food supplies were now dwindling and our enthusiastic tracker taught us how, on just one teabag and one bouillon cube per day, to survive in the bush for days. Of course, there had to be enough water available to be able to make three cups of tea from the single teabag and a broth from the cube.

In the morning, we backtracked to the Matetsi River where Johnny Johnston left us.

I later heard that the newspapers had honoured him for having been lowered by helicopter to rescue a stranded tourist from the Victoria Falls.

Some stress during an ambush

We had been ordered to patrol back along the Matetsi River. Our stick consisted of Corporal da Silva who was a Porra, Mellet, Toughey, Hayward from intake 137, and me. We traversed some distance upriver without incident and towards evening, da Silva selected a suitable ambush site and we laid up close by until nightfall.

After dark, we quietly crept into position lying on a ledge with our feet against a steep cliff facing out over the river which gurgled lazily through a series of small pools. It was between two of these pools that we sited the killing-ground. I was placed on the right flank and Hayward on the left flank with his MAG. Da Silva controlled from the centre of our position.

The hours drifted by slowly and the guard was changed every two hours. After 23h00, Da Silva woke us up with an urgent nudge. The night was pitch dark. We could just make out the silhouette of the cliff top which towered high above us, framing the few bright stars which failed to light up the canyon.

Footsteps squelched through mud and I gripped my weapon tighter. Da Silva held an illuminating grenade, a relic from the Second Great War. When the squelching sounds were in front of us, he challenged the intruders. There was no response so he pulled the pin out of the grenade and lobbed the device as far as he could. It ignited with a dull plop and emitted a not too bright light which immediately set some reeds alight. There was no movement in the killing-ground but we all fired into areas of likely cover as we had so diligently been trained to do.

My rifle fired two rounds and then jammed. I re-cocked the weapon and fired another round. Bang! This was followed by another stoppage which I rectified by cocking the weapon again. I loosed off another round which was followed by another stoppage. Every now and then a tracer round hummed high above us, ricocheting off the granite walls. This continued for about a minute and then da Silva ordered a ceasefire. It turned out that I was not the only misfit to have experienced stoppages that evening. Da Silva, Mellet and Toughey had experienced the same. Not too much noise had emanated from Hayward's machine gun either but he hadn't experienced any stoppages.

There was a fire raging on the other side of the riverbed and da Silva became concerned that it may endanger us as we were trapped in the canyon. He ordered the riflemen over the river to put the fire out with Hayward in position to cover us. There we were, all dancing around, stomping out a grass fire. Fortunately, there were no enemy present for we would surely have made good targets.

Once the fire was out, we re-crossed the trickle of water in the river bed and returned to our ambush position. The smell of burned grass and singed hair hung heavily in the motionless air. We all settled down again and da Silva resumed his guard. A few minutes later, a spine-chilling scream rent the air from our left flank. I thought that a terrorist was stabbing or strangling one of us, just like we had seen them doing in the movies.

The sounds were emanating from Hayward's throat. Mellet jumped up with his rifle at the ready but he could not see anything in the pitch dark night. Hayward just lay on his back and screamed. Unable to cope with the suspense of gunfire in the dark night, he had suffered a temporary nervous breakdown. Mellet dropped to his knees and placed his hands on Hayward to feel what was wrong.

When Hayward felt Mellet's hands he screeched even louder. Mellet calmed him with a heavy slap to the ear and we moved him to the centre of our position where he seemed to feel more reassured that he would live through the night.

Everybody calmed down and we attempted to resume sleep. That was not immediately possible as adrenaline was now coursing through our bloodstreams.

'All the rifles had stoppages and now our gunner has lost his nerve,' I thought. 'I hope we don't meet up with a real band of gooks tonight...'

The next morning, we reported the ambush and the stoppages, but were ordered to continue with our patrol. We walked all day and passed the dangerous path that we had originally used to descend towards the Matetsi River. Hayward seemed to have recovered from his spell of terror and was in high spirits. His mood was frivolous and he even showed me how to clean his MAG by hanging it by the sling and swinging it back and forth in a pool of water. When he lifted the gun, torrents rushed out of the many apertures and he declared that but for a spot of oil, his gun was good for another few days.

I was starting to become a little concerned about my new friend Hayward.

The South African Police constable gets robbed
Hunger was becoming a growling problem. Is that a pun, I wonder? Our bouillon cubes and teabags were finished, our cigarettes had long been

smoked and it was a crestfallen stick that proceeded with their patrol that glum morning.

We had been ordered to rendezvous with the South African Police. They were dressed in their distinctive camouflage with floppy hats on their heads, but carried the same types of weapons as ours. When we asked them for food, the police lieutenant just shrugged and assigned a constable to our stick, explaining that the man was under orders to assist us as he knew the area well. We left, walked a short distance, and stopped for a smoke break, but we didn't have any cigarettes left, did we? I politely asked the policeman if he had any, and he took a packet from his pocket and generously offered me one. Voicing my thanks, I took the packet from his hand, offered one each to Toughey and Hayward, and placed one between my own lips. These we lit and puffed contentedly. The packet disappeared into my greedy pocket.

The bewildered policeman objected and demanded that I return his cigarettes. Toughey asked him if he had any more. He protested again but Mellet opened his pack and spilled the contents. Tins, biscuits, and chocolates tumbled out and five starving soldiers scrambled madly to grab at any source of nutrition. With groaning pleasure, we gobbled the tastier choices of his three-day ration supply with much salivating and lip smacking.

The unhappy policeman gawked at us, open mouthed, with his hands and arms twitching in protest. We divided his cigarettes equally among the smokers. This amounted to a pack each and we charitably included the now passionately protesting policeman.

That evening we borrowed and shared his blankets, bivouac, and raincoat, and left him with his thick combat jacket for warmth. He was not a very happy policeman, but at five to one he was surely outnumbered. The next day, the six of us patrolled without event, and were all uplifted to our respective bases before nightfall.

On return to base, we reported to the armourer who investigated the stoppages we had experienced. He announced that we had damaged our rifle magazines by using them as bottle openers. The feed lips of the magazines were so bent that they were interfering with the mechanisms that ejected spent cartridge cases. How the magazines had not been problematic while zeroing the weapons was a mystery. (This was possibly because we had subsequently used the magazines to open bottle tops!)

He replaced all the magazines with new ones and issued a severe warning that anyone found with a magazine damaged in this manner would, from then on, experience a short visit to detention barracks.

So there, Mr Snelgar, the use of my bayonet as a utensil has now been justified. Thank you!

First bush trip to the north-east

In October 1974, 1 Independent Company was assigned to the north-eastern border for a six week tour and we all left Wankie in convoy. The old Bedfords rumbled and whined as the drivers pushed them to the limit. The vehicle I was travelling on had an unbalanced prop shaft which throbbed us to sleep as the slipstream tore past.

We based up at a drill hall in Salisbury for the night. I found a callbox in the building and telephoned Julia, an old acquaintance from my apprenticeship days. Her apartment was just two blocks away and I sneaked out of the drill hall to visit. After a welcome meal at a small restaurant we returned to her pad where we chatted and listened to music.

It was getting late and I made a move to leave but she invited me to spend the night. We hopped into her bed and she turned into a horny toad. My virtue was hungrily devoured by the greedy monster hiding in the furry patch down under.

Ah, the fudd!

Early the next morning, we repeated our endeavours to destroy each other's pelvises. I was conscious of a very slippery Mr Willy bouncing around in my denims as I ran all the way back to the drill hall and arrived just in time to throw my kit onto a vehicle. Mr Havanar scowled at me but did not ask where I had been.

Our convoy was routed to the Chikwizo Tribal Trust Land, adjacent to the Mozambican border. We were ordered to prepare for deployment as contact had been initiated at a place called Kanyoka School, located on the bend of one of the Ruenya River's tributaries. Our convoy drove up to the deserted school and laagered in an all round defensive position. There were some terrorists holding up under cover of rocks and trees down in the dry river bed. A reaction force had already been deployed and a K-car was orbiting the river. There was a sheer drop from the school grounds to the river and it seemed as though the K-car was flying at our level when it went by. It was so close that we could clearly make out the features of the pilot's headgear.

9 Platoon was uplifted and dropped to assist fireforce by acting as stop groups. A radio transmission reported that a man by the name of Dawie Visser had been injured by ground fire when a round had passed through the floor of the helicopter and shattered his left humerus. The helicopter deployed the remainder of Dawie's stick and then returned to our laagered position, leaving Dawie in the care of a medic.

Our turn!

Another helicopter uplifted us to a point on a rise overlooking the contact area from which we were to sweep towards the contact zone. The helicopter shuddered as it strained to slow down and the pilot nodded his consent for us to deplane. Corporal da Silva arranged us in an extended line and we advanced down the slope towards the river.

The K-car continued its orbit. It had now sighted the enemy and the 20mm cannon opened fire. This was the first time I had witnessed anything other than small-arms fire. The gunner fired off three shots at a time. The crack of rounds passing close by as they sped through the sound barrier was immediately echoed by the high explosive shells detonating amongst rocks deep down in the valley. The heavy thud, thud, thud of cannon fire from the helicopter orbiting some 800 metres above us reverberated in our ears. What a show! It could not have been reproduced with such magnificence in any cinema.

We continued our sweep until the K-car commander halted us with orders to remain under cover and act as stop groups. Bullets cracked overhead sporadically and we involuntarily ducked each time, but these rounds passed by harmlessly. The K-car killed some of the terrorists and the remainder disappeared into the bush. Trackers were transported in and 9 Platoon followed up. We returned to the vehicles where everyone discussed our first real action excitedly.

Old soldiers, for sure?

Dawie Visser never returned to C Company. There was mention that his arm had been completely disabled and that he was seeking compensation from the military.

Vengeance for the village headman

Early one evening, our section was waiting in ambush when our attention was drawn to some shouting and screaming followed by some shots, all emanating from a village over a rise. Quiet ensued and we tensed ourselves to engage if the enemy passed our way. The screaming and sounds of consternation were replaced by mournful wailing and ululating which continued most of the night.

At first light, we legged it over the rise. Gooks had indeed been there. They had bayoneted the village headman in the back and then thrown him onto the fire where he had burned to death. The cowards had left after threatening the villagers with the same sell-out treatment if they ever colluded with the security forces.

Looking at his map, Lieutenant Havanar deduced that the terrorists would most likely rendezvous at the convergence of two rivers about three kilometres from the village.

Captain Snelgar ordered us to sweep through the area and placed Bravo and Charlie sticks on the opposite banks of each river as stop groups. These were close by, patrolling in the same direction as our stick. Radio messages confirmed that the two stop groups were in position as we swept the area towards the union of the two rivers.

The grass was thick and difficult to pass through without leaving signs. We crossed the spoor of about six men as we swept the territory and followed them as they curved towards the river's junction. The terrain sloped downward slightly as we cleared the area, moving in an extended line towards a small woody outcrop. It was from here that the first shots were fired at us.

The air churned as invisible projectiles swarmed past our heads. We dived into the grass for cover. Kneeling, I loosed off the 20 rounds in my magazine in three brisk bursts and saw the bullets chipping away at rocks and trees. I rapidly changed my magazine and continued to spray the outcrop. A whoosh overhead, immediately followed by a tremendous explosion close behind us indicated that the enemy had fired an RPG7 rocket at us.

Picking my shaking body up off the ground from where I had hastily thrown it, I sent up a silent prayer of thanks for the rocket operator's inaccurate aim.

Several shadowy shapes fled through the trees. Some had rifles over their shoulders and were firing blindly, hoping to hit us. Two of these men fell as their bodies were penetrated by bullets.

We advanced cautiously, firing single shots into the copse to ensure that any men still in position would not dare expose their heads to return fire. Then we cautiously stepped into the mass of boulders and trees as one.

Scuff marks and ejected cartridge cases indicated where the firing positions had been. A discarded RPD machine gun with a still-smoking barrel lay on the ground. An abandoned RPG7 rocket launcher lay next to a backpack full of fresh rockets. Tubes of propellant poked from its pouches. There was also an abandoned SKS rifle, its bloody bayonet folded away under the barrel. One man lay where he had fallen, his blood seeping rapidly into the rocky ground from wounds to his torso and lower back. Blood from a second injured man trailed off into the long grass. After moving through and clearing the contact zone, we regrouped in the grass. Havanar sent our stick's two riflemen back into the contact zone with me to cover them so that they could make sure the downed enemy soldier was indeed dead. I protested the unfair order as I knew that there would be trophies for the taking and I would not be able to extend my greedy hands in order to claim ownership.

I was then ordered to search for spoor close to the rocky outcrop. Most of the survivors had bomb-shelled over the two rivers in different directions. There was a trail of blood, bright red in the mid-morning sun, indicative of at least one gook with a serious hole in his body.

We were informed that a G-car with trackers on board was winging its way to our location. We were to follow-up immediately. In the meantime, the two riflemen were rummaging through the abandoned kit and pocketing some fancy souvenirs. I fumed at the injustice but Mr Havanar would not let me back into the contact zone.

The dull thud of a mortar shell leaving its tube caused us to glance wide-eyed at each other and then yell for cover. I hugged the ground amid the thick grass and the shell thumped down onto the ground some 40 or 50 metres from the rocky outcrop. The next shell fell closer as Mr Havanar and I ran to the rocks for cover. I heard the next mortar bomb being fired from the tube and made an assumption that it was being fired from a low rise on the north

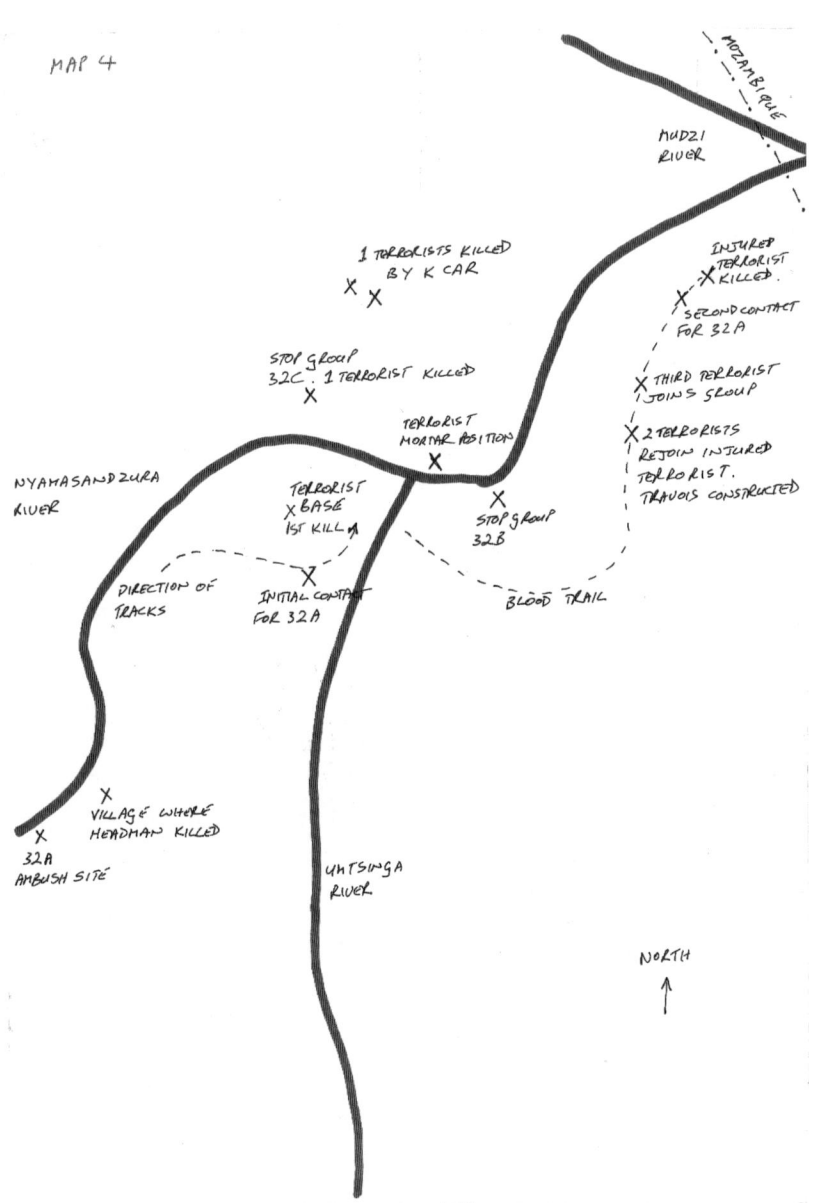

MAP 4

MOZAMBIQUE

MUDZI
RIVER

1 TERRORISTS KILLED
BY K CAR
X X

INJURED
TERRORIST
X KILLED.

SECOND CONTACT
FOR 32A

STOP GROUP
32C. 1 TERRORIST KILLED
X

THIRD TERRORIST
X JOINS GROUP

TERRORIST
MORTAR POSITION
X

X 2 TERRORISTS
REJOIN INJURED
TERRORIST.
TRAVOIS CONSTRUCTED

NYAMASANDZURA
RIVER

TERRORIST
X BASE
1ST KILL

X
STOP GROUP
32B

DIRECTION OF
TRACKS

X
INITIAL CONTACT
FOR 32A

BLOOD TRAIL

X
VILLAGE WHERE
X HEADMAN KILLED
32A
AMBUSH SITE

UHTSINGA
RIVER

NORTH
↑

bank of the river, 300 metres down from where the two rivers merged. I placed the Bren gun's bipod on a low flat rock and fired in the direction from which the gooks were mortaring us. My tracer curved down over the river and bounced amongst the boulders there.

The last bomb fired at us was reasonably accurate. It fell close to the cluster of rocks and exploded with a loud boom. This confused me and I sat down on the ground for a minute but the effect wore off quickly. No more bombs were lobbed at us.

A K-car flew overhead and, directed by Mr Havanar, fired 20mm explosive shells in the direction from which we had been mortared. The gooks scattered and three of their number ran directly into stop group Charlie who killed another of the enemy. The helicopter then orbited the area to search for more terrorists. Gunfire resonated as the gunship fought a running battle with the fleeing men. One more enemy soldier was killed by the gunner.

Naturally, everyone in our stick claimed to have shot down at least one of the two gooks dropped in our initial contact. We all rejoiced at having made our first kill. Mellet and Toughey teased me mercilessly about not having been allowed near the abandoned terrorist position and patronized me by displaying their spoils.

A G-car landed in the grass and disgorged a tracker and several policemen. Prior to follow-up the copper in charge insisted on searching all our gear. He rifled through our packs and removed an AK-47 bayonet, some magazines, and two gook combat caps from Mellet and Toughey's kit.

They were furious and remonstrated with the lawman saying that it was unreasonable not to let them keep the equipment as keepsakes. I smirked at my two comrades and Mellet threatened to flatten my face if I did not instantly 'wipe that stupid grin off my ugly mug'. We left the police to process the contact area.

The tracker walked forward between two riflemen with his eyes searching the ground. I was positioned behind Doug Havanar who walked behind the tracker. We tracked for over two hours, following the blood trail which did not abate in quantity of blood lost. I marvelled at the fortitude of the injured man we were hunting. He was being accompanied by two others.

We came across some small mopani trees that had been hacked down.

From there, the tracks changed to show that the terrorists had constructed a travois and were dragging the injured man behind them. We could clearly see the drag marks made by the stick construction on which the injured individual lay. An hour later, the tracker informed us that a fourth individual had joined the three that we were tracking.

The terrain changed slightly. The ground became stonier and was interspersed with clumps of mopani trees. There was a small rise ahead on which another outcrop of granite boulders provided an ideal position for our quarry in which to rest. Our follow-up patrol reformed into an extended line and we moved up the rise towards the protrusion of rocks.

A shot rang out and we all dived for cover on the stony ground. The skin left my bare elbows in a smear on the hard stones. Shoving the butt of the Bren into my right shoulder, I leaned forward on the bipod, and pulled on the trigger. I aimed low and loosed a single burst of 20 rounds into the outcrop of rocks. The rounds kicked up a cloud of dust and I changed the magazine. Mr Havanar shouted an order for us to charge the enemy position and I rose up in readiness to charge forward. The tracker, who was in front of me, leaped up and ran back past me with a wild look in his eyes. He dropped down a short distance back towards where we had just patrolled and lay as close to the ground as he could. My forward charge faltered as I hesitantly crouched down, amazed by his unpredicted manoeuvre. I discharged more rounds toward the rocky outcrop. By now the fire from the terror group had ceased. They had obviously fled the scene.

My lieutenant was screaming at the tracker to charge forward. The man then leopard crawled forward. Havanar told him to remain where he was and not to fire his rifle, and again ordered his stick to charge forward. We did, and I observed the tracker charging forward with us. I was astonished at how strangely the human mind works when under duress. Together we all assaulted the low rise and I saw the stick construction that the terrorists had dragged through the bush. It contained only some bloodstained cloths that had been used as bandages. The occupant had left at speed. The power of the adrenalin working through his system amazed me.

I suppressed a sudden urge to laugh at his misfortune. Imagine being shot and assisted to safety by your comrades only to be shot at again that same day.

We quickly regrouped and followed his spoor. We found him just below the summit of the rise. Blood had spewed out of his mouth. He had died in full step and collapsed in a floppy bundle of dirty limbs and dust. He had taken a round through the side during our first contact and the stress of running must have ruptured some blood vessel deep inside his body.

We followed up until twilight and then slept on the spoor. At first light, we continued to the Mozambican border. We were not granted permission to cross the border. Instead, we ambushed the tracks for two days, hoping to contact other insurgents.

The police collected the dead terrorists and transported them back to the village where they had killed the headman. Their bodies were displayed to the villagers in a vain attempt to illustrate the security forces' ability to destroy the enemy.

Payback in its extreme, don't you think?

Living off the land

It was another mundane patrol and we were ordered to move to a certain point on a nearby road for uplift. We gathered at the edge of a deserted kraal and waited for our vehicles. We had finished our rations the previous morning and we were all starving. I spotted a cucumber in a field and snatched it up. Without skinning or washing the vegetable, I ate it, seasoned with salt licked from my forearms. Salty juice flowed blissfully down my chin.

There were more cucumbers lying on the ground, attached to a scrawny brown vine. The other three men helped themselves to the remainder. As I finished my snack, I saw one last cucumber lying in a furrow. I darted forward, picked it up and bit deeply into the flesh.

Yuck!

The underside was rotten and brown with worms, and it tasted foul. I spat it out to a chorus of laughter and mockery from my stick about being punished for my greed.

A native man rode by with a scrawny chicken cooped in a bark cage tied to the carrier of his pushbike. We bought it from him at an exorbitant price. One of the men strangled, gutted, and plucked the bird while I started a fire. A rough spit was hastily constructed and we had the chicken roasting on open flames within a few minutes.

The sound of vehicles reached our ears just as the chicken started to sizzle and smell good. Gears grated as the drivers halted their trucks and the escorts shouted for us to embus immediately. We ignored them. We were unaware that our captain had accompanied the uplift. He stood up and angrily shouted at us to embus instantly, or else...

His threat was muted by four simultaneous, 'oh shits'.

Desperately, we ripped the half-cooked bird apart and ran for the trucks, dragging our kit. We climbed the sides of the vehicle with bloodied hands and undercooked chicken grasped in our teeth, and then ravenously ripped the chicken pieces to shreds and gulped them down without chewing. The escorts stared aghast. Captain Snelgar just grinned and threw us each a ration pack from the bag at his feet. He seemed impressed by our resourcefulness and suggested that we consider joining the newly formed Selous Scouts.

We were redeployed for another three days. My stomach rumbled and groaned within me and I thought it might be the rotten cucumber that I had bitten into. When our stick leader called a halt and then bolted to squat behind a bush I knew we were in for the runs.

We quickly drank anti-diarrhoea tablets and managed to avert most of the plague.

The blister beetle
Lieutenant Havanar signalled us to move out. We all stood up and dragged our webbing and packs onto our backs. I felt a warm spray on my left leg as we followed our stick leader into the murky dusk in the usual marching order. Warm liquid ran down my leg into the sock rolled up above my takkie uppers. It felt warm on my leg for a long time.

We ambushed all night long without any success and the next morning I crawled out of my sleeping bag and inspected my leg, which had been irritating me. What a shock! The whole front of my leg, from the top of my knee down to my ankle, was a mass of red blisters, some broken and leaking watery blood, others tight and fat with pressure. The liquid on my leg could only have come from a blister beetle, which sprays a defensive acid when disturbed.

The patrol continued without incident. When we got back to our base, I reported to our medic, Yogi Bear (so called because he was the spitting image of the cartoon character). He treated the festering skin with some ointment and gave me a course of penicillin. This relieved me from the next patrol and I looked forward to skiving at base camp for a few days but this was not to be. CSM Williams quickly rostered me for guard duty by night and skivvy details during the day. I quickly grew to hate the continuous bitching and unnecessary orders. 'How many sandbags can a man fill in three days?' I thought.

When my stick returned from patrol, I fought to rejoin them so that I could avoid these needless daily duties. The doctor told me not to patrol as the rotting skin on my leg had shown no sign of healing. I went over his head and reported to my corporal, saying that I was fit for duty.

When our tour was over, we found ourselves on the Bedfords en route back to Wankie. My leg had grown worse due to the fact that I had not been able to keep the sores covered and clean while on patrol. Yogi Bear fought with me but I was his favourite and my charming smile broke his resolve. He obtained permission for our vehicle to pull in at Llewellin Barracks so that I could visit the hospital there.

We were milling around the same regimental police charge office in which I had spent the night after the harrowed engineer saga. Lieutenant Havanar disappeared into the office to sign us in. A narrow eyed sergeant from the regimental police espied us and marched over. He rebuked us for being so gungy and improperly dressed, and ordered me to attention. Why always me, will I ever know?

I pathetically straightened my back, leaving my left leg bent, and placed my hands on my hips. The sergeants face flooded crimson with rage and the spider veins in his cheeks seemed to swell purple as he raised his voice and shouted at me. I lost my cool and shouted back. Remonstrating that I had a leg injury and could not stand to attention, I declared that we were not his stupid rookies. Continuing my outburst, I highlighted the fact that we were on our way back from the bush, something he had never experienced himself, and that he should leave us *makonyas* alone as we answered only to our own officers. Then I took a deep breath to recover vented oxygen. Taken aback at my outburst, he stepped back a pace and struggled to find words with which to address this sedition. The fact that all my colleagues were laughing did not help him to maintain his composure.

Havanar exited the office with a murderous scowl, approached the enraged sergeant and ordered the fuming man to stand down and bugger off. The sergeant cringed and slunk off with his tail clamped firmly between his buttocks. I felt a new twinge of warmth for my platoon commander.

At the hospital, a military doctor with eyes that were magnified through lenses as thick as the base of a beer glass, examined my leg and made an appointment for me to visit a specialist. The appointment fell right in the middle of my pending R & R. I protested but was told to shut up or I would be kept at Llewellin until the appointment date. So I kept as quiet as the proverbial church mouse until the vehicle was well on its way back to Wankie where I squabbled with my medic and platoon commander to no avail. Fortunately the sores began to dry out and I cancelled the appointment. No one ever questioned me regarding the prognosis. It took about six months for the sores to clear up completely, and another 20 years for the scars to disappear.

Botswana border patrol

My stick was ordered to patrol the Botswana border fence north-east of the Kazuma Depression. We were to assess the condition of the fence and check for signs of anyone having jumped the border.

It was a monotonous patrol and on the afternoon of the second day, we came across a small hutted area occupied by two men. They were government employees and their job was to maintain the border fence. Seemingly, they had not conversed with anyone for some time due to their remote location. They offered us a meal and a hut to sleep in that night. This would be a welcome relief from ration food and possibly also a reprieve from the mosquitoes that attacked us every evening.

All that our hosts requested was that we hand over some rations in return for a banquet that we would never forget. We agreed and our only condition was that they would join us for supper. This would allay any suspicion of toxic substances having been added to the meal.

The meal consisted of *sadza* and a stew made up of our rations bolstered with some of their home-grown vegetables. Chillies added a very enjoyable kick. We sat around the fire with salivating mouths as these men cooked this most amazing meal. The unique taste tingled on our palates for hours afterwards. Toughey and I shared our cigarettes with them and their appreciation of this luxury was evident. Some time after 22h00 we dossed down in the hut provided for us and all slept soundly without so much as one mosquito bite between us. This might have been due to the confines of the hut or more possibly, the bite of the chillies?

The next morning as we were preparing to leave, the more senior of the men approached us politely. He said that the two of them would be willing to carry our heavy packs to our next waypoint, and hinted that some fresh meat would be an acceptable reward for their efforts. Da Silva was hesitant but Mellet finally persuaded him with a promise to fashion for him, a trophy from the skin of whatever we shot.

We marched away from our luxurious camp feeling euphoric. The two Africans trudged on uncomplaining, each bowed under the combined weight of two packs. Some distance from the camp, we noticed a herd of sable antelope. They lifted their heads and observed us fearlessly as we walked past. The senior African man craftily mentioned that there were many of these in the area and one would not be missed. His hint achieved the desired result. Unable to resist the urge, Mellet shot a magnificent bull between the eyes. The gratitude on the faces of our two new friends was totally indescribable. Their eyes shone with joy and I am sure their mouths watered in anticipation of their next meal. Unfortunately, we would not share it with them.

Mellet instructed one of our porters to remove the scrotum. The man skilfully sliced the piece of skin off the animal and then asked us for some salt, which he rubbed into the fresh side of the skin before giving it to Mellet. The two native men then set about skinning the animal and we realized that they now considered their duties as porters over. Thanking them, we all shouldered our own packs and continued on our way.

The freedom with which Mellet had fired at the sable inspired in all of us, a need to shoot at something. Da Silva and I fouled Toughey and Mellet's attempts at hunting by sending bullets cracking over the heads of their targets an instant before they fired. The result was that these two hunters fired some wild shots. Da Silva and I teased them and called them bum shots. That mad Porra and I laughed so much that we had to remove our heavy packs and lie down for relief. Mellet and Toughey scowled at us.

We observed circling eagles or vultures high in the sky above us and further amused ourselves by firing rounds at them without trying to hit them. The birds jerked in mid-air and then resumed normal flight every time a round passed close to them. We whooped and rejoiced at these near misses and the sport provided us with some much needed entertainment.

That evening when da Silva radioed his report back to base, he was asked if we had heard any shooting. Da Silva replied that we had heard none but would keep our ears and eyes open. We shrewdly cleaned our weapons prior to collection, just in case they were inspected and found to be freshly fired. It would not, we reasoned sensibly, be a good idea for the whole stick to be sent off to the box. Our worries were unfounded as there was no mention of any shooting by anyone. Such were the stresses of the national serviceman in the later part of 1974.

I often lie on my bed at night thinking about my life as it was nearly 40 years back. The meal prepared by the two fence guards is one of my most delightful memories.

Mellet pushed an old jam jar into the bag of skin. When it had dried, he removed the bottle and was left with a well-formed dice cup which he gave to da Silva. Sometimes payback can be beneficial.

Public violence

"Walsh, the captain wants to see you, NOW!"

I mooched over to the camp headquarters and waited to be ordered in. Williams was there and but for a murderous glare, he ignored me. His brain cell failed to connect me to any offence that he could gripe about. The orderly reported my presence and I was left to wait for a while.

"Walsh, enter," came the order from inside.

I marched in, halted, and turned smartly to the right to face my officer, smiling beatifically to create an aura of innocence on my angelic face.

"You bloody little hooligan!" he thundered. "You are a skate and a gangster…a hoodlum!"

The smiling angel fluttered off my face and a dark and gloomy noose was placed over my head. It transpired that a minor incident which had occurred while I was on leave from Llewellin Barracks had finally caught up with me.

While on R & R, I had met up with John and some of his friends with whom I had not previously been acquainted. When the pubs closed on Friday night we roamed the town in search of adventure and noticed that there was a function being held at the Civic Centre. There were only coloured people at this gathering but this did not worry me as my old friend, Aaron Renders, was there. We quickly got chatting and recovered old ground, reminiscing about the time during which we had worked together in Salisbury. We sipped a beer and I met his girlfriend.

While we were chatting, we heard a scuffle and both of us looked up to see a lanky coloured man punching one of John's friends who reeled backwards through a glass panel. Aaron leapt over to the gangly coloured and ordered him to cease fighting. A small crowd of grumbling coloured people gathered around. We decided to leave. I said goodbye to Aaron and we roared off in our cars.

Our drive took us past a bus shelter under which a group of Africans were huddling together for warmth. John's friends stopped their car, charged towards the sleepy natives, and started assaulting and throwing dustbins at them. John and I protested and stopped the attack as soon as we realized it was malicious. Then we all piled back into our cars and drove off in search of more entertainment.

One of the Africans in the sleepy group recognized John and reported him to the police. John was arrested and turned state witness the next morning. The police phoned my father, who drove me over to the police station to give a statement. Even though I was not involved in the assault I was charged with public violence for having been present.

Bummer!

My old man was excessively cheesed off with me and complained that my lifestyle was too carefree but he still contacted his older brother, my Uncle Frank, who ran a law firm in Bulawayo.

I explained to Mr Snelgar that I was quite innocent as I had merely been caught up with a bad element. He concluded that justice would run its course and told me that I should hope for a life sentence in a civilian jail rather than ever returning to his unit if I was convicted. The inferred punishment that he would inflict upon my skinny little body and reprobate mind for disgracing the army was left unspoken.

I was to make my way to Bulawayo for an appointment with one of my Uncle's lawyers, which I did. We prepared the case and then I hitchhiked to Fort Victoria to attend court.

I pleaded not guilty to the charge. After a short deliberation, the judge stated that he could not see why I had been charged at all. He dismissed me with a severe reprimand to choose better company and told me that he didn't want to see me in front of his bench again, or else! John's friends were all fined for their crime.

I made my way back to 1 Independent Company at Wankie and presented myself to my commanding officer. After congratulating me on my successful defence, he stated that it was OK for soldiers to engage in this kind of activity, but being caught was a crime. His view sounded like a more serious version of Akkie's.

"I'm watching you, Walsh," he said, as I marched out of his office.

Detention barracks

Four men were sent to detention barracks during our stay at 1 Independent Company.

The first was, inevitably, Nick Toughey. I cannot remember his sin but he was sent to the box for 14 days. On his return, we were due for a pass, and Toughey and I hitchhiked to Bulawayo for the weekend. On the Saturday morning, we walked past a barber shop. The bored barber was leaning against his striped pole and Toughey, ever the funny man, thrust his mostly shaven head towards the barber's face and asked how much for a haircut. The barber flicked his eyes at me, saw me laughing, and understood the funny side.

"For you free but for your sidekick a dollar," he laughed.

The next was Russell Hardy. He was on his way to muster parade one morning and somehow became confused while readying his weapon for inspection. He aimed his supposedly safe rifle at a truck tyre and squeezed the trigger. The tyre hissed a long spurt of water from the bullet-hole (the tyres of our operational vehicles were filled with water to help dampen the blast of landmines). Hardy just shook his head and handed his rifle over to his platoon commander. He knew he was going to DB.

The third man was Roy Salisbury, who attacked Lance-Corporal Godwin. I do not know what triggered the incident, but Salisbury fought easily after a certain amount of drinking. Mr Snelgar sent him to the box for 28 days. It is also possible that the incident in which he had clobbered the engineer with a beer bottle at Llewellin, showed on his record. This could have resulted in a stiffer sentence.

The fourth soldier to be sentenced to a period of detention was Corporal Pete Robbins. He had arranged for his stick to be dropped off at their pickup point and bunked off for three days. When Captain Snelgar caught wind of this, he ordered Robbins to return to his designated drop off point for redeployment. Robbins had to admit that he was not able to return within the time constraint imposed and was sent to Brady Barracks for a while to consider his future as a territorial soldier.

Strange to note here is the fact that all three men who were with me when the engineer complained about three little guys beating him up were sent to detention barracks. How did I manage to escape the box I wondered?

I hoped that it was not payback delayed.

Guard duty at Victoria Falls Bridge

Every week, a section was sent to perform guard duties at the bridge which spanned the boiling Zambezi River just downstream from the Victoria Falls. The section was divided into two sticks, each of which was on duty for 12 hours.

The border between Zambia and Rhodesia was denoted by a thick white line painted halfway across the bridge. We were not allowed to touch this line. If any number of Rhodesian soldiers walked onto the bridge, an equal number of Zambian soldiers would do the same.

I often walked up to the line and leaned over the rail to gaze down at the swirling waters far below. A Zambian soldier would then march up to the line and stand there with his weapon at the high port across the front of his chest.

The Zambian soldiers always looked very serious but it had not always been so.

A South African Policeman had spoiled it for the Zambian Army while engaged in conversation with an affable Zambian soldier. Their conversation turned to guns and the South African asked the Zambian if he could have a look at his AK-47. When the trusting Zambian smiled and handed the weapon over, the policeman didn't even look at the rifle. He just tossed it over the side of the bridge.

Thus, Zambian soldiers were forbidden to converse with us.

We would stand there and tease them about their impeccable turnout and anything else we could think of. If we asked to look at their weapons they became even stiffer and glared at us menacingly. This always made us laugh.

We always made sure that the MAG fixed on a tripod in our bunker was manned when any of us went onto the bridge; just in case one of our jokes was unacceptably offensive to these most solemn of men.

We also alleviated our boredom by dropping bottles off the bridge onto the rocks way below on the floor of the canyon. I would watch, fascinated as the bottles fell and then turned into puffs of shiny dust on contact.

Our time off duty led us to the many hotels in the town. We would sit at the bars in our uniforms and buy one beer each. The drinks were very expensive and we just sat there sipping to kill time. Many hotels provided a buffet. To partake of these expansive (and expensive) meals one had to be in possession of a ticket. We each took turns to buy a ticket which admitted one. Once in, the ticket was passed to a comrade outside who then gained admission, and so on.

I think the hotel management knew what we were up to but they never said anything to us.

Firepower demonstration at Deka

Our futile efforts to win the hearts and minds of the local population included firepower demonstrations which were designed to convince the natives that we had the means to destroy the enemy.

CSM Williams shanghaied some of 8 Platoon's members to assist with one of these exhibitions. We loaded a pile of bricks, some cement and some wooden benches into our Bedford trucks. Then we drove to a spot on the Deka road where we constructed a wall, about hip high and two bricks thick (about as intelligent as our sergeant-major, we joked). Various targets and dummies dressed in old camouflage clothing were hidden in the outlying vegetation. The tribes-people started arriving at 11h00 the next day, some hours before the demonstration was scheduled to start. By 13h00 they were still trailing in. A vexed Mr Williams, who after living in Rhodesia for many years had not gotten used to African time, screamed at everyone to sit on the benches. I am sure his screaming impressed these people who had walked miles at the insistence of the military. The interpreter hastily told the 300 odd visitors to sit down on the dusty ground, and arranged the chiefs and dignitaries on the benches.

Williams bayed at his troops, telling them to fall into formation. A section of men charged through the open air theatre, screaming and firing their weapons at the dummy targets on their path. When the charge was complete, the tribes-people were ushered forward to inspect the damage we had wrought. They politely clucked their tongues and aah-aahed at the damage inflicted.

Next, we showed them the newly built brick wall, emphasising its solid construction. Our guests were told that we would now shoot the wall down to the ground with only one machine gun. They were ordered to sit down again. One soldier positioned his MAG and fired a succession of rounds at the wall. Brick and mortar turned into powder and chunks as high velocity bullets chiselled the masonry apart. Our audience was again ushered forward to have a close look at the destruction. A dummy placed behind the wall had been torn to shreds.

More clucks and aah-aahs from our indifferent audience.

"No place for any terrorist to hide," said our sergeant-major triumphantly. The interpreter translated his words.

I then fired a few two-inch mortar bombs at an old hut some distance across the road. This collapsed after a close hit. Rifle grenades were fired at targets with great effect. Da Silva instructed me to fire my 28R antitank rifle grenade through the branches of a tree above my target.

"The grenade should burst in the air and make a magnificent impression on our audience," he reasoned.

This was in defiance of Mr William's instructions but I did so. When the grenade exploded in the treetop, Williams' brain cell fused and he screamed at me and called me a string of ugly names. The wily da Silva just grinned at me.

The closing display was a white phosphorous rifle grenade fired in the mortar role. The projectile flew high and exploded at its zenith. White trails plumed out of the smoky cloud high in the air. Much more clucking and aahs from the crowd.

One of the rifle grenades had failed to explode and we had some fun watching a nervous Williams place a block of explosive next to the offending grenade, push a detonator in and ignite the fuse. The contrivance exploded with a satisfying bang.

The interpreter dismissed the tribes-people and we cleaned the area and left for Wankie base before it grew dark.

I wondered if all the clucking tongues and aah-aah sounds had been a true measure of the demonstration's effect on the people. I doubted it. The terrorists had a much more effective way of gaining support. Killing old men and raping women and children certainly made more impact on people's hearts and minds than our puny display of firepower.

The Baobab Hotel
The Baobab Hotel was situated on a high hill on the outskirts of Wankie. The management welcomed us as long as we behaved and did not unduly disturb any of the tourists staying there.

There was a liberty run every night during which the duty drivers transported personnel to the hotel in the early evenings. The trip there was normally uneventful. The old Bedford trucks struggled up the steep road that circled the high hill on which the hotel had been built. The drivers coaxed the old ladies up with much gearing down and unnecessary revving. They then left to fulfil other transport requirements and returned at 23h00 to collect the bleary eyed troops that came staggering out of the hotel's public bar.

My problem came with the drive home. The drivers enjoyed the run down the hill and competed with each other to establish some kind of speed record. I was petrified of the return journey. This stress provoked in me, the need to drink as much alcohol as I could afford in order to generate the Dutch courage I needed to face the trip home (*mampara* for sure). Inevitably, I would be drunk when time came to return to base.

Such a misunderstood fellow was I.

Fishing at Deka

Deka was a fishing camp, popular with many Rhodesian and South African fishermen. They arrived in October before the rains when the Zambezi River was at its lowest and the tiger fish were on the bite.

The road to Msuna passed over the Deka River close to the Deka/Zambezi junction. A damn had been built there and the water backed up under the bridge. With permission from our commanding officer, we parked our vehicles on the bridge, pulled the pins from some surplus M962 grenades and tossed them into the water. There was a short delay before the munitions exploded, making several geysers of water erupt high into the air. Others, from charges exploding deeper down, just bubbled furiously. The water churned dark brown from disturbed bottom mud and the scales of many fish reflected sunlight into our eyes. We hurled ourselves off the bridge into the water as one and started catching fish. This was a simple matter of steering them to the edge and flicking them out of the water as most were dead or dazed.

We loaded the fish onto our vehicles and transported them to the local chief, where we gave them to the people as a gesture of good will, leaving 100 odd Kariba bream on the vehicles for our dinner that evening.

Payback for a good days fishing I'd say!

Buggered on the mountain

I had been ordered to attend relay station duties for a week and found myself on a huge hill in the bush with a signaller and two other riflemen. The signaller performed all the radio duties and the rest of us did odd-jobs like cooking and making tea. We did not normally perform guard duties as we considered it safe high up on the mountain and the signaller slept with the radio handset close to his ear. Any calls made on the correct frequency would wake him and he would then relay any messages as required. Not standard procedure, but it worked for us.

An Alouette relayed us in two lifts and we were left alone on top of the huge mound. The wind was cool and night imminent and we hastily erected a tarpaulin while the signaller assembled his equipment and established communications. The view was breathtaking as a crimson sun settled down below the horizon, leaving a bright pink smudge in the dusty sky. It had been a long day and we all drifted off to sleep early.

In the morning, we woke up to a disgusting smell. A swarm of stinkbugs had invaded our camp and a number of them had released stinkbug odour when we had accidentally crushed them. They crawled into our sleeping bags and clothing and floated in our tea. It would have been impractical to exterminate or even remove them and we were occupying the only possible campsite so we were stuck with our unwelcome guests.

Strangely, I noticed that the smell of stinkbugs was just like the taste of English cucumbers.

After three days, we received an urgent message from our commanding officer. He ordered us to be ready for uplift by helicopter within the hour as our company was relocating. We broke camp hastily and I emptied out the jerry cans of water, keeping one back on advice from the signaller, who knew from past experience that the order might be rescinded. If all the water had been emptied out it would be a thirsty team left up on the hill.

That is exactly what happened. Our call sign was radioed and we were told that uplift was no longer required. We were to continue in our current role for the next four days as planned. I opened the last jerry can to obtain water for tea. As I filled my fire-bucket, the ugly bloated body of some huge cricket burbled into the vessel. It stank like a dead animal and I heaved until my stomach muscles ached. The rest of the team cursed me as though this inglorious event had been my fault.

I recovered from retching and swore back at my team with a sweating brow. We sat glaring at each other and pondered how to survive on one can of defiled water. It would definitely have to be boiled and treated with purification tablets. The tainted water still emitted a fetid bouquet, even after we had done this. We made tea and mixed jungle juice into it, but nothing disguised the smell and taste of that cursed dead insect. We all survived the putrid ordeal with a nasty case of the runs.

What a bugger up it really was.

Some leave in Salisbury

While on pass, I hitchhiked up to Salisbury to visit Ron. His parents were away working on a contract in Botswana and I met him at their house in Goromonzi. We arranged to meet David at the Round Bar. The Round Bar was exactly that. A huge round bar built into the centre of an oval room, adjacent to the Le Coq Dorr night club.

Here, we all swilled an appreciable amount of alcohol, and David met a pug-faced blond girl whom Ron named Miss Piggy after the *Muppets* character. Ron and I wept at our inspired humour. David concentrated his limited charms on her, and later suggested that we all leave and go to his place. Why he invited us two drunkards along, I have no idea!

It took a while for Ron and me to disengage ourselves from the Round Bar. We were enjoying our booze and ordered some more drinks. This was a luckless move as a stocky soldier from the RLI joined us and staked a claim on Miss Piggy. He attempted to enrapture her with stories of his proficiency as a soldier, so Ron and I called him Audie Murphy, after the American hero. When we asked him what medals he had been awarded, he hedged a little, changed the subject, and attempted to entice Miss Piggy away with him for the remainder of the evening.

When he visited the restroom, we downed our drinks and raced down the stairs onto the pavement outside. We thought we had a limited chance of being followed by the valiant Audie Murphy but we had not realized how resourceful our artful rival was. Storming down the stairs, he accused Miss Piggy of being unfaithful to him and ordered her to join him at his side.

David advised him to get lost. Audie Murphy then walked up to David and started throwing punches at his face. David stepped back and walked rearward in a circle, blocking the ever more irate Audie Murphy's blows. They circumnavigated the pavement and danced past where I was standing. I let loose with an exceptional boot to Audie Murphy's midriff, complete with a victory shout and clicking of fingers like a Spanish dancer. *Olé!*

The assailed man bellowed in agony and fell to the pavement writhing and winded. I hurriedly put forward to my friends that we should leave before he got his breath back. Fate thought differently. A chilling war cry rent out from across the street where someone had witnessed the termination of Audie Murphy while getting out of a taxi. He charged at us.

"Yaheeeee!" he shrieked as he ran, "All for one and one for all!"

Why the hell was he quoting *The Three Musketeers*? And what was he doing running across the street towards us? He was dressed in a black shirt and long pants and he had a colourful cloth tied around his head. My last thought was that he must be a ninja.

"No one hurts the brothers!" he shouted.

Then I was lying on the stained pavement looking up at the pigeons roosting in the gutter of the concrete arcade above. They looked back down at me, nodding their heads in mock deference to my stupidity. Audie Murphy repaid me with a few kicks to my ribs and then walked off with his arm around Miss Piggy's shoulders.

'Sorry David,' I recall thinking, 'but you ain't gonna score with her tonight!'

I lay dazed for a considerable length of time. David and Ron had each received the same treatment from the ninja who had dropped them both onto the pavement with a few nifty *kung-fu* kicks. Audie Murphy had left them alone though. When I sat up, the pavement and street were deserted, except for a sleeping Ron and a bloodied David, who sat nursing his nose. My jaw objected if I tried to clench my teeth and my side ached a little but I was otherwise unharmed. I reached over and shook Ron who groaned awake and together we three stooged over to David's apartment where we spent the next hour nursing our wounds with some of David's whiskey.

The next morning Ron and I bade David farewell. On our way out, Ron tossed a half-empty jar of Vaseline that he had found in the bathroom at David. He said not a word but we both bawled with laughter at the implied Miss Piggy replacement. A red faced but grinning David closed his front door on us.

We hiked back to Goromonzi and discovered that the premises had been broken into. Among the other stolen items was my neatly packed bag. Ron would not let me use his toothbrush so I settled for a strange looking bristly brush in the family toothpaste glass.

We hung around the house while the police investigated and took fingerprints, and then left for town. Our objective was to end up at Club Tomorrow to see if we could score a couple of chicks. There we met some good friends of ours from the RLI.

Are we ever going to escape these blokes this weekend?

Mike Watson, Harry Whitehead, and Fl Mylie entertained us as we sat at the bar. We told them about the thrashing we had received the previous evening and they laughed heartily at our lack of functionality, especially since one of theirs had issued us with such a good hiding.

Mike then told us about one of his RLI mates who had asked a girl to dance the previous weekend. She had refused this honour and promptly accepted a dance proposal from a long haired civilian. The soldier stole her handbag and disappeared into the gents where he quickly defecated into it. Then he returned it to its original position and sat back to watch the action.

The girl returned to her table with her new boyfriend and sipped her drink. She then daintily reached into her handbag for a packet of cigarettes and pulled out a hot smelly turd. She screamed, flicked the clinging excrement onto the floor, and shot off to the ladies, clutching her soiled handbag. Mike said that the RLI soldier had laughed so much that he had nearly wet himself. We too, laughed at the appropriate lesson that the snobbish girl had learned.

Our boisterous laughter halted all conversation in the bar and the other patrons stared at us. By now we did not care what people thought of us. We acquired some drawing pins and pushed them through our earlobes to try and be cool. The other customers continued to stare at us but they were now grinning at our antics. The evening dragged on and then suddenly, I felt tired and homesick. I excused myself and took a taxi to the outskirts of Salisbury.

The taxi dropped me off near a Shell garage where I spent my last coins on a fizzy drink and packet of crisps. The road was deserted. It was around 01h00 and I was freezing. There was a low picket fence behind me. I stomped on it to break up the wood and soon had a comfortable blaze going. Just before I settled down to sleep for the night, a car pulled up and a wizened old man asked me if I wanted a lift.

"Yes please," I replied, and jumped into the passenger seat next to him. I looked back at my merrily blazing fire as we drove away. I hoped that I had not caused some poor citizen too much inconvenience.

I politely engaged in conversation until I could no longer keep my eyes open and then courteously excused myself, dropped my chin onto my chest and fell sound asleep. Some time later, I was roughly shaken awake by the old man who was now shouting at me. There was a lot of smoke pouring into the car from the location of the gearlever and he was blaming me for having started a fire with a cigarette. I tried to explain that I had not lit a cigarette in his car but he would not listen. He stopped the car and ordered me out. I stepped out of the car into the cold darkness and he slammed the door and sped off. There was such thick smoke pouring out from under his car that the outline of his rear parking lights was obscured.

'What a strange man,' I thought. Surely he should have been taking action to extinguish the fire.

I stood next to the road shivering as dawn tinted the eastern sky a tinge of pale yellow. Well after sunrise, I was picked up by another motorist who dropped me off opposite the post office in Fort Victoria where there was a public callbox which I used to call my parents reverse charge. My mother collected me an hour later. As I climbed into her car she exclaimed that I surely needed a bath and asked why there was a brass drawing pin in my right earlobe.

I saw the old man standing next to his car as we drove past Standard Motors. The hood was up and a couple of petrol attendants had their heads buried deep inside, looking for some explanation as to what had been burning and why. He glared at me as we drove past and I smiled and waved at him.

Prinnie

My days at Llewellin barracks were anything but a tea party and they were made considerably more unbearable by one person in particular, a certain Prinnie.

Prinnie was also called up with intake 138 and from the moment he found his army feet, his confidence grew and he became proud and loud. He vociferously professed to be a Christian but I could not figure out what made him tick. I found most of the other guys easy to get along with but our Prinnie wavered between great highs and unfathomable depths. Whenever I was alone with him he treated me well but as soon as other company gathered, he used me as a target to prove that he was clever and witty.

I did my best to avoid him.

During our second tour to the north-east, our platoon was waiting for pickup on an isolated road in the Mudzi area. A single Bedford arrived with escort, turned around and waited for us to climb aboard with its motor idling.

As we embussed, an escort passed each of us a bottled cool drink from a wooden crate which had been placed on the back of the truck. These were greatly appreciated. The effervescent contents were quickly drained and the empties returned to the crate. Prinnie was being childish and loud as usual, but we all ignored him for the most part.

We were all pretty switched off as our national service was nearly at an end with only a couple of weeks left before a much dreamed of demobilization. The driver pulled the nose of the vehicle around through a shallow curve in the road. There was a long puddle of rainwater in the right furrow and he drove straight through it.

An astute communist terrorist had cunningly inserted a Russian TM-46 antitank landmine into this puddle. Prinnie was sitting directly above the right rear wheel which made contact with the firing mechanism. I love big bangs but this one was just a bit much. The concussion crashed through my ears with a noiseless deafening. It felt as though I was being forcefully squeezed by some giant hand as violent air rushed about me. We were all punched up into the air and then dropped down onto the conveyor belting above the vehicle's sandbagged floor amid the clutter of tumbling backpacks and hard firearms. I lay there, disoriented and unable to hear for a moment. Then I struggled to my hands and knees, all the while shaking my head, trying to grasp what had happened. Smoke and water vapour swirled all around me, hampering my vision, and the air was filled with the nasty smell of charred rubber. I was aware of a mad scramble while my mates all recovered weapons and jumped off the vehicle as we had been trained to do.

Then some dizzy hearing returned and I heard a strange wailing sound. After recovering my Bren gun, I looked around and saw Corporal Prinnie lying over the flattened cool drink crate. His buttocks were immersed in broken glass and splintered wood and he lay quite still, leaning back on his elbows. By now every troopie had debussed and was taking cover in the bush surrounding the damaged vehicle. I took one long hard look at Prinnie, who was still emitting exotic noises, and considered what I could do to help him. The thought that the landmine would have initiated an ambush was now very real in my mind and, boy, was I immediately switched on. The terror of being shot while silhouetted for any enemy to see was very real and I did not like Prinnie very much anyway. Launching my Bren over the side of the Bedford, I vaulted the rail followed by an accusing cry. This all happened in less than five seconds but seemed to last an eternity.

My Bren was pegged into the soft ground by the barrel and I extracted it before running for cover in some nearby brush. This sprint was made in agonizing fear of someone having planted an antipersonnel mine just where I was about to stand. There were no other explosions or shots and my fear abated. The relief of being alive and well sparked some jokes and frivolous banter. This was especially so because our faces and bodies were all black with soot and mud. It was also fortunate that I had not had to fire my gun as the barrel had been blocked by a core of compressed sand. Firing the weapon would have caused the barrel to burst. This could have injured me and would surely have prompted great embarrassment as I would have been mocked by my comrades for being a wanker. My stick was sent to do a quick clearance patrol and when we returned, Prinnie had gone.

Prinnie had been casevaced by vehicle to the field hospital in Mtoko and then on to Andrew Fleming in Salisbury. I never saw Prinnie again as we demobbed on completion of our national service a few weeks later.

Payback may not always be planned and intentional but it usually happens if you do not treat your fellow man well. My disdain of Prinnie's plight while injured was payback for his hypocrisy during the year I'd had to spend with him.

Two years later, I rolled my Ford Anglia. There was a case of beer in the back of the car for the weekend, my mate. The doctor on duty the next day extracted quantities of broken beer bottles from my back and buttocks.

Payback is no respecter of persons, so it seems!

Marathon madness

Some bright spark suggested that the soldiers of 1 Independent Company run an inter-platoon relay race from Wankie to Victoria Falls. This would create excellent publicity for the Rhodesia Regiment and be a good send off for our demobilization.

Whoever comes up with brilliant ideas like these needs to be discouraged by firing squad!

So we ran. Victoria Falls lay 100 kilometres south-east of Wankie and three teams comprised of members from each platoon had to run a total of seven kilometres each.

I was wearing a pair of civilian shoes made of rough hide. We called them veldskoens, a bastardization of the Afrikaans word *veldskoene*, roughly translating as bush shoes. My socks were all ruined so I ran without any. I had lost all feeling in my big toes by the end of my stint.

The CSM drove by in his Land Rover while I was busy running my last kilometre. He shouted words of encouragement until he saw my veldskoens and then rebuked me, using a string of extremely foul words.

At the time, only officers were allowed to wear veldskoens as part of their uniform. He ended off by saying that he still could, and would, send me to the box even though I had almost completed my national service. These were the last words he ever said to me and I haven't missed his one track brain cell since then.

When the relay race was over, I removed my veldskoens with a sigh of relief. My two big toenails were a terrible red colour. A week later they turned coal black. I marvelled at this and knew that they would fall off in due course as it had happened to me once before at school.

This they did, and I pinned them onto the notice board at work where they hung for a few weeks until my mother noticed them. She unpinned my trophies with a snort of disgust and sent them flying into the waste paper basket.

So there, mum.

That's payback for sending your little boy off to the army with such a cumbersome suitcase!

Chapter 4
Bulawayo Technical College

On completion of my national service I signed a contract of apprenticeship with my father. I was immediately enrolled at the Bulawayo Technical College where I studied my trade for a year. I recall a few interesting incidents.

A rose bed ploughed

One Friday evening I was socializing with my classmates Des Viljoen, Ken Shed and Attie Pieterse. We gathered at Grey's Inn and guzzled a number of beers. Later that evening we decided to shower in preparation to visit a discotheque. Ken lifted us to the hostel, weaving his small car all over the road amid a din of music and laughter. He was driving recklessly and missed the student driveway, having misinterpreted my instruction. Instead, he overshot and turned into the housemaster's driveway.

I shouted at him to about-turn but he swerved and drove through the beautiful rose garden growing in front of the housemaster's patio. Mud and rose petals sprayed up into the air as the vehicle slewed through the manicured flowerbeds. I caught a fleeting glimpse of Mr Roberts and his wife who were enjoying a cup of tea on their patio. They gawked open mouthed, daintily grasping raised porcelain with extended pinkies, as the revving car careered past.

The vehicle veered drunkenly, crashed through a light barrier, and skidded into the student parking area, its windscreen flecked with mud and plant matter. I craned my neck and looked out of the car's rear window. By the feeble light of the luminaire mounted above the hostel's entrance, I saw Mr Roberts' bony knees pumping up and down under a pair of baggy khaki shorts as he ran towards the now silent car, screaming at all of us to get out. I obediently threw my door open to exit the vehicle. I was sitting behind the driver and Mr Roberts was running up to open the driver's door. He crashed hard into my opening door, fell cursing onto the gravel chips that lined the driveway, and turned his malevolent attention from the driver to me. I blundered out of the car and muttered an apology and some words about bearing full responsibility for what had happened. This was because I had been guiding Ken and felt as though I was accountable for the incident in some way.

Mr Roberts was furious and shouted at me with his face an inch away from mine. I felt his spit flecking my cheeks like a stinky blast from a claymore mine charged with sweet tea. I closed my eyes and stopped breathing until his tirade was over. He threatened me with expulsion and, ignoring the other occupants of the car, turned on his heel and angrily marched back through his destroyed garden. I imagined a dark thundercloud floating above his dismal head.

I was expelled from the hostel the following Monday. I didn't know why I had been singled out for punishment. Possibly because I had opened the car door as Mr Roberts charged past.

I dragged myself over to the hostel and packed my gear into my old army pack which I threw over my shoulder. Then I trudged through town to where Kevin was staying at the Toc H. They had a room available. I booked in and lived there until my college days were over.

I have often wondered where I had previously transgressed to warrant payback by expulsion.

Mrs Havanar's chickens

A weekend home in Fort Victoria found us at Kevin's home late one Saturday night. I was quite fond of his mother and Uncle Eric, who was Kevin's stepfather. With both parents in bed, we wound up the stereo and danced to music. I became tired of the noise and knocked on the main bedroom door. I entered without waiting for permission and found Mr and Mrs Havanar sitting upright against the headboard.

They may have been praying for us to leave.

I instructed Mrs Havanar to move over, kicked off my shoes, and slid into bed next to her. There we three sat quietly until I asked what we were talking about. Uncle Eric was a little concerned that I might be trying to feel up his missus and kept checking to see whether I was behaving. Mrs Havanar and I chatted for a long time about things I cannot remember. She did mention having prepared food for a church function in the morning and hoped we would not eat all her snacks.

Later on in the evening, Kevin popped his head around the door which I had left ajar. By this time, Uncle Eric had turned over and was trying to sleep under the duvet. Kevin realized that I was alone in bed with his old duck and wanted to thump me. Phillip and Mogg the Dogg listened as I tried to reason with Kevin.

"She's my old lady!"

"I'm not trying to shag her," I protested.

The Dogg and Phillip bawled with laughter in the passage.

Uncle Eric sat up and straightened things out with Kevin. I climbed out of the bed and pulled on my shoes, all the while thanking Mrs Havanar for such a stimulating evening. I saw relief on Uncle Eric's face as I left. The door was closed behind me and I heard the key turning in the lock.

Kevin switched the kitchen light on and opened the fridge. His hungry eyes glowed as he saw six roast chickens waiting to be devoured. I protested, but the lads each ripped a chicken apart and started stuffing their mouths.

"Don't worry, Toc," mumbled Kevin through chock-a-block cheeks, "my mom will make more in the morning!"

Such simple reasoning is life!

The Exorcist

Des and I went to the cinema to see *The Exorcist* one evening. I sat horrified at the young Linda Blair's antics as she turned her head through circles and vomited on terrified priests. We parted on the pavement in front of the cinema. Des stalked off towards the college hostel, and I walked through the deserted city towards the Toc H.

Light from yellowed streetlights diffused through trembling branches, casting quivering shadows on pavements and walls. My pace quickened and I turned my neck constantly (just as Linda Blair had) to see what evil was creeping up behind me. Sounds I had never heard before afflicted my ears and I started to run. The sound of shoes clapping hard on asphalt followed me and I ran as though there were demons on my heels. I could have sworn there were. Puffing up to the front entrance which was subtly lit by the dim Toc H lamp, I wearily climbed the stairs to my room.

I collapsed on my bed and closed my eyes. Feeling safe and a little stupid about my irrational fear, I remembered a similarly terrifying experience from when I was at school. I was camping out at the Great Zimbabwe Ruins with some friends one weekend and we had run out of cigarettes. Mike Armstrong and his two younger brothers and I decided to walk to the hotel to purchase a pack. The dirt road wound up alongside the silent golf course and the rising moon silhouetted the acropolis. Some dogs were howling from a nearby kraal.

Spooky!

Mike was carrying the only torch and we were all joshing and pretending that there were ghosts or wild beasts creeping up on us.

"What's that," I shouted to scare the others.

My hand passed through the beam of Mike's torch as I pointed forward. I saw its shadow on the road surface in front of me and sheer terror thudded in my chest.

"It's a hand!" I screamed and clutched at Mike's shoulders.

Mike moaned with horror and pirouetted back and forth with me hanging onto his shoulders. Petrified, he shone the torch all around trying to pinpoint the source of my dread.

"Get off me, you stupid bastard, get off!" he struggled and swore.

All the while he was trying to manoeuvre me in front of him so that I would be the first to be taken by the ugly thing.

His two brothers had long since disappeared. They had run back down the road, all the while wailing curses at me.

When I realized that the shadow had been my own, I let go of Mike's back, shaking. I laughed to try and make it seem as though I had tricked them all deliberately, but my tremulous voice belied my arrogance. Mike called me a halfwit and told me to stop fooling around. I realized then, that he had been as scared as I was. His torch beam continued to flit all around us as he searched for any sign of evil, all the while complaining to me in a quaking voice.

Deciding that the night was far too dangerous, we turned back to our camp and craved nicotine until morning.

So I lay on my bed and started giggling about these crazy things.

Hell's Angels

With my spell at college complete I was due to report to the drill hall at

Gwelo within the week and I decided to spend the weekend in Bulawayo for one last thrash before submitting to the military machine again. Kevin had just moved into a large two-bedroom apartment on Main Street and I moved in for a few days.

On the Friday afternoon we went to see *Jaws* which had just started showing at cinemas nationwide. Afterwards, we paid a visit to Greys Inn to quench our thirsty tongues. After we had poured a number of beers down our gullets, we started discussing a scene from the movie in which Quint crushes an empty beer can in his fist. We were both very impressed by this show of strength.

At the time there were no cans on the market in Rhodesia, just bottles. When Kevin had drained his umpteenth beer, he crushed his glass in his fist without cutting his hand. I was so impressed that I emptied my glass and attempted to crush it like Kevin had done. The glass resisted my puny strength and those gathered around the table sniggered at me. Undeterred, I circled the glass with both hands and squeezed. Once again, the glass resisted and our companions chuckled more loudly. Frustrated, I picked the glass up in my left hand and smashed it on the table top. Glass flew everywhere and the base stabbed a deep cut into the ball of my hand. I swore and pressed the wound onto the denim covering my thigh to stem the flow of blood. A dirty handkerchief was procured from the laughing crowd and I used this as a bandage.

Kevin was now fired up by his success and challenged me to a game of chicken, in which two people push their forearms together across a table. A glowing cigarette is placed where the two arms meet and the person who pulls away first is declared the chicken.

When I refused to participate, he crushed his cigarette out on my forearm.

I could not believe that he had done this and instead of immediately flicking the glowing coals off my skin, I just sat staring at the smouldering mass with my mouth open. A strange keening noise whistled through my nose. When I swept the ash away, the skin came off my arm. A tang similar to the smell of burning bush pigs pervaded my nose. (This I had smelled before while passing by natives who were burning the hair off a slaughtered pig before butchering it.)

On Saturday morning I woke up and examined my injuries. There was a thin red line running under my skin from the cut on my hand up to my elbow. My arm throbbed incessantly and a scab had started growing over the cigarette burn.

Someone really inconsiderate was working with a jack hammer close by.

I scrounged a crepe bandage from Kevin's rudimentary first aid kit and bandaged my inflamed hand.

An aspirin slowly calmed the jack hammer down.

On Saturday afternoon we bumped into a group of Hell's Angels who had motored up from Johannesburg the day before. They seemed to accept our company, most probably because we were as wild and inebriated as they were.

Of the six men, one was a lawyer, another was a doctor of medicine, and the rest were engineers and accountants. These were well educated men who lived for some excitement over weekends. One of the men, Fuzzy, had struck up a friendship with a pretty local lass who seemed to enjoy partying.

"I pick up a new bitch in every town," he said, leering.

We drank beer at Greys Inn. Later that evening when we were properly tanked up, the group decided to visit Talk of the Town. This was a popular discotheque frequented by many young people from Bulawayo, and fondly referred to as Talkies. Each Hell's Angel rode his own motorcycle or 'boney,' as the gang referred to them.

The girl sat on Fuzzy's pillion and I jumped onto Johnny's bike. Kevin hitched a ride with one of the others. These madmen revved up their engines and we roared off down Grey Street. No attention was paid to any traffic lights as they raced their machines. It was totally exhilarating. We swooped down into all the drainage dips in the street and ramped up into the air as we crested each rise. One of the gang loosed a series of shots from his .44 Magnum. What a gas!

As we entered Talkies, the bouncers stressed that they did not want any trouble and the Hell's Angels just told them 'not to look for any then'. We left the discotheque at midnight and flew back down Grey Street, taking a detour past Downing's to buy some bread and pies which we devoured on the pavement.

The next stop was Kevin's apartment.

We were all sitting around the dining table chatting when Fuzzy disappeared into Kevin's bedroom with his bitch. I sat a little red faced and tried to ignore the muffled squeals. Fuzzy sauntered out of the room and another Hell's Angel stood up and walked in, unbuckling his belt as he went. The Hell's Angels all grinned at each other.

Kevin and I were offered turns with the girl but we both refused because neither of us relished the idea of being with a girl so soon after she had been sullied by another.

When the Hell's Angels were satisfied she freshened up in the bathroom, joined us around the table and merged into the conversation as though what had happened was an everyday event, but she avoided eye contact with me.

Replete, the gang decided to go to Club Vegas for some hell-raising. I didn't tag along pleading total disinterest as I was now in a lot of pain from the infection in my left arm. The Hell's Angels all left on their boneys and Kevin went into his bedroom to clean up. I laughed at his efforts to remove the soiled sheets. The next day he implied that the sheets would have dried stiff as cardboard and been irremovably glued to the mattress had he left them on the bed that night.

Suddenly I do not feel well anymore!

Kevin drove me to the outpatients because my arm was now too painful to move. A student doctor examined the cut on my hand and stated that it should have been stitched closed but it was too late for that now. I hollered in pain as he inserted a pair of tweezers into the protesting gash and pulled out a chip of glass. Then he anointed the wound, applied a fresh bandage, and attended to the burn on my forearm, after which, he administered a tetanus injection and prescribed antibiotics.

"Bloody *mampara*," he called me.

Later that day we heard that the Hell's Angels had driven out to Matopos Hills and one of them had been killed when he crashed his motorcycle.

When I met up with Kevin at the end of that year, he told me that the young lady who had so willingly entertained the Hell's Angels on his bed had suffered some kind of breakdown. We surmised that this may have been related to her evening of debauchery. She spent a while recovering in the local mental hospital, Ingutsheni.

What if she had fallen pregnant I wondered? She might have had twins or triplets. Maybe I would even have read an article about her as a mother of sextuplets in *Scope* magazine. I wondered if, when the kids grew up, one would have been a lawyer, another a doctor and the others engineers and accountants?

Chapter 5
Kotwa: continuous call-up

A waste of bullets

This was my first patrol with Charlie Company, Tenth Battalion, Rhodesia Regiment. I had been off duty for a year and was really not sure how it would turn out. My stick comprised of a recently promoted lance-corporal, his brother in law, and a rifleman. No machine gun! Retraining was not on the menu for this camp which was not normal as we usually spent three or four days at a battle camp.

Weapons were zeroed at our small range on Kotwa base and then we were ready for patrol. I enjoyed the firing immensely but realize today that it was insufficient for my needs. We were inadequately prepared for patrol. In my ignorance, I conformed to what I had experienced during national service. Thus I was armed, in total, with one white phosphorous grenade, a rifle, and 100 rounds of ammunition.

We patrolled uneventfully and on the second day, as the sun was beginning to slide slowly out of the sky, our lance-corporal was considering where to lie up until dark.

Walking in single file along the western side of a river behind my stick leader, I saw him suddenly turn and wave his right hand in a very excited manner. He then pointed urgently, first at his rifle and then at the other side of the river bed. Both riverbanks were lined with dense reeds so I could not see what he was excited about, but assumed that he had sighted an enemy. His unconventional sign language also didn't amuse me. Enemy presence was normally indicated with a thumb pointing down.

There was great indecision in our stick and we took cover next to the reeds while the two brothers in law, one of whom was second in command of the stick, conversed. Talk about nepotism. I was getting a little vexed as I expected us to at least attempt an attack, and suggested that we advance in the same direction as the gooks and cut them off.

The enemy was advancing parallel to our direction on the eastern riverbank. Not wanting to cross the dry riverbank and expose ourselves to a hidden assembly of unknown numbers, we cautiously continued forward in single file.

The reeds opened to reveal a low *kopjie* immediately in front of us. My two leaders ran to the left of this rock and I have no idea where the third rifleman disappeared to. I advanced up a gulley in the centre of the *kopjie* until I reached the ridge at the top and peered over. The granite on the other side of the ridge dropped sheer to the river bed.

There I spied one communist terrorist with a large pack on his back, toting an AK-47. He was running through the long shadows on the other side of the river bed, weaving as he ran, and was about to disappear into the foliage on the riverbank. My rifle pointed over the ridge, which was just above chest height. I stood on my toes, hastily aimed at the fleeting dodger, and loosed off a series of fast single shots. He fell, rolled, and continued his dash for cover, melting into the blurry flora.

I felt exhilarated for I was sure that my first round had found its mark and the man now lay bleeding to death. I emptied the magazine into the bush where he had disappeared. Tracer bullets streaked through the darkening undergrowth at great speed and I ducked down below the ridge to reload.

I was aware of numerous rounds snapping overhead as I peered over the ridge again, and fired into the reeds on the opposite bank. Hopefully I would score some hits on anyone hiding there. Then I realized that the sound of gunfire was getting much more forceful and that the air around my head was alive with violent movement.

Bullets were cracking loudly past my head in quick succession and I could feel the air buffeting my cheeks and ears. Some shithead was firing at me and I had no idea where he was. My head and shoulders must have made a beautiful silhouette against the glowing sunset that afternoon.

I threw myself down behind the granite ridge, replaced the empty magazine, and then hastily doubled over to the edge of the ridge on my right to take a better firing position. I emptied the magazine in the direction I thought the fire was coming from. The noise died down and an eerie quiet descended on the river. I waited for a short minute and then, realizing that the gooks had all absconded, backtracked to join up with my stick.

They were all huddled together on the opposite base of the *kopjie* and asked me what the hell was going on. It seemed I'd had a contact with the enemy on my own, with zero support from my mates.

The evening was now closing in on our world and we backtracked to a small thicket and radioed base. Major Clive Currin, our commanding officer, informed us that trackers would arrive at our location at first light and that we were to commence follow-up action on their arrival. We bomb-shelled close by to wait the night out, each facing outwards in a defensive position.

A distant crackling sound, not unlike gunfire, fell on our ears. The sound gradually grew louder and the strong smell of burning vegetation drifted downwind towards us. A red glow from the direction of our contact zone rapidly fuelled a staggering sunset of its own. An eerie glow cast flickering light through the rocks and trees and strange shadows darted before our eyes. Fire; and heading in our direction too!

This must have been started by the tracer rounds I had discharged into the bush. The vegetation was dry and thick and the flames seethed down on us even though the wind was not blowing hard. Fortunately our kit was still packed, and following our gallant leader, we gapped it for the dry river bed to escape the heat.

The opposite bank was also ablaze, probably also ignited by my tracer. The brightness of the fire afforded us clear vision for a quick escape but we also knew that if any enemy were present, we would surely draw some fire.

No one shot at us that evening as we crouched on the sandy river bed. When the flames had passed, we searched for shelter among some rocks close to the river.

The freezing winter air soon cooled us down. We didn't use sleeping bags in case we had to make another fast move that night, so it was a cold and restless night. This was exacerbated by the sound of burning trees and dead logs cracking and popping off all around our position, and sounding just like gunshots.

As I drifted off to sleep, I realized that I only had 40 rounds available. This was definitely not enough ammunition to endure another contact. I vowed to make sure that I was carrying at least 150 rounds in future. I also determined never to fire indiscriminately. Choose likely cover and fire calculated shots, I affirmed.

At first light, we walked to the nearest native village which was a motley collection of thatched roofs located close to the contact area.

The sound of vehicles grew closer as we arrived at this complex. A stick of trackers debussed from the vehicles and our stick leader guided them in by radio. The villagers all stood outside their huts, solemnly waiting for the inevitable questioning.

My civvie street mate, Voc, was the leader of the tracker team. After asking what had transpired, he instructed us to remain at the village while the trackers determined the line of flight. They returned a while later, stating that they had seen the tracks of four men heading in the direction of the village we were now standing in.

There were no tracks leaving the small village complex as the area had been disturbed by the hooves of many cattle, herded away from the village towards Mozambique. The terrorists had fled the area and ordered the villagers to cover their tracks.

While being interrogated one of the male villagers voided in his trousers. He urinated first and then came the unpleasant smell of well digested *sadza* and gravy. He apologized profusely for all the disgrace his incontinence had caused and no, he was sorry but had seen no soldiers, heard no shooting yesterday evening, and had no idea how the cattle had mysteriously left the village the night before. We left him bruised and humiliated, and I am sure, a little more disinclined to support Ian Smith's 'illegal white regime'. The police special branch arrived and assured us that the man would sing soft sweet songs to them within an hour. I shuddered to think what methods they would use to coax information out him.

And where were the kills, and why were there no blood trails to follow, Voc had asked. He was told to ask me as I had done all the shooting. When he realized that I had missed an open target he jeered at me, called me a wanker, and suggested that I apply for a kitchen post as I would surely be able to cook better than I could shoot.

Thus ended an unsuccessful first continuous service patrol for yours truly. I should have been some kind of hero. Now I was just a shit shot.

Shame!

"A waste of bullets," Voc had said.

Assault on the flintstone vehicle

I complained to Voc about the worrying leadership on the previous patrol. The stick was broken up and I found myself slotted into Sergeant Les Krause's stick for the next patrol. He was the oldest person in our platoon, possibly in his mid-thirties, and his confidence put me at ease, both in the bush and at base camp.

Voc was not required to track after my first patrol. He joined our stick and we were buddies for the duration of the call-up. Patrolling was easy under Les' command. We patrolled with caution and spent many hours observing from high ground. Sensible soldiering Les called it. I agreed with him!

Nights were stressful as Voc snored hard and loud. I always had to wake him several times and insist that he turn over. This helped little because as soon as he fell into a deep sleep, he would start snoring again, regardless of how his body was positioned.

We were all in a jovial mood as we returned to our base camp in the rear of our troop carrier one afternoon. Voc and I sat together at the tailgate of one of the vehicles. The Grundy climbed into the cab via the turret situated in the cab roof and joined Morgie the Raider, who was driving.

Fooling around with my rifle, I removed the magazine, cocked the rifle, and pulled the trigger.

Click.

Replacing the magazine again, I went through some comic sequence which had some of the guys amused and others looking on, waiting for the inevitable.

Our vehicles rolled on and we passed one of many locally manufactured carts which we called flintstone vehicles. These were made of logs and sticks, held together by fencing wire and cow hide, and they had carved wooden wheels which revolved around wooden axles. This particular contraption was being pulled by a donkey and driven by an elderly African man who looked straight ahead and acknowledged us with a half-wave. I suppose he did not want to draw attention by making any sort of eye contact.

As our vehicle passed him by, I squeezed the trigger of my rifle as I was still playing my silly game. I had outdone myself this time as there was a round chambered. The rifle discharged and the round kicked up dust between the cart and the donkey before ricocheting through the dense bush. The donkey danced a little skit and the geriatric native jumped and then regained his composure. They both continued to plod along as though this was a normal, every day event.

I guess the man was terrified of the army, but could not have run away without risking being shot at. And then we shot at him anyway. He probably thought we were trying to force him to run so that we could shoot him legally. It must have been a really terrifying moment for the old codger.

My spent cartridge case ejected as designed and bounced off the vehicle roll bar into the shorts of one of the men. He thought he had been shot and screamed with fright as the hot brass burned his thigh. His shriek was rather girlish and it greatly amused the other men to watch him cursing and wriggling in an attempt remove the offending object while strapped down to the seat by his restraining harness. We all laughed loudly.

Almost immediately, the covers on the turret exploded upwards on their hinges. A rheumy eyed Grundy thrust his head out and a cloud of pungent smoke billowed out of the cab. The smoke pluming around his neck made him look like some medieval fire-breathing creature. This added to the humour and the men doubled up with laughter.

"What are you shooting at?" he shouted, his eyes shiny and bloodshot from the effects of recently smoked cannabis.

The Grundy was obviously stressed by the shot. Possibly he thought that we had been attacked. He was also confused by all the laughter. When Voc told him what had happened, he developed a major case of the giggles and disappeared back into the cab. Then we heard Morgie the Raider screaming with laughter and they continued so until we arrived back at camp.

The Raider and the Grundy were puffing on a sly one that day, they were.

Les Krause just shook his head in amazement and grinned at the comedy of it all. I am glad that he was the senior NCO present or I would have spent time in the box.

Rifleman Steven Byrne

When we returned from our patrol we heard that a single discharge had killed one of 7 Platoon's men and injured his commander. This was indeed bad news but when I heard that it was Steven Byrne that had been killed, it shocked me as we had done our national service together at Wankie.

The new company clerk had not seen active service before and had somehow fed a round into the chamber while cleaning his rifle. The round discharged and flew some hundred metres through the area where 7 Platoon was bivouacking.

Steven Byrne had been sitting in his bivouac. The round entered his back and exited just below the heart. The bullet continued its trajectory and smashed through Sergeant-Major Hodnot's thigh. Gary Pheasant, assisted by our signaller, Digger, bandaged Steve's wounds and the medic attended to Hodnot's injury. An aircraft was dispatched to evacuate the two injured men but Steve died in transit.

Steven and I had enjoyed some good times together and I thought it a needless waste. He was a bright and amiable young man.

Kotwa mortared

Kotwa base camp lay sleeping peacefully with the guard patrolling when the muted thump of a mortar firing a bomb sounded some distance from the camp. The guard yelled for stand to and ran for the closest trench. The mortar bomb arced overhead and exploded some distance from the perimeter. More bombs were fired but they exploded ineffectively outside our camp's perimeter.

8 Platoon was in camp for our day off. Every soldier exited his sleeping bag like a marathon runner off the starting blocks and raced for the safety of the trenches.

Voc ran for the mortar pit situated in the centre of our camp. He lobbed two shells in the direction from which the enemy was firing. His first bomb fell within a few metres of the terrorist mortar position, causing them to abandon their equipment and flee.

Small arms fire zinged through the trees overhead and every man in a trench on the perimeter under attack returned fire. The terrorists continued firing until Voc's second bomb fell close to their position. Then they also fled the scene.

Shorty, the African batman, was the first to enter his trench. He jumped in and lay curled in the bottom of the hole followed by five soldiers who threw themselves into the excavation with no concern for anyone who might have entered before them. Shorty was thus flattened by five pairs of big smelly feet.

The Grundy was the owner of one of those pairs of feet. He had seen Shorty enter the trench, and as he jumped in, he threw his webbing at Shorty and instructed him to remove a magazine and be ready to hand it to him. The Grundy fired his 20 rounds and shouted for the replacement. Shorty thrust it into his lowered hand. The Grundy reloaded and continued firing. Shorty passed magazines to the Grundy and another soldier in this manner two more times. When the attack was over, we stayed in the trenches until our commanding officer had decided that it was safe to return his camp to normal.

Thus was Shorty the batman introduced to the rigors of combat?

Les Krause injured

The following call-up, I was attached to a new platoon commander, Warrant Officer Gary Pheasant. We called him the Pheasant Plucker...hey c'mon, use your imagination. It's wordplay! Gary was an old family friend and I felt very comfortable under his command as he was a reliable, courageous and trustworthy leader. He had already proved himself competent as a platoon sergeant during our national service.

Les was transferred to 7 Platoon and injured in a contact with terrorists. He had halted his stick for a short rest and an insurgent had fired a rocket at the resting men. The projectile had struck Jigger van Wyk's pack and exploded, destroying the pack and severely injuring Les' arm. He was casevaced and I did not see him again.

An old man on a bicycle

8 Platoon was at base camp enjoying our one day rest. That afternoon while preparing for patrol, we heard a distant bang followed by the popping of gunfire. Increased activity thus ensued in the vicinity of the operations tent. Realizing that we were the troops most likely to be used for reaction, Gary ordered us to complete our patrol preparation and then disappeared into the

ops tent. Sure enough, he ordered us onto the vehicles when he returned.

7 Platoon had been returning to base for their rest day when one of the vehicles hit a landmine. The firing we had heard was the platoon's reaction to the land mine. It had become standard practice to fire into likely ambush positions in the event of a landmine explosion. We were to conduct sweeps and determine whether there were any fresh tracks to follow.

We saw a helicopter taking off as we arrived on the scene. The crew had deployed an engineer to check the area for any more mines, and two medics from the RAR who were attending to an injured local in an adjacent field. He had been shot by one of our men.

7 Platoon were all gathered around their vehicles and the engineer was now busy clearing the road. We debussed and performed a thorough sweep but found no tracks. Rain from the night before had washed all the evidence away.

The medics were still busy in the field when the engineer declared the area free of mines. Rifleman de Wit was the centre of attention as we approached the place where 7 Platoon had congregated. He was boasting about his well-aimed shot. De Wit had debussed and seen the figure of a man riding towards them on a bicycle 200 odd metres away. He had aimed and fired a round through the centre of the man's chest. It was a good shot considering that he must have been shaken by the explosion and that his target was moving and bouncing over a bumpy pathway. I thought it strange that the man had carried on riding his bicycle towards the vehicles after such a loud explosion.

Kudu Naude (so called because of his large front-facing ears) and I strolled over to where the African medics were still attending to the injured man. We moved up behind the medics quietly and they were not immediately aware of our presence. I observed one of them struggling to change an empty drip. The other had his arm under his patient's head and was speaking as though to comfort the dying man, who was lying on his back. We could see that he was very old.

He was possibly hard of hearing which may have accounted for his strange behaviour in continuing to cycle after the explosion. His chest was swathed in crimson bandages and there was fresh blood congealing on his lips and in the cracks and wrinkles of his cheeks.

He was softly calling, "*Mambo, Mambo,*" which is a polite Shona word used to address important superiors.

He must have been calling to God for help.

We asked the medics if they needed any help. One of them became tight lipped and the other turned fiercely and asked what more damage we wanted to do.

"Do you want to shoot me as well?" he enquired vehemently.

His bitter words expressed his frustration at this unnecessary shooting. He told us to leave and we did.

When Kudu and I returned, we were ordered to guard the damaged vehicle until the wrecker arrived from Mtoko. The others all left for base and we took cover in the bush. I saw the medics in the field stand up together. One of them threw something down onto the ground. It was a gesture of anger and frustration that told me the old man had died. They packed their gear and walked down the road away from us to await their transport. Not once did they look in our direction. The old man was left in the field for his relatives to attend to. Why the helicopter had not uplifted him to hospital was a mystery to me.

I felt strangely ashamed to be associated with this murder. The memory of the old man's helpless words still stirs strange emotions in me to this day.

The seagulls visit Kotwa

Voc and I had just showered after a harsh patrol and we were relaxing around our trench, waiting for the canteen to open. We were despondent because we had worked strenuously for very little reward by way of contact with terrorists. Voc, rather pointedly, said to me that he was going to smoke a joint with Morgie the Raider that night.

So now what?

I enjoyed a good party but on principle I had not partaken of any drugs. Going against my ethics was going to be an issue of mind over matter. I did not matter and nobody minded me too much, therefore I did not mind and their opinion did not matter anyway. Decision made, I told Voc that I wanted to join him and he replied that I was in.

We ambled off to the canteen to enjoy a beer and wait for nightfall before meeting at the appointed spot. Evening dragged into a moonless night with the Milky Way glowing brightly above us. Voc and I met with Morgie and some others in the centre of the base camp area where we sat in a close circle facing each other. A half-moon had now slunk up over the horizon and was sluggishly pulling itself up into the sky. Amongst some idle chitchat, Morgie produced a cigarette shaped object and placed it between his liverish lips. A match flared briefly in his cupped hands and he inhaled smoke into his lungs.

Ahhhh!

He breathed out slowly, took another long drag and passed the joint.

The joint reached Voc and he sucked on it a few times before passing it on to me. I placed the soggy item between my thumb and forefinger, pursed my lips over this assembly and drew in just like the others had done. My lungs shrieked. I coughed hard and the joint flew out of my grip and onto the sand.

Was I ever popular!

I hastily retrieved the joint amid contemptuous ridicule and pulled on it again. There was more strained coughing but I managed to retain hold of the *zol* and hold the smoke in my lungs before exhaling noisily. I passed the joint on to the man next to me who puffed away gratefully. Serenity returned to the group and my sin was forgotten for the time being. We sat and listened to the quiet evening and my mind drifted...

Voc's voice penetrated my murky brain.

"Hey, Toc, where are you?"

I looked at him dumbly.

He chuckled and passed me another joint. A series of voices warned me not to screw it up again and I puffed on the joint a few times, a much wiser young man. I passed it on with some comment like, 'cool man, good stuff *ek sê*,' as though I had been doing it for years.

This made everyone laugh and I gazed at them dumfounded before I saw the humour and began to laugh myself. It was a strange laugh which welled up from deep within. It sounded hoarse and it was uncontrollable and certainly did not belong to me. I laughed like a child, until my sides ached but I still could not stop.

This was great fun until the Pheasant Plucker strolled over to see what was so amusing. A dig in the ribs from Voc brought my laughter up short.

"What have you been drinking?" Gary asked me.

I tried to say 'nothing,' but my tongue did not work properly and some alien language garbled out of my lips. This became worse when I tried to correct myself. The circle of men roared with laughter again and my boss chuckled with them.

"Keep an eye on him," he ordered Voc.

When all the joints had been smoked and everyone in the circle had relaxed, we just sat there and buzzed. Morgie reclined with his elbow on his combat cap and his legs stretched out in front of him. He said that he was now waiting for the seagulls to come.

Between some suppressed mirth and silly giggling I said, "What seagulls?" and was told to shut up and wait. I was vacillating indecisively about whether to shut up or not, so I just sat there trying to be sensible. This was just impossible as my thoughts were changing frequently under the influence of the drug. My mind wandered again and then I heard the sound of *kivikies* high up in the atmosphere. *Kiewiet* is the Afrikaans name for a plover and in Rhodesia, we referred to them as *kivikies*. One species flies around at night making a noise that sounds like '*kiep kiep*'.

"Ah," exclaimed the Raider, "my seagulls have arrived."

We all lay back in awe and marvelled. Voc said that we should keep our mouths closed or we might taste bird shit. For the second time that night inspired laughter pealed out over our campsite. I vaguely wondered whether we would all be charged with disorderly conduct in the morning. This added strange fuel to my mirth and once again my sides ached with a great and pleasurable pain. When the group grew quiet I thought some more and said, "No Morgie, those aren't seagulls they're *kivikies*."

"No," he quipped, "they're seagulls. They've just flown from Beira to make me happy."

Beira was over 200 kilometres away! "No way," I tried to argue, but was simultaneously told to shut up by half the group. I sat and fretted a little and thought some.

'Seagulls,' I thought. 'Idiots!'

The laughter pounced on me again and I laughed and laughed and the circle of men laughed with me. Our sides ached terribly and our cheeks shed tears of merriment but we could not stop.

Eventually some of the men became hungry and meandered off to see what they could scrounge off the sleeping cook. Voc said that he was also hungry and giggling together, we ambled off with the Raider to our bivouac to raid our ration packs.

It be true then, the munchies will rule supreme.

Fireforce. A first and only time

On assembly at the drill hall in Gwelo, we were informed that 8 Platoon was going to do fireforce duty at Mtoko FAF 5 for the next six weeks. Now this seemed like good news. We liked the idea of spending every evening dry, warm, and comfortable at base camp after being choppered around to shoot at gooks. Our convoy arrived at Mtoko airfield the next afternoon. We were briefed regarding fireforce operating procedures and told to report to the airfield's apron by 05h00 every morning.

We were deployed many times during the next six weeks, only to discover that the enemy had fled the scene prior to our arrival or that there had not been any enemy present to have warranted a callout in the first place. We called these fruitless callouts, 'lemons'.

I was issued with a Bren gun which I carried for the next 18 months.

Flight Lieutenant Stevens

Flight Lieutenant Stevens flew to FAF 5 at Mtoko from New Sarum air base. After landing, he was promptly dispatched to assist an internal affairs call sign that was receiving mortar fire from across the Mozambican border.

At the same time, our fireforce team was returning to FAF 5 after having suffered a lemon. Stevens confirmed over the radio that he had the enemy mortar position in sight and was turning in to attack. While attacking the position, Stevens radioed to say that he was taking fire, and then to say that he had been hit and was going in. His radio transmission had then ended.

Our flight was redirected to a remote airfield at Fombe which was a landing strip about ten kilometres south of the Ruenya River, close to the Mozambican border. Here, we awaited orders. Some Hawker Hunters arrived overhead and fired into the valley to calm the jungle bunnies down while our helicopters left to assist in the search for the crash site.

We heard the sound of multiple 30mm cannons firing as our pilots retaliated to enemy aggression. A most awesome and thrilling sound it was with the screeching aircraft and rolling gunfire. We all hoped that the blue jobs would take more than a few out! Such was the aggression of these wonderful airmen who endeavoured, wherever possible, to destroy the enemy and assist infantry on the ground.

We were informed that the air force had identified the most probable crash site, but thick vegetation and high altitude made confirmation difficult. We were ordered to prepare for an operation to destroy the remains of the aircraft and recover the pilot's body. Later that afternoon, a Dakota landed with an RAR mortar team on board to provide backup if required. Also on board were two engineers who were assigned to our team.

Later in the afternoon we could still hear the shriek of Hawker Hunter jets as they endeavoured to validate the crash site. By this time, they had been given an order only to fire if fired upon. We overheard one pilot requesting to burn a very favourable target over the radio.

"Negative. Do not engage," responded the controller.

"I read you strength three. Confirm affirmative to engage, over," solicited the airman.

"Negative, do not engage, I repeat, do not engage," repeated the frantic controller. He was obviously scared of the reprisal that an international incident would elicit from his superiors.

The day started to die and all the aircraft left for their respective air bases.

We bivouacked in the bush adjacent to the airfield that night. Early the next morning, the Alouettes arrived to uplift us into enemy territory. Our stick was split up to accommodate the two army engineers who were to be responsible for destroying the aircraft wreckage. I ended up in the lead aircraft with Gary, the engineers, and the explosives they had to carry. The cool morning air blowing over us as the machines clattered and whined their way over the border allowed us to disguise shivers of apprehension about our first external operation, which had been devised hurriedly without much of a plan.

The pilot indicated that we were close to the drop-point and we prepared to deplane but the thick bush and rocky ground below prevented the helicopter from landing and we had to jump. This was a hard call considering the combined weight of our arms and kit. We had all drawn extra grenades and ammunition on account of the remote location of our objective. I was the first out followed by the engineer who had been sitting next to me. On the other side of the helicopter, Gary was followed by the second engineer. The reduced load made the helicopter lift higher off the ground each time a soldier jumped and the unfortunate engineer who jumped last had an extra few metres of height to overcome.

After we had all crashed and rolled into cover followed by troops from the other helicopters, we assessed and found all to be healthy bar some minor scrapes and bruises. The blues leader wished us well and left us to our fate. Gary organized his platoon and we advanced in single file through thick thorn bush and hilly country towards our objective, some 15 kilometres ahead.

I noticed that the engineer walking behind me was having some difficulty keeping up. I attributed this to the weight of the explosives he was carrying. It also gave me some comfort as I was unnerved by the possibility of his load detonating in the event of a contact. After a while he called me to halt. I informed my commander and dropped back to ask what was bothering him.

He said that his leg was broken. I was impressed at his fortitude for we had advanced some distance already, but I had to suppress my mirth as he lifted his trouser leg to reveal one splintered and cracked wooden prostheses.

Broke his leg, my foot!

We all took defensive positions while four men used their machetes to hack out a landing zone. Another engineer was choppered in. He loaded our casualty's pack onto his back and we advanced cautiously.

Ahead of us was the Matisi River, a tributary of the Ruenya River which flows from the Inyanga mountains in Rhodesia towards the Zambezi in Mozambique. A section of the Matisi River ran along the border where we were to cross over into Mozambique. The platoon formed a defensive position on the west bank of the river and we prepared to cross. Fortunately it was the dry season and the river was a trickle. Well, a trickle compared to full flood.

Alpha stick was the first to cross in pairs. Gary and I went first while

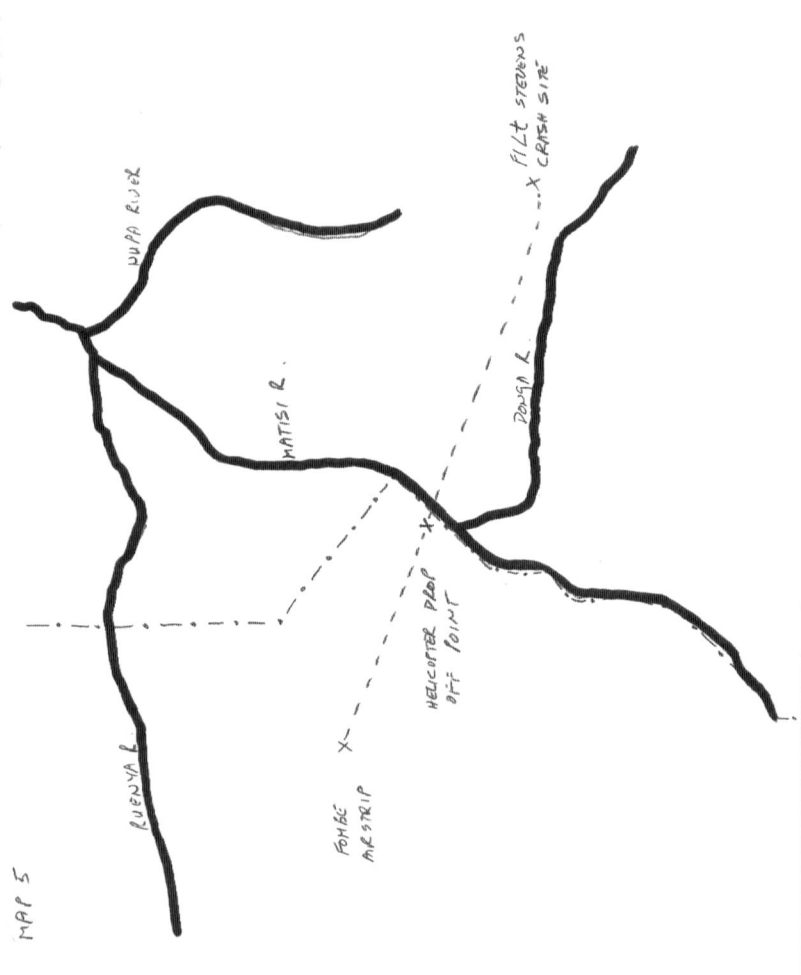

MAP 5

Blackie and Kudu covered our advance. This was one of the 'privileges' of being a member of the platoon commander's stick. I soon found myself up to my nose in strongly flowing water. My leader disappeared underwater with his rifle and webbing held over his head and I pressed on in good faith despite his madness. My skinny arms could only just hold the weight of the Bren gun above water level, so I wore my webbing as I did for normal marching orders.

I had used plastic bags to prevent rain from damaging my rations but these did not protect them from water pressure and my cigarettes and teabags suffered an unspeakable drowning. The water rose up over my head and I surged forward with my lungs full of air. Fortunately, I was heavily weighed down. Being swept off course would have resulted in some frantic shedding of equipment on my part. On and on I marched through the murky water, stumbling over slippery rocks, until my up-thrust nose broke the surface and I breathed for the first time in many years.

Just ahead of me, Gary was crouched in the water next to the bank, gesticulating at me to take cover. 'Up yours mate,' I thought, 'just where do you think I should hide? Grow a shell and act like a turtle?'

Stealthily, thanks to the sound of the flowing water, I made my way to the bank and peered over the side into the bush. There were some Frelimo soldiers walking along a well beaten path flanking the river. A very brutal looking group they were too.

I sneaked my Bren over the top of the bank, ready to fire on these chaps as we would have done back in our own country…but we had just left our own country! A strong hand squeezed down on my shoulder and the Pheasant Plucker silently ordered me not to shoot by shaking his head. I realized my folly. The enemy had all the advantages now: firepower, numbers, and lay of the land. We were in a vulnerable position without any nearby air support.

The enemy 'band of brothers' passed on and we slunk out of the river to check before giving the all clear for Blackie and Kudu to cross. The immense weight of my gear dragged me back as I raised myself out of the water. I removed my webbing which was full of water and left it under cover to drain before taking up a better position. Gary radioed back and told the others to try another crossing. They were fortunate enough to find a slightly shallower drift. We covered their movement and the platoon made their way across the river safely. When the entire platoon had crossed and all were accounted for, we advanced deeper into enemy territory. After the advent of the Frelimo troops, Gary changed our advance formation to double file so that we would have the advantage of being able to concentrate more fire power at a single point while still having good control. If the patrol walked into an ambush, the troops flanking the ambush would return fire while the other file took a defensive position in case of flanking operations by the enemy.

Some hours later we vectored onto the crash site. The airplane looked as though it had dived nose first into the ground at a shallow angle and come to rest after a short skid. Huge gouges in the earth bore witness to this.

All that remained of the aircraft was a blackened pile of ash and twisted wreckage. The black mess was arranged in an airplane-shaped silhouette with two large lumps in line with the shape of the fuselage. These were the push me, pull me arrangement of engines. We found the pilot between them. We soldiers just stood and gazed at all this, quite aghast at the scene.

"Jeez, just look at him," exclaimed Corporal Wilsenagh.

The poor man was charred to the bone. The only consolation was the realization that he would have died instantly on impact and been spared the agony of being burned alive. A large, dark cavity in the back of his head bore testimony to this.

I was ordered up onto an outcrop of high ground to keep a lookout. Other sections were sent to do clearance patrols to ensure the safety of those working at the crash site. There was some consternation when an attempt was made to load the corpse into a body bag. The limbs were so burned that they just pulled apart. Eventually the body was successfully contained and the engineers set about mining the engine blocks.

The clearance patrols were called in and they made their way back to the crash site to defend the helicopters which were now singing their way to our location. The first section broke cover slightly to my north-west and cautiously advanced in my general direction. Then, just in front of the first returning section, a second section emerged from the thick bush. I stood up to shout a warning, but before I could utter a sound, both teams saw each other and reacted. Rifles were thrown up into firing positions and some of the men threw themselves onto the ground, but there were no bangs. I was grateful then, for their discipline, and the skills of our section leaders.

A landing zone was hastily cut a short distance from the crashed airplane. The Alouettes flew in one by one and ate up four soldiers each before clanking their way back into the sky. Once again 'privilege' prevailed and Alpha stick was the last to be uplifted. I found myself in a defensive position around the landing zone with Gary and one engineer. The other engineer was setting fuses on the engine blocks.

The helicopters alerted some distant Frelimo soldiers. They fired mortar shells speculatively, but none of the bombs fell too close to us.

Our lift flew in and landed hastily. The pilot signalled for us to get in which we did. He wanted to take off immediately and Gary had to press him to wait for the second engineer. That poor pilot got visibly agitated as the mortar bombs sounded in the close distance, their explosions becoming louder and louder. Then the explosives engineer calmly strolled into view. We all motioned for him to hurry but he casually climbed into the cabin, grinned at the pilot and gave him the thumbs up. This slow walking was a safety protocol to avoid falling whilst beating an urgent exit from the blast zone. A fall while running could have resulted in a damaged limb or unconsciousness, pending a possibly fatal bang.

We surged into the sky and roared off, climbing as fast as that noisy bird could. The engineer then asked the pilot to circle the crash site to confirm detonation, for if it failed we would have to land and try again. The pilot's facial features became a little more strained at this unwelcome news. Circling high up with sufficient radius to evade the effects of the blast, we all looked out of the orbiting helicopter in the direction of the imminent explosion.

It was beautiful. There was an instantly expanding circle of movement as the shock wave thumped out over the vegetation. It was as though a massive invisible hammer had walloped down and raised dust and debris far into the sky. Birds rose into the air for miles around. And then a colossal clap reverberated in our ears and rolled off into the distance. It was deafening over the sound of our engine and rotors.

Some congratulations on this wonderful display caused the demolition man to glow at his success. Then this intrepid man asked the pilot to put him down again so that he might inspect his workmanship. Our pilot removed his mouthpiece and lipped a vulgar word at him.

The poor man just sat there having had his moment of glory ripped away. This combined with the relief of a successfully completed mission sparked our humour and we roared with laughter.

The nonplussed man sat there with a lopsided grin, as if we had all just pissed on his battery.

Follow-up on Fireforce

It was fairly late in the evening and Blackie and I were sitting in the troopies' pub keeping Rory the chopper technician company. Suddenly one of our men burst through the door.

"Howzhit, *ou man*," we greeted him.

He instructed us all to stand to and prepare to move out. Blackie and I rushed over to our bivouac area where we met the rest of our platoon. They were loading their kit into two strange looking police vehicles which we later learned were Isuzu trucks that had been stripped of their bodywork and armoured with steel plates. They were called Hippos and acted like them too! We crawled into a cold steel shell and sat on hard benches with our weapons pointing through small square openings on the sides of the vessel. The vehicle bounced and shook and we commenced a very uncomfortable ride. So much for the anticipated comforts of fireforce!

Blackie and I both mused over the fact that earlier, we had tanked up with Lion Lager and not yet broken the seal. Our bladders stretched tighter and tighter. There was no opening through which we could pee without spraying the others on board. This would undoubtedly have resulted in some injury to my person and Blackie was too large to negotiate the confines of the moving vehicle.

En route, we were informed that terrorists had attacked a farm house in the district and we were to follow-up as soon as possible. Our vehicles were preceded by a Pookie landmine sweeper and trailed by a mine-proofed police Land Rover. After two hours of brutal travelling, the vehicles lurched into the farm yard. Blackie and I immediately debussed and each hosed down a rear wheel of our Hippo, long before the platoon had completely exited all the vehicles.

There was a police dog in the Land Rover, an Alsatian that debussed with his handler. After sniffing our freshly hosed down tyres, he lifted his own leg against each wheel and then stood triumphantly next to his master as the reigning alpha-male. He sniffed the air arrogantly and wagged his tail at us slowly.

The farmhouse had taken an RPG rocket through the wall just above the back door's lintel and there were numerous pepper marks where bullets had chipped the brick and plaster walls. Broken glass and splintered wood lay on the kitchen floor but the farmer and his wife seemed to have been unharmed. They had been moved to safety by another farmer and we did not see them at all.

Gary informed us that we were going to attempt a nocturnal follow-up using the dog as a tracker. 'Ha,' I thought, 'now we are going to nose around the bush like a bunch of *nag aapies.*' This would suit my crazy platoon commander down to the ground, I thought.

The dog handler walked his animal up and down so that it could pick up a scent, but the hound seemed confused by all the soldiers in the farmyard. His owner then exclaimed that we were on tracks, and we proceeded in standard tracking formation with yours truly behind my noteworthy stick leader.

We walked up and down and around and around until a decision was made to rest up for the night as the dog was obviously bewildered. This was a relief as it is infuriating to follow someone who has no clue where he is going through the bush, worse so at night. But we had to accompany the tracker to provide protection in case he was successful and did make contact with the enemy.

We were on our way before sunrise, following the tracks of approximately 15 men. The dog could not fasten onto the scent of the fleeing criminals and was withdrawn from the follow-up along with his master.

'Ha,' I thought, 'who is the alpha-male now?'

A helicopter flew a team of four trackers in from the RAR support group and we immediately split into two teams of two sticks each so that we would be able to leapfrog ahead of the flight path in an effort to pick up tracks closer to our prey. We followed up in this fashion for over 40 kilometres. Our stick was the last to be leapfrogged forward late that afternoon. We regrouped with the others and the helicopter left en route to FAF 5 for the close of day.

The bush was very thick and we were reduced to walking behind the trackers in single file. Picking our way through the undergrowth, we fanned out into a large open clearing and advanced down a bare slope in an extended line. The shadows were growing long and the air was cooling. I felt a little invigorated, a second wind possibly. My thoughts wandered and I lost myself in some fantasy world involving better things than waltzing through thick bush on a sweltering day.

My left peripheral vision abruptly noted one of the trackers suddenly dancing a quick step backwards, and crouching as though there was great danger ahead. His eyes were wide and rolling in fear and I saw the tracker on his flank displaying the same symptoms.

My mind clicked like a switch and I was instantly alert. I was aware of Gary lifting his rifle, aiming and firing a shot. At the same time, I glanced forward and noticed a bouncing triangular hat, similar to those worn by Chinese coolies when they work in rice paddies, moving through the undergrowth. It dived into cover as Gary's shot cracked up ahead. Firing my Bren from the hip, I directed shots into the bush where the bouncing coolie hat had gone, correcting fire according to the fall of my tracer bullets. Twenty rounds were fired in a short instant and I dropped to my knee to change the magazine.

I heard my mates firing to the right and left of me and we stood ground, blasting bullets into likely cover. The RAR soldiers were no longer in my line of vision but I wasn't too worried about them. Winning the firefight was our primary objective and we did so with some of us standing and others kneeling. Our red tracer winged its way forward and rival green tracer cracked viciously across the clearing towards us. The terrorists abandoned the will to win the firefight and fled.

With a fresh magazine in place, I continued firing and discerned a great thumping in my left ear, not unlike shots passing my head, but with much greater concussion. My magazine was empty again and I reached into my chest webbing for a replacement. I can remember my head thudding with great force. It was like being hit on the temple by a heavy flexible bat.

As I turned to my left, magazine changing not an immediate priority anymore, I saw Gary running up to my position and thrusting the rifle of the

Field reservist Del Vincent on the right with glasses.

Funeral procession for D. Vincent.

Depot Rhodesia Regiment intake 138 at Llewellin Barracks

Top row left to right: Dawson, Robbins, Stanford, Marr, Lodge, Newman, Kriel, Wood, Kruger, Pretorius, Harding, Bennett, Will, Havekes, Kruger, Grobler, Wilsenach.

Second row from top, left to right: Worthington, Le Blanc Smith, Uys, Riley, Mullins, Morris. De Vos, James, Smith, Sawyer, Little, Cloete, Poley, Prinsloo, Seymour, Medeiros, Holland, Frasier-Grant.

Third row from top, left to right: O'Brien, De Kock, Dee, Hanekom, Cowell, Roper, La Grange, Menzies, Devine, Jocks, Beer, Murray, Conradie, Toughey, Macleod-Elliott, Price, Tullett, Marriot, Da Silva, Nicca.

Sitting on bench, left to right: Waghorn, Eckard, Wantenaar, Sgt Ferreira, C/Sgt Van den Bergh, C/Sgt McKinnley, WO1 Fraser, Capt Cook, Capt Drake (OC), Capt Robertson, 2Lt Marais, WO2 Pelser, C/Sgt Foulkes, Sgt Graham, Huyser, McCormack, Cruger.

Kneeling left to right: Galinos, Van der Horn, Walsh, Wiggell, Hadkinson, Gorrett, Kashula, Fyfer, Edridge, Timveos, Fotheringham, Tingtinger, Dixon, Smith, Swart, Kefalas, Tziralle, Hill.

Sitting front, left to right: Worselly, Botha, Johnston, Layfield, May, Meiring, Macedo, Tamblyn, O'Donnell, Woodford, Moutinho, Roberts, Salisbury, Wolpole, Sanderson, Jeanson, Rogers.

7 Platoon, 1 Independent Company, Wankie.
Rear from left to right: Sgt G. Pheasant, L/Cpl K. Menzies, Rfn F. Wiggell, Rfn P. Roper, Rfn W. O'Brien, Unknown, Unknown, Rfn Woodford, Cpl C. Beukes, 2Lt P. McGraw.
Front from left to right: Rfn M. Saunders (signaller) Unknown, Rfn M. Roberts, Rfn J. de Vos (driver) Rfn W. Hadkinson, Rfn G. May, Cpl N. Difford.

8 Platoon, 1 Independent Company, Wankie.
Rear from left to right: Cpl da Silva, Sgt Wood, Rfn K. Mullen (driver), Rfn H. de Beer, Rfn G. la Grange, Rfn N. Mellet (signaller), Rfn N. Toughey, Rfn A. Seymour, Rfn D. Will (driver).
Front from left to right: Author (it's those skinny arms again), Rfn K. Waghorn, Rfn M. Kashula, L/Cpl A. Fotheringham, Unknown, L/Cpl F. Fyfer, Rfn C. Frazier (signaller) Rfn R. Salisbury, Cpl H. Prinsloo.
Front: 2Lt D. Havanar.

9 Platoon, 1 Independent Company, Wankie.
Rear, standing from left to right: Unknown, L/Cpl R. Eckard, Rfn P. Hill, Rfn R. Harding, Unknown,
Cpl F. Jocks, Cpl W. Wilsenach, Unknown, Rfn G. Cloete, Rfn I. McCloud-Elliot.
Front, standing from left to right: Rfn K. Tamblyn, Rfn Timveos, Rfn J. van der Horn, L/Cpl P. Swart,
Rfn Tingtinger, Rfn K. Layfield, Unknown.
Front from left to right: Sgt K. du Preez, 2Lt Jenkins.

School of Infantry, intake 138
Left to right: Unknown (posted to RLI), Chunky Beukes, Karl du Preez, Nigel Difford, Doug Havanar,
Paul McGraw, Gary Pheasant (kneeling).

Swimming at Deka base camp.

Mock ambush. Frank Wiggell closest to camera.

1 Independent Company at a drill hall in Salisbury en route to Mudzi. Standing: Gary Pheasant with Frank Wiggell behind the trailer. In the vehicle from left to right: Ting Ting, H. Prinsloo (sitting high up on the toolbox), Roy Salisbury (in front of Ting Ting) and Freddie Jocks with sunglasses (background). Group of five sitting right at the back of the vehicle from left to right: Nick Toughey, Author (sitting high on the right side of the vehicle), Chris Rogers, Ken Menzies, Mike Saunders.

Bush braai. Left to right: M. Roberts, Ken Menzies, R. Cowell. Note Gary Pheasant's rifle in the foreground, loaded with a 28R anti-tank rifle grenade.

Mudzi area. This is a Bedford with its cab modified for protection against landmines. Note Gary Pheasant's rifle hanging from the right side of the vehicle. The vehicle drove off with Gary running behind it, screaming for the driver to stop. We learned the hard way. On the vehicle from left to right: Driver de Vos (sitting on the crash bar) Unknown, Gerry May (sitting on the extreme left of the vehicle) Standing: Unknown, Ken Menzies (with his back to the camera).

Base camp, Mudzi. Left to right: Gerry May, M. Saunders, de Vos.

Lt G. Pheasant being presented with the Bronze Cross of Rhodesia

CITATION

WARRANT OFFICER CLASS 2 GARY MICHAEL PHEASANT

THE BRONZE CROSS OF RHODESIA

From February 1976 to March 1977 Warrant Officer Pheasant commanded various platoons of his unit in action. On 8 February 1976 in the North Eastern Operational Area a BSA Police vehicle was ambushed by a group of terrorists. Warrant Officer Pheasant led the follow-up and on cantacting the terrorists opened fire and personally killed one terrorist. Due to his initiative, aggression and determination, eventually seven terrorists were killed and three captured. On 16 August 1976 after a contact where two Security Force members were wounded, Warrant Officer Pheasant followed spoor for approximately ten kilometres. He made contact with a group of terrorists and of these four were killed and two captured. On 16 September 1976, after terrorists attacked a farmhouse, starting at first light with a small number of men, Warrant Officer Pheasant followed spoor for approximately forty kilometres. Near to last light contact was made with terrorists in very dense bush and Warrant Officer Pheasant showing typical tenacity and determination, closed with them and personally shot one terrorist at three metres. On 4 November 1976 after terrorists blew up a bridge it was ascertained that two groups of terrorists were responsible. Warrant Officer Pheasant and one man followed one group for about twenty kilometres. Reinforced by eight fresh men he continued the follow-up and after a further two kilometres made contact. Ten terrorists were killed. Sleeping on the spoor of the other group that night, Warrant Officer Pheasant followed them from first light next morning until he had ascertained that the terrorists had fled from Rhodesia. Warrant Officer Pheasant had displayed outstanding qual ities of leadership, determination and personal bravery of a high order.

(J.S.V. Hickman) Lieutenant General,
            Commander of the Army.

...this contact lasted for some four hours."

On September 8, 1976, 2 Lt. Stobart-Vallaro observed a number of terrorists moving into dense undergrowth. The next day, in a series of contacts, four terrorists were killed and two captured, among whom were senior enemy commanders.

"On March 6, 1977, along with two soldiers and a tracker he followed a large group of terrorists for a considerable distance.

"In the initial contact, although wounded by enemy bullets and shrapnel, 2 Lt. Stobart - Vallaro personally killed three terrorists from a range of five to 10 yards.

"He then directed fire force deployment on to the position and a further six terrorists were killed."

He had been in contact with many terrorists in the Eastern operational area.

Sgt. John McKelvie, 1 Battalion, Rhodesia Light Infantry.

Sgt. McKelvie was involved in 14 contacts during the period May 1976 to February 1977.

In all he displayed considerable initiative, leadership and gallantry, and together with his men, accounted for over 60 terrorists.

"On November 9, 1976, Sgt. McKelvie and seven men were dropped by helicopter into an area in which a large group of terrorists were based. The helicopter was subsequently grounded.

"Despite the lack of air support Sgt. McKelvie and his men killed 18 terrorists in three hours.

"Sgt. McKelvie's conduct during this contact was exemplary."

Five more terrorists were killed and one captured.

On November 24, 1976, Sgt. McKelvie and seven men were again dropped into an area containing terrorists. Sgt. McKelvie and his men were later joined by additional men. They captured 13 terrorists and captured two.

Sgt. McKelvie's gallantry and example and disregard for his personal safety have been of the highest order and his professional dedication and determination have been an inspiration to all who serve with him."

Bronze Cross
of Rhodesia

CAPT. DAVID ANDREW SAMUELS, 1 Battalion Rhodesian Light Infantry.

On March 6, 1977, in the Eastern border area, Capt. Samuels and a small number

Citation Rfn D. White

On October 31, 1976, in an attack on two enemy camps which contained large groups of terrorists, Lt. Schrag led the assault with great determination forcing them to break and run.

When under close range fire from two terrorists hidden in a river bed, Lt. Schrag charged in alone and killed both terrorists at a range of less than 10 metres.

He then led his platoon in a sweep of very thick cover where a further four terrorists were killed.

Enemy small arms and mortar fire was intense.

"His total disregard for his own safety and brave conduct was an inspiration to all who witnessed it."

2 Lt. Graham Derek Bedford Murdoch, 1 Battalion Rhodesian Light Infantry.

On December 16, 1976, 2 Lt. Murdoch discovered at first light that his stop group had been positioned in the middle of an occupied but previously undetected terrorist base camp. The group came under heavy fire.

In the course of extricating his men, he killed five terrorists.

"One of his stop groups was pinned down in its original position and its commander was killed. With no regard for his personal safety, 2 Lt. Murdoch crawled back the contact but retralised the terrorist position.

"He was wounded during the contact but remained in full command of his men and directed three air strikes on to the terrorist position before leading his men in an assault on the position, which resulted in its capture.

"2 Lt. Murdoch displayed exceptional gallantry and leadership while operating under extremely arduous conditions. His personal example was an inspiration to his men and greatly contributed to the successful elimination of the terrorist camp."

W/O Gary Michael Pheasant, 10 Battalion, Rhodesia Regiment.

On February 8, 1976, in the North - eastern area, a BSA Police vehicle was ambushed by a group of terrorists.

"W/O Pheasant led the follow-up and on contacting the terrorists opened fire and personally killed one terrorist.

"Due to his initiative, aggression and determination, eventually seven terrorists were killed and three captured.

"On August 10, 1976, after a contact where two security force members were wounded,

Company), Rhodesia Regiment.

On April 30, 1976, in the Eastern operational area a contact initiated by 2-Lt. Carloni and his platoon killed three terrorists and captured two others.

He called for air support and directed the positioning of the fire force, and in the subsequent action a further seven terrorists were killed and one captured.

On May 10, 1976, two terrorists were killed.

On November 28, 1976 in the same operational area, his platoon made contact and killed eight terrorists.

2-Lt. Carloni skilfully deployed fire force on to the position resulting in a further 10 terrorists being killed.

On January 5, 1977, although mortared by terrorists at 4 a.m. his platoon put the terrorists to flight and a large number of terrorist recruits were prevented from leaving the country.

On March 9, 1977, an Internal Affairs patrol was ambushed by a group of terrorists.

2 Lt. Carloni and seven of his men followed them, killing five.

Thereafter, 2 Lt. Carloni so effectively positioned fire force troops that every remaining terrorist was accounted for.

"In these and other contacts 2 Lt. Carloni always displayed calmness, bravery and aggressive leadership."

L/Cpl. Noel Ross-Johnson 6 Battalion, Rhodesia Regiment.

On the night of February 7, 1977, during a heavy mortar and rocket attack on a base, Cpl. Johnson on his own initiative and with complete disregard for his own safety, climbed the 100ft. radio mast from where he directed retaliatory mortar fire on to enemy positions. One enemy mortar position was neutralised.

Again, while under mortar attack on the night of February 9, 1977, he repeated this action, and another mortar position was neutralised.

On February 10, 1977, during daylight, Cpl. Johnson again climbed the radio mast and had small arms fire directed at him.

He climbed the radio mast again on February 12 and directed our mortar fire.

Cpl. Johnson observed the enemy advancing to positions from which direct small arms fire could be brought to bear on the camp.

"He engaged the enemy with rifle fire, preventing some of the groups from reaching their fire positions.

grenade Tpr. Hyde, with no regard to his own personal safety, leapt on to Sgt. McKelvie, forcing him to the ground. The grenade exploded, causing no casualties.

Tpr. Hyde saved Sgt. McKelvie from death or injury.

RFN. DEON MACALASTAIR WHITE (posthumous) 10 Battalion Rhodesia Regiment.

At 5.45 a.m. on October 28, 1976. Rfn. White on the extreme right of an exposed position saw terrorists moving past at a distance of 12 metres.

He alerted the soldier on his left and stood up opening fire.

With complete disregard for his own safety Rfn. White continued to fire standing in full view of the enemy and exposed to their fire, while his companions withdrew to cover.

By holding continuous fire Rfn. White drew all the immediate heavy enemy fire to himself and it was estimated that his action killed six terrorists.

A further five terrorists were killed and Rfn. White sustained a gunshot wound from which he died.

★ **Military Forces Commendation (Operational)** ★

W/O II BENJAMINI MAKURIRA, 2 Battalion, Rhodesian African Rifles.

On October 31, 1976, two terrorists, one armed with an AK rifle, the other with an RPK light machine-gun broke through a stop line and dived into thick cover.

W/O Makurira chased the terrorists and killed them both when they turned to fight him off.

He handled his platoon with skill and determination showing bravery and a great devotion to duty.

SGT. LIONEL MARTIN YEOMAN, 3 (Independent) Company, Rhodesia Regiment

On October 9, 1975, Sgt. Yeoman was deployed as a medical orderly in response to a call for casualty evacuation in the Eastern border area.

He immediately made his way under fire to the injured persons to render first aid, at the same time deploying a machine-gun to engage the enemy.

"To neutralise the enemy position Sgt. Yeoman repeatedly exposed himself to fire in an attempt to indicate the enemy position to an armed helicopter, on each occasion placing himself in extreme danger."

7 Squadron receiving freedom of the town on 17 May 1980. My father, the deputy mayor, congratulating the Officer Commanding 7 Squadron, Squadron Leader Ed Potterton, on attaining freedom of Fort Victoria. Background: Mayor D. McEwan and his wife Ross.

Rotary International 75th anniversary. Left to right: Stan Hall, Sue Johnson, my father (president) and mother, Butch Coaton.

Delville Wood survivor. Left to right: Bridesmaid, best man, my grandfather C.J. Vincent alias C.J.S. Vincenz when he married my grandmother, Elizabeth Hobson.

Certificate of Baptism

IMMACULATE CONCEPTION CHURCH
44 ALBANY STREET, EAST LONDON 5201 [South Africa]

This is to certify that CHARLES JAMES SANTAGATI VINCENZ

Born on 9th. February 1896 was Baptized on 1st. March 1896

by the Rev. J. Bernard Schmidt.

Date 13/5/77 Signed

Parish Priest

ST. F.C.P.

Copy of baptism certificate for C.J.S. Vincenz.

The rescuers. My father posing with the dogs that rescued him from his wild bees. Poodle Ethel, Labradors Lucy and Barney with Kenge the bull terrier.

Alouette helicopter taking my sisters for a flight from my parents' home.

Old soldiers photographed in 2012. Left to right: Gary Pheasant, Nigel Difford, Author (not so skinny anymore).

Dale Venters, national service patrol officer.

Dale playing with his motorbike. Girl unknown.

Friends at Stop 1. Stop 1 was a pub thrown together at one of the single-quarter messes in Mashaba. We frequented the venue many times. Rear standing from left to right: Malcolm Kincaid-Smith, Unknown, Alan Dongworth, Dietz, Martin Cremer (Big Balls) Kneeling: Plum Graham, Colin Kirkham.

Colin and Jean Kirkham at their wedding. One of the few couples that honoured their vows. I take my hat off to you, Kirkham, being married to Jean could not have been that easy.

An evening at Club Tomorrow, Salisbury. This photo was taken late in 1973 while I was still working as an apprentice in Salisbury. From left to right: Author, Kevin Thomas, a grumpy Ron Williams, Gail Tonks, Phil Nel.

Boy Scouts. This photo was taken at a jamboree held in Lourenço Marques (now Maputo) in 1971, two years before I left school.
From left to right: Mike Armstrong, Ian Wallace, Andrea Dracos, Author, Tom Fulton.
During this time Mike was given the nickname Vuurhoutjies (matches in Afrikaans). He is now fondly known as Spook. Ian was called the Lone Stranger due to his habit of taking long walks to sulk after being teased. We called Andrea Dragon and no one dared give Tom a new name as we feared a good thumping. Absent from photo is Grant Gallagher.

Ron Williams posing sometime in the late seventies. And I thought I was skinny …

Kevin Thomas at his wedding. Left to right: Kevin's sister Lorraine, Kev, Christine, and the best man.

Relaxing at Kyle Boat Club sometime in the nineties. Kev and Marlene Thomas with my two children Hilton and Shannon.

Author, Ron Williams and Kevin Thomas. I had not seen Ron since 1981. We had a great reunion.

tracker behind me up into the air. This unconcerned soldier's rifle muzzle had been less than six inches from behind my left ear. I think Gary was expecting my head to change shape and I am grateful for his quick action.

"Cease fire," I heard Gary shout through buzzing ears.

We stopped firing and advanced forward into the river bed. As Gary and I slid down the sharp sandy slope into the river bed Gary wheeled and fired shots into an injured terrorist who was cowering in a small gully. I was grateful for his action as I had no magazine on my gun. The terrorist just groaned once and died on the spot.

There, lying on the ground next to the man was a triangular coolie hat plaited from reeds.

Through the river bed and up the opposite bank and hillside there were trails of men who had hastily leopard crawled to safety. The terrorist band had unwittingly been split into two by this hill.

Then there was the sound of a helicopter returning to give us assistance. The pilot had heard Gary's standard procedure radio call, 'contact, contact,' alerting all on our frequency to our contact with the enemy. The helicopter gunner immediately fired at targets ahead of us and quickly expended his ammunition. I looked up as the machine bellowed overhead and saw the gunner huddled over his special gun sight. The smoke from his fired bullets wafted back in the slipstream like a strange grey rippled cloud formation which was instantly swirled into thin air by the rotors.

The pilot informed Gary to say that the gunner had shot down some terrorists. Their bodies were lying in a river bed a few hundred metres to our left flank. Low fuel forced the pilot to return to FAF 5.

We advanced to the ridge in front of us and peered down into the area where the dead men were supposed to have been lying. We observed no one. It was later established that the men, who had been lying in the open, had played possum and fled as soon as the helicopter had left.

We swept through the dark shadows of impending evening but saw no more evidence of enemy soldiers, except for the mass of kit and weapons they had left behind.

That evening, we bedded down in a circle formation not far from the contact sight. There was a flurry of panicky shots later that night as the RAR soldiers fired at movement. They had probably been exposed to much more action than we had and we forgave them for their nervousness. Even so, Gary instructed them not to fire any more shots unless they had specifically been ordered to do so. If there was movement, their only duty was to alert one of our own leaders and let that man decide on appropriate action.

As I sit writing this story, my left ear sings a shrill song to me. This is not dissimilar to the urgent zinging of the cicada beetle which rouses the Rhodesian bush in December, an inadvertent reminder of my brief experience on fireforce.

Some classy chicks

Gary and I had been planning our leave together and he stated that he was going to take a classy lady out to dinner at the Monomatapa Hotel in Salisbury. He asked me if I wanted to accompany a friend of hers and I did.

That was fine, Gary informed me, but these were not the ordinary run-of-the-mill skanky chicks that I hung out with. These were real elegant ladies, they were. I would have to mind my manners as I was likely to offend, in which case Gary would not score, which could evolve into unpleasantness for one junior member of his platoon.

And so I received a series of etiquette lessons from my venerable platoon commander. He probably learned all these fancy manners at the School of Infantry. These tried and tested methods (chewing with your mouth closed, opening doors, and doffing hats) were all quite interesting but I knew most of them anyway. My parents had been strict about how I presented myself in public.

I had to compliment my partner and make sure she felt comfortable. I couldn't make any derogatory comments about her hairstyle, shape, or size, intentional or otherwise! I had to open every door for her while bowing slightly and indicating with my arm that she should proceed and I would follow. I had to pull out her chair and make sure she was comfortable before seeing to my own seating. I had to sit up straight with no slouching, and avoid biting my fingernails or scratching in my nose.

"Not good for the image," said Gary.

The knives and forks were also an issue as etiquette dictates only one correct way to use them. Gary explained how to place food on the fork and lift it to your lips. Swooping down to snatch food into ones gaping mouth as it was falling off the fork was a terrible sin. When the meal was finished I was to place my knife and fork together on one side to indicate that the waiter could remove my plate.

"And don't get too drunk," he said.

And so on.

The anticipated evening arrived. We went to collect the stylish ladies in Gary's whiny Ford Zephyr and arrived at the Monomatapa with great aplomb. The girls did not wait for us to open doors. Instead they charged off into the hotel, barging through the doors, giggling and squealing all the way. They did not wait to be seated at the table. Instead, they dragged their own chairs out, sat down, and then pulled the chairs into position under their classy rumps.

The meal was served and we watched in horror as these two chic girls heartily shovelled food into undisciplined mouths. They used any utensil that came to hand, including fingers tipped with pink varnish, which were sucked noisily and wiped dry on serviettes and the tablecloth. Buckets of cool wine were smacked down through giggling red lips. Gary and I just grinned at each other, realizing that we could just sit back and enjoy the evening without fear of social class rejection. So much for uptown girls, give me a shady lady any day.

What a hoot!

We drank, we swore, we killed

We had reported for duty the night before and there was no rush for us to attend to anything until summoned for orders. After washing and brushing our teeth, we greeted the men who had arrived that morning, some looking fresh and alert, others red eyed and hung over. At 08h00 we stood to attention for roll call on the parade square. Our company commander, Major Currin, had been called to other duties and we were under the temporary command of a certain Captain Campbell. He was a short, seedy looking man who arrogantly declared that he had heard all about our ill-discipline and was not prepared to take any of our crap.

Mr Campbell also stated that our order for departure had changed. Charlie

Company would board a normal civilian train at Gwelo station that night and arrive in Salisbury at 06h00 the next morning where our vehicles would be waiting to transport us to Kotwa. We were told that we had better bloody well behave ourselves, or else. Furthermore, we were not to hang around the drill hall and be an embarrassment to good soldiering but bugger off and keep a low profile until the evening departure.

Big mistake, sir!

After we were dismissed, the men hurriedly attended to trivial duties like drawing ammunition and kit. Some eagerly contacted their women to collect them at the drill hall. "Probably to get in another quickie," we teased, jealously.

The wankers all went shopping or site seeing or something. What the hell was there of interest in Gwelo anyway?

The more unsettled members of 7, 8 and 9 Platoons strolled to the local hotel in dribs and drabs and arrived at opening time. The beer flowed and small groups slunk in and out of the bar to smoke *boom*. Some girls arrived, the music from one soldier's portable tape deck blared, and the party hopped. Sometime after midday, the regimental police arrived and ordered us to report to the drill hall immediately. As one, we roared abuse and threats at them.

"Oink, oink oink, weeeeeeeee!" we snorted at them.

This may very well have been one of the most satisfying moments of my undistinguished military career. The pigs left with their curly tails drooped and went to rally the support of our various platoon commanders.

Some of the men were more sensible than others and a great debate ensued as to whether we should leave or not. Duimpie was all for laying an ambush for them with his machine gun at the hotel reception. Mother said that we should all go back to the drill hall and beat them up or unprintable words to that effect. It was all a little hazy after that but most of us staggered the 300 odd miles back to the drill hall before our brass arrived at the hotel.

On arrival we were fallen in. Some office-bound sergeant-major with a thick blonde moustache started shouting and threatening us with all sorts of unpleasantness. None of us gave a hoot but he carried on regardless until he ran out of words. He inspected the swaying ranks in front of him with an angry eye. Realizing that his words were having no effect, he singled out a grinning Mother and proceeded to make an example of him.

"You! Get out here now and bring your weapon."

Dutifully, Mother bent down, grabbed the carry handle of his MAG and strolled to stand impudently before the unsuspecting NCO. Our leaders, those of whom were not swaying with us, were standing in a group to one side. They all knew that there was now going to be some real entertainment.

The sergeant-major ordered Mother to raise his weapon above his head and double march around the drill hall. This Mother did, in perfect military order, thighs parallel to the ground and gun high above his head. After orbiting the drill hall for the first time, he thundered past and greeted us in his familiar slang:

"Hey you *okes*, check me out, *ek sê*. This *ou* thinks he can rev me but I can take his shit. This is just like PT. He doesn't know us *okes* from C Company."

We all cheered him on and a sweating but triumphant Mother sustained his PT without slacking. If his arms grew tired, he dropped the gun to his shoulders while out of his aggravated tormentor's sight and then lifted it high again just before turning the last corner of the drill hall. This NCO was dealing with a real *makonya* here. Mother started singing a song to annoy this slacker NCO and we continued to cheer him on and laugh at his antics.

'Our sergeant-major's got a finger up his arse, but his mouth still stinks like shit!' he sang.

The sergeant-major fumed.

When he realized he was fighting a pointless battle, the sergeant-major ordered Mother to join ranks once again and handed us over to our own leaders with a ribald curse.

Our grinning platoon commanders then took over and kept us on a tight rein until it was time to board the vehicles for the station. Not tight enough however, as some men managed to sneak out and purchase grog from the local bottle stores and the party continued in the tents. I am not sure what time the train arrived. I vaguely remember stumbling into a compartment with three or four others, bottles clinking between our clutched fingers. This included Mother, who entertained us all through the night. Other groups of men visited the dining car and consumed more alcohol. No military police out here. The civilians on the train hastily disappeared into their compartments and locked the doors, no doubt fearing for the chastity of their womenfolk.

The smell of marijuana permeated the train but no one cared.

On arrival at Salisbury station, the train vomited out a deluge of drunk and aggressive troops. The air turned a hue of pale blue from the foul language that we so casually allowed to flow from our lips. And loudly too! Mother had written vulgar words urging all to kill the enemy onto the front of his combat cap.

There were some Africans on the platform and Mother promptly handed his MAG to a colleague and charged the small group, voicing his intent to commit murder. He was followed by some others carrying their rifles! The black people's eyes widened in amazement. Fear took hold and they ran as though there were wild animals at their heels. And there were! They all ran leaping over piles of luggage and platform trolleys and disappeared into the street.

When he returned, a sweating Mother stated that he had been unable to catch any of his foes. Some of the soldiers laughed and said that they were probably still running for the border. The remaining civilians, who were all white, had retreated to one side of the platform. There they grouped, observing us with a mixture of trepidation and fear. If this was the thin red line saving their country from being overrun by vicious communist terrorists, what hope was left?

The vehicles were ready for us and we were rerouted to one of the drill halls in Salisbury. There, waiting for us, was the incorrigible Captain Campbell. This man was not amused. It was then, while we stood to attention rocking back and forth on our heels, that he rolled out his most famous speech, which we shall remember for the rest of our days.

"You have shown us that you can drink, and you have shown us that you can swear. Now show us that you can kill."

With that we were ordered to embus the vehicles. Our convoy rolled its ponderous way out through Borrowdale on the highway to Kotwa. Most of us did not even notice that we had left the bright lights as one by one, we dropped off into deep slumber with the wankers and satiated married men on guard.

Wisely, Captain Campbell did not take any action against his disorderly company. Instead he sent us all on the first ten-day patrol. Gingerly, we complied without too much sarcasm or complaining.

Possibly, a bond of mutual respect had formed between the dissident troops and their new commanding officer.

Rifleman Deon White, BCR

I only knew him for five months but as a soldier, Deon White impressed me with his attention to detail and the great care he took to conduct himself appropriately. While the rest of us patrolled in shorts and T-shirts, he insisted on wearing full denim camouflage. This, he said, was to afford him as much camouflage as possible. He always had a smile on his face, never complained, and was eager to help in any situation. Fondly known as Chalky, he was the machine gunner for Charlie stick.

On 30 October 1976, our stick, call sign 32A, was mobile at the crack of dawn, sweeping westwards along the Mudzi river. The two other sticks comprising our platoon were also operating close by. Our task was to cross-grain during the day and then ambush certain predetermined points by night.

Special branch had warned us that there would be an increase in traffic along the Mudzi River during that period. Bravo and Charlie sticks had married up to combine their firepower the previous night.

At around 06h00, Gary climbed the only small hill in our immediate vicinity to establish communication with base and deliver a situation report. After reporting in a very professional manner using correct voice procedure and keeping strictly under cover, he suddenly leapt up and cheered, 'Yeehaaaaa!' like a madman.

I had been suspecting, for a while, that he was insane.

He then tore down the hill, howling and applauding like one possessed. Reaching our position, he gleefully exclaimed that Bravo and Charlie sticks had just reported killing eleven gooks. This was great news, especially for Gary, who had been instrumental in placing his men in the correct position. One of our own had been injured in the subsequent exchange of fire.

Bravo and Charlie sticks had laid ambush together behind a small hump of ground in an extended open area facing a track which curved down the edge of a steep and rocky hillside covered in coarse mopani shrub, thorn trees and loose stones. At about 05h00 that morning while the men were packing their kit away, a large group of terrorists had walked down the track heading for the border, obviously not alert. In retrospect, we assumed they had thought themselves safe with the border less than ten kilometres away.

First to see the enemy, Chalky had alerted his section by opening fire. His first burst had dropped several of the surprised and confused foe. With great pluck, Chalky had then broken cover and run a short distance to divert enemy fire from his section. He had dropped to the ground and continued firing at the enemy while his section organized themselves and started returning fire.

During the contact, Chalky's gun had jammed and he had raised himself up and opened the top cover of the gun to clear the stoppage without any regard for his own safety. A round from one of the terrorist weapons had whipped across the top of his head and he had fallen to the ground unconscious. Within a few minutes, all the remaining insurgents had been dropped by the other section members, who had now regained control of their wits. The remaining members of the section had then charged the enemy position and killed any gooks that were still alive. Lou Boom had excelled by firing his Bren gun from the hip, exterminating one injured terrorist who had been about to fire at them from where he was hiding in the undergrowth.

Sergeant Henry Friend had radioed for a helicopter to casevac Chalky while members of the section bound his wound and administered first aid as best they could. The helicopter had arrived on the scene, uplifted Chalky and flown him directly to Andrew Fleming hospital in Salisbury.

Bravo and Charlie sticks were uplifted as their presence in the area had now been compromised by the ambush. Gary decided that Alpha stick would ambush the road again that night as the locals would assume that we had been removed from the area, having seen empty troop carriers enter their area and leave with men on board.

Our ambush was silent through the night and in the morning we walked through the previous day's contact site. We could see where our comrades had laid ambush and the spot where Chalky had fallen. There were cartridges strewn over the whole area. We walked up the track and saw blood thick on the ground where the rebels had fallen. The police had removed all the bodies and transported them to Mtoko for identification. When we returned to Kotwa base from our patrol a week later, we learned that Deon White had succumbed to his injury and died.

He was buried with full military honours and the members of his section were present at his funeral. Sometime later, the authorities awarded Deon White the Bronze Cross of Rhodesia posthumously. No one I knew was more deserving of this honour.

I just wish he had been there in person for the President to pin the medal to his chest.

Bobtreps

Just after sunrise on 4 November 1976, one four man stick from 8 Platoon and Voc, who had been reassigned as a platoon tracker, found ourselves in vehicles on the main tarred road between Kotwa and Mtoko. During the night, a gang of insurgents had detonated a land mine on the high level road bridge which crossed a tributary of the Mudzi River. We were on our way to investigate.

When we arrived at the bridge, we saw that a manhole-sized cavity had been blown through the tar and concrete; an imaginative attempt to destroy the bridge using a landmine. Next to the hole, a flat rock had been placed over a communist stick grenade. Tied onto one of the concrete safety rails was a dirty, fluttering piece of paper onto which the words, 'BEWARE OF THE BOBTREPS,' had been scrawled. Obviously one member of the gang had a sense of humour even though his spelling was below par. We easily inferred that he had been referring to booby traps and even though we joked about his limited ability to communicate through the written word, we hastily withdrew from the bridge. We didn't want to set off any more sophisticated devices that may have escaped our attention due to the obvious deception of the booby trap. In the mean time, Voc located spoor and a line of flight was established. Leaving the 'bobtreps' for the engineers to sort out, we proceeded with follow-up.

The spoor indicated that a group of 20 men were fleeing straight for the Mozambican border, 50 kilometres away. The group was in a hurry and their spoor obvious, so we followed at an immense pace, frequently breaking into a trot in our efforts to engage them before they crossed the border to safety.

After eight kilometres, the gooks split into two groups. Not wanting to lose the opportunity to make contact with these terrorists, Gary split his team into two. The Grundy and Kudu followed one group under the leadership of Voc, who was carrying a radio. Gary and I followed the second group. We had no problem following the spoor as the bush was thick and the terrorists, in full flight, had made no attempt to anti track.

Fifteen kilometres on, the two terrorist groups married up and continued their flight. Gary and I re-joined the other members of our team and continued following.

October/November is the hottest time of the year in Rhodesia and the heat was dry and unbearable. We crossed the Mudzi twice that day, but the river was dry and our water supplies were running low. We could not spare time to dig for water and some of us started to show signs of heat fatigue. There was a small track about five kilometres ahead and fresh troops were requested to meet us there.

Two of us were fatigued and another had damaged his knee. The Grundy, Kudu and I were relieved by a fresh stick, one of whom was Blackie. All the team members drank their fill of water and replenished their canteens from the tanks on the vehicles. The malingerers then climbed onto the vehicles and were driven away while the follow-up team continued on the trail.

Five kilometres on, they made contact with a group of ten terrorists resting up in the early afternoon. The terrorists were sleeping in open formation without having posted a guard. The vegetation had thinned out and our troops arranged themselves in an extended line and opened fire on the dozing enemy. The contact was short. All ten were killed in less than a minute.

When the contact was initiated, Blackie loosed off his 28R rifle grenade in the mortar role. This crashed down on the other side of the contact area just before the cease fire was ordered. The explosion was terrific and startled all the men on the follow-up as they thought they were being rocketed.

Those of us on the vehicles also heard this explosion which was followed up with news of the contact by radio. We were overjoyed when we heard that ten enemy had been killed. I was also disappointed that I had not pushed on with the follow-up, but I knew that my energy had been depleted and I would have held the follow-up team back. After a rest and some salt tablets flushed down with jungle juice, we quickly regained our energy.

The other ten terrorists had not rested but continued their flight. Gary continued with the follow-up as soon as the police arrived to process the contact site. They slept on the spoor that night and carried on early the next morning but were unable to catch up with the remainder of the group. It was surmised that the other half of the group had heard the contact and redoubled their efforts to cross the border that night.

A police unit immediately transported the bodies to Nyamapanda police station for identification. As the contact had taken place within a few kilometres of Nyamapanda, the police had returned to their station before we reached the main Kotwa/Nyamapanda road.

We rerouted to Nyamapanda to visit the dead. We debussed the vehicles and walked to the rear of the police station where the dead men were laid in a row side by side on the neatly trimmed grass. Some were dressed in blue denim and others in a mixture of Eastern European uniforms and civilian clothing. They were all youths and most had been shot through the head.

The Grundy and I left our small group, who were gazing at the bodies, and each stood over a dead man. The unfortunate comrade over whom I stood had taken a round through the right temple and the deformed bullet had removed most of the brain and the left side of his skull on exiting. There were still pieces of curved skull bone attached to the head by woolly strips of tatty skin.

I tapped a drum roll on the side of his hollow head and the Grundy removed pieces of brain from the other dead man's head and squashed the mass in his fist. Fluid oozed out from between his fingers. Kudu and the others all expressed revulsion and retreated to the vehicles. A young policeman turned his face away, retched his afternoon tea onto the ground and then retreated into the charge office to avoid these ruffians from 10th battalion. After washing our hands, we returned to Kotwa in time for dinner.

8 Platoon was showing Captain Campbell that we surely could kill! Well done, boys.

The Goff camp

The Rhodesia Defence Unit was camped a few kilometres down the road towards Nyamapanda. The coloured people of Rhodesia were fondly referred to as Goffs. Therefore their base was referred to as the Goff camp.

They were a versatile and volatile people with a language of their own, similar to the slang spoken by the RLI. They had strange names too, such as Mad Dog Jones, who was one of their drivers. Mad Dog was well known to us as he traded in *dagga*.

We were enjoying our dinner one evening when we heard the sound of a fire fight coming from the direction of the Goff camp. Radio contact with the Goff unit's commander revealed that no support was needed from us.

The following day, Mad Dog told us that all the Goffs had been sitting in the huge marquee that served as their canteen shelter. The main mast of the marquee had snapped and the tent had collapsed onto the unfortunate Goffs, injuring some, while others had been hurt by gunfire from within the tent. The breaking mast had sounded like a gunshot, causing the Goffs to react and fire their Sterling machine guns at each other. Fortunately no one was killed in the fracas. We assumed that all the Goffs had been smoking it up and smiled at the story. What a fright they must have had.

'Hey, who you gunning for *ek sê*?'

Mad Dog Jones wrapped up his story by exclaiming that these Goffs were a mad bunch.

We all stood in agreement with Mad Dog Jones.

Billy the Kid did not hang

Lou Boom discovered a lone billy goat kid on the way to his stick's pickup point. He felt sorry for the beast as it seemed afflicted and decide to care for it back at base camp, after which, he planned to take it home as a gift for his little sister.

Back at camp, he conscripted the services of Guttergoose Gunn, our camp cook at the time. Guttergoose promised to feed the animal and make sure that it had enough fresh water at all times. After a visit to the medic to determine what ailment was causing the goat's diarrhoea, Lou Boom forced some medicine down the wretched animal's throat and christened his new friend, Billy the Kid.

That evening, Billy the Kid was tethered to the small tree which straddled our bivouac. Fortunately, having outdone ourselves in the bush canteen that evening, we were immune to the kid's noise. The next day, all of us except Voc, who was still assigned as a platoon tracker, were deployed on patrol. Thus, Voc waited at camp for an incident that would require his keen eye in search of enemy footprints.

The kitchen was close to our sleeping area. Later that night, Guttergoose Gunn crept out of his sleeping bag and loosed Billy the Kid from the kitchen tent peg to which he had been tethered. The small goat had grunted and farted all night and Gunn had been deprived of much essential beauty sleep. He led the skinny animal to the tree next to our bivouac and tied it there, unaware of our slumbering Voc.

Voc was a sound sleeper but awoke to the niggling and grumbling of the goat in the very early hours of the morning. He lay there listening to the wee animal bleating in its misery until the sun peeped over the horizon. He then crawled out of his sleeping place and went to urinate next to the tree.

Billy the Kid and Voc eyed each other suspiciously. Voc then scraped his spurs on the sidewalk and reached for the trenching tool propped up against our bunker. He took aim with a keen eye. Billy the Kidd was a mite too slow for the local sheriff and one edge of the shovel chopped him between the eyes.

Dang it all!

The diminutive beast fell to the ground with a short squawk and was miserable no more.

Some days later, Lou Boom returned from patrol and immediately asked Guttergoose Gunn about the health and whereabouts of his pet. When he learned of the goat's violent demise he was quite upset, and threatened Voc with some hostility.

Voc accused Lou Boom of planned bestiality and shook the trenching tool at him as a silent warning of intent.

Later that evening while swigging Lion Lager, Lou Boom and Voc had a long-winded discussion about the lousy lives of goats in general. It was a comical discussion fuelled by hops brewed to perfection and it made absolutely no sense at all. Morgie the Raider and I just sat and grinned.

Thus was Billy the Kid dispatched to the happy paddock?

Water, water everywhere, but beware the drops you drink
(The ancient mariner sighs in his grave.)

Our water was kept in three or four bottles which we carried on us. What amounted to a two day supply could be stretched to a maximum of four days when absolutely necessary. On a follow-up, this amount of water could easily be consumed in a morning. We patrolled for between seven and ten days at a stretch and this implied that we had to seek alternate water supplies.

One of the ailments all bush-bound Rhodesian troopies had to contend with on a regular basis was diarrhoea. Fresh water was hard to come by in the field, especially in winter months when no rain fell. We were reasonably sure of being able to drink flowing river water without any side effects. Also, if the water was extracted from freshly dug holes in a river bed we would not experience any adverse consequences. However, if the water was stagnant and not treated with sterilizing tablets or boiled, the drinker was guaranteed a session of the runs.

And how that man would run!

The theory that flowing water was good to drink without treatment was totally dispelled from my mind one glorious morning as we sat resting on the banks of the Mazoe River. The stick reclined under the dense foliage which grew right up to the riverbank. Hence we were able to refresh our water supplies without risking exposure.

A barefoot tribesman strolled out of the bush onto the opposite riverbank. He was dressed in an unbuttoned short sleeved shirt and a pair of short trousers. He started crossing the shallow river, moving diagonally across to a point a few metres downstream. Then he stopped midstream in knee deep water, unzipped the front of his trousers and pulled out a huge black reptile. Pulling back an ominous hood, he proceeded to wash vigorously. This action stimulated some activity within his circulatory system and his penis swelled erect.

Without a bother in the world, he continued walking downstream under the shade of the huge trees overhead like a spry unicorn looking for something to stab. By now our mirth was irrepressible and much chastisement from a giggling Gary could not quell the peals of laughter that floated downstream towards the aroused fellow. The tribesman snatched a quick glance in our direction, sheepishly tucked his nomadic projection into his pants and continued on his way. That vision still worries me and I like to know that the water I drink has been properly treated.

Tap is fine but bottled is preferable.

These stomach upsets could harass us at any time and seemingly, after many days of drinking potable water, a luckless victim's stomach could suddenly cramp and he would have to rush to find suitable amenities for relief.

It was difficult to determine the state of one's bowels at any time and an unwary abdominal squeeze could vent a surge of processed rations. These accidents brought forth lewd ridicule from the other men. Such mockery usually came from the headquarter element as they seldom patrolled and had clean water available all the time. Therefore they were usually exempt from such humiliation. But be careful for you never know when it could be your turn. Morgie the Raider was one such headquarter element as he was a driver and had only to contend with camp cuisine.

One fine morning on ten day pass, Morgie the Raider woke up in his bed at home. With his wife snuggling up close against his back, he was enjoying life to the utmost. He felt the need to rid his system of a little poisonous gas and lazily lifted his leg.

What a mess!

The Raider sprayed hot microbes all over his wife's lower body and the bed sheets. Sis, what a stink. She swore at him and hurtled to the bathroom.

Morgie the Raider was a man who did not embarrass easily yet he snickered self-consciously. With a red face, he limped over to join his missus in the shower. He slid shamefaced into the shower next to her as she forecast the details of an impending conjugal drought.

Shame, Glynn!

As I reflect back I remember that the Raider and Glynn gave me a large nut and bolt for my 21st birthday. This was to secure my head to my neck just like Frankenstein. Open mockery it was and they also accused me of wearing a permanent mask because they teased that I was so ugly!

I told them payback was due, so there...heehaw.

The village idiot

Creeping past a village one twilit evening, we were greeted by a man who approached us from under an indistinguishable tree right in front of our patrol leader, as though expecting us.

"*Manheru, changamire,*" he greeted, and our leader promptly shot him through the head. The rest of us opened fire in the general direction from which the curfew breaker had appeared as we did not know whether there were any terrorists preparing to fire at us.

The fact that he had stood up and greeted us suggested that he had been expecting visitors that night, possibly terrorists, since we were obviously military. Maybe they would still appear?

We walked away from the village and doglegged around to take up an ambush position with the dead man in the centre of our killing-ground. We sneaked in silently and prepared for the night, which passed uneventfully with the exception of a cow that bellowed all night. In the morning, we walked to the village to question the inhabitants.

"No," they were adamant, "he was not expecting anybody last night. He just does not understand."

We had shot what we referred to as a village idiot. There seemed to be at least one of these in every village, many of whom had been shot while breaking curfew. I often wondered whether they were in fact as simple as their families made them out to be, or wandering about on the outskirts of their villages on dark nights with more nefarious business in mind. This 'village idiot' story, I suspected, was a ruse to prevent us from investigating more deeply, and it is possible that this deception stopped us from scrutinising many of the villages that were assisting terrorists.

As we left, we walked past the cattle kraal where we discovered that the bullets fired the previous night had hit some of the cattle. Some of them were still alive and a soldier at the front of the section shot them as he walked past. When I ambled past the cows, I observed that one of them had a strange sizzle in its head. I went closer and saw a tracer round lodged in its skull. The phosphorous of the tracer was still burning and glowing through the small bullet hole in the faint early morning light.

Carpenters never cut themselves

Once again finding ourselves at base camp for our one day rest after having showered and changed, Lou Boom, the Grundy, Voc, and I were sitting in our bivouac passing time.

At the beginning of the call-up, Lou Boom had decided that he was not going to use any soap or toothpaste for the duration of the tour. We did not bath or brush our teeth for ten days while on patrol anyway, he reasoned sensibly, so what the heck! He sat in a corner cleaning his machine gun with a cigarette dangling from his lips. His hair and beard were matted and I am sure he had more flies buzzing around him than the rest of us. He grinned and chuckled to himself a lot that afternoon and I wondered if he had prescribed himself a tranquilizer to alter his view on life!

Voc and I sat discussing our forthcoming trip to Durban which we were planning to take on our next ten day break. We had an open bottle of cane spirit between us, and we were mixing this with jungle juice in our fire-buckets.

When the bottle emptied we would chase the out devil. To get Satan excited enough to leave we would first rub the bottle feverishly with our hands. When it was warm enough, a lighted match would be inserted into the neck and, WHOOSH, the evil one would depart. These were the most exciting exorcisms. More intriguing, were the ones where a gentle blue circle of flame slowly burned down the inside of the bottle.

I was busy exorcising in this manner at home once, but the neck of the bottle had been broken off during a slightly inebriated accident. My right forefinger slid over the broken part of the bottle and sliced off a circular section of skin. Jean Graham examined this section of skin while I sucked on the wound. She exclaimed that there was a layer of fat on the cut side. I was amazed as I had thought I was so skinny as to be fatless! 36 years later I can still see and feel the scar on my finger.

To relieve boredom we would whittle our own dog-tags from small pieces of wood. These articles were invariably cut in the shape of a tombstone with the craftsman's name and blood group carved onto the front. Some were stained with boot polish but most just had a plain grubby appearance from being handled by grimy fingers.

The Grundy reclined in the back of the shelter on his sleeping bag. Back home, he was employed in the construction business. His job was to install wooden shuttering in preparation for the pouring of concrete, thus, he considered himself an expert worker of wood. He was busy carving a tombstone for himself with his nearly empty fire-bucket at his feet.

Many soldiers had been issued with a clasp knife and this was the Grundy's tool of choice for this most intricate of operations. He produced an oilstone and sharpened the knife, using slime hawked out of his throat as a lubricant. When he had completed this task, he illustrated how sharp his knife was by slicing through a section of the groundsheet. We were immensely impressed.

The current round of drinks expended, I scratched in some opened ration packs for some more mix. Voc stretched over to retrieve the Grundy and Lou Boom's fire-buckets for a refill. We poured like apprentice wizards and tasted the fusions with much lip smacking and moustache sucking. Voc returned our friends' replenished vessels to them.

The Grundy received his and gulped back several huge slugs of the liquid with relish. Lou Boom giggled sagely and shook his head as though he knew a great secret and was much wiser for it. He chuckled again and prophesied that he would die from laughter when the Grundy cut himself.

"Ha," retorted the Grundy, "carpenters NEVER cut themselves!"

He smirked and called us a name or two. Lou Boom just chortled and carried on assembling his gun. Voc grinned at me, called the Grundy an arsehole and suggested that I go and warn the medic that he was about to get his stitching skills tested. We lit up a round of cigarettes and sucked happily on our drinks as the Grundy continued shaving his piece of wood.

Then an awful hiss through clenched teeth merged with a stifled squeal was followed by a string of crude words. The Grundy had cut deeply into the palm of his hand. Lou Boom whooped with delight at the fulfilment of his prediction. Blood spattered onto the groundsheet and splashed all over the Grundy and his sleeping bag. He clasped his incised hand with the other and rolled into a painful bundle, swearing.

Lou Boom shouted, 'I told you so,' and cackled unchecked, like a hen that had just laid her first egg. I was now sure that he was under the influence of more than just cane spirit but he refused to let us in on the secret, the stingy sod. His grinning face revealed a set of blemished teeth covered in what appeared to be a furry yellow coating.

Our injured hero grasped a towel to stem the flow of blood and then stepped out of our army home with an ashen face. He aligned himself with the medic's tent and toddled off for help with misty eyes. After an hour he returned with a crisp white bandage covering his left hand. In his right hand, he clutched a container full of potent pain killers.

"Not for you bastards," he stated, when he realized that our attention was focused on his new hoard of treasure.

"C'mon, hand over," we demanded.

He rationed us each a few Propons which we promptly swilled back with generous shots of blend. The effects of the spirits fortified by whatever was in those pills quickly made us tingle. We sat there grinning like lampoons and talked nonsense.

Later, some background talking stirred us and we realized that it was afternoon snack time, during which our cook provided a lovely treat that we all looked forward to: jungle juice with chunks of cheese and raw onions in enamelled bowls.

Nothing to drink for us, thank you. Well, we had our own variety of jungle juice, didn't we!

Evening drew nigh and I felt a little jaded. I fumbled out of the tent, went to the perimeter of the camp and donated a synthesis of lumpy cheese and onion floating in a gravy of spirited yellow liquid to the ants. Then I hurtled off to the camp long-drop and decorated the inside of the thunder-box with a fresh coating of aromatic light-brown. I attributed these strange emissions to the after-effects of the Grundy's pain killers.

Feeling rather groggy, I groped my way to my sleeping possie through the darkness. The others were all finishing dinner but I was in no mood for food. Soporifically, I poured myself another dose of jungle juice, lit a smoke and waited for my friends. They returned and mocked me about my unstable intestines. Then we mooched of to the canteen where we spent the rest of the evening.

Early the next morning I woke up before the others. The Grundy and Lou Boom were curled up in their sleeping bags and Voc lay on his back, snoring loudly. I lit a cigarette and lay on my back, puffing contentedly and contemplating what lay ahead for the day.

The sun was struggling to break over the horizon. When it eventually forced light through the entrance to our shelter, I saw an opened clasp knife on the groundsheet by the Grundy's bed. Next to it lay a half modelled piece of wood. The Grundy had tried to start a new craze in Charlie Company by tinting his tombstone a shade of cherry red.

It was not a trend that became fashionable.

Durbs, here we come

Four of us decided that we should motor down to Durban during our next R & R. Located, as it was, on the South African East Coast, Durban's weather would be superb in midsummer. With the Rhodesian dollar firmer than the rand, it was a no brainer. And all them curvy chicks on the beach, what kind!

The trip to the border was uneventful. We motored along with a rifle poking out of each window, like a speedy little hedgehog. At Beitbridge, we checked in at the police station which had a facility for storing weapons as we were not allowed to take these over the border. This formality complete, we passed through both custom posts without incident. The road down to sunny Durbs by the sea was now open all the way.

'Head south,' the television advertisement had told us, and we did.

We stopped in Messina to procure a few dozen beers and Voc's Fiat shot down the freeway to Durban. The speed limit in South Africa at the time was 100 kilometres per hour but we knew that any ticket issued to us would not be traceable by the customs officials at the border.

Voc had an eight track cassette player installed in his vehicle, but only one tape. This was a collection of rock 'n roll oldies and we knew the words to the songs by heart by the time we cruised into our destination.

'You-keep-on-knockin'-butcher-can't-come-in,   come-back-tamorrer-night-an'-try-it-agin.'

Voc pulled into a service station at Mooi Rivier to refuel. The rest of us popped into the small kiosk and bought snacks while Voc supervised the attendant. Refreshed, we continued our journey. A joint scored from the garage attendant was quickly set aglow and the journey became a blur of music, snacks and belly-bruising laughter.

On arrival, we checked in at the Rydal Mount Hotel, two to a room. There were no sea views from our cheap rooms but we did not even bother looking out of the windows. We met Ryan, who was a trooper from the RLI also on R & R, and accepted his company easily. The next day was Saturday and by law, no one was allowed to purchase liquor in South Africa on a Sunday, so our primary mission was to make sure that we would have enough stock of our favourite grog. A quick trip to the bottle store did the trick and we sneaked our stash into our hotel room.

Adjourning to the beach, we spent the rest of the day swimming in the warm water and sipping slyly from covered bottles. That evening, we were to test the town and see what action was available. The five of us found ourselves in some night club, but it was early and the entertainment had not started yet. Mother, Ryan, and I were starting to flow with the go (hic) and ducked off to the bar as the service at the tables was a little slow. On our return, we saw that Voc and Trevor had moved tables and were now sitting in front of the stage with two cute girls.

Not wanting to be outdone, the three of us bounced up onto this stage and started stripping our clothing off seductively in time to the *Rocky Horror Picture Show* soundtrack.

'It's just a jump to the left and then a step to the right, with your hands on your hips...'

Our small audience laughed and cheered us on. Thus encouraged, we stripped and piled our clothing onto the floor. When we were down to our underwear, the tolerant club manager quickly jumped onto the stage and said that we had provided good entertainment and he would sign a contract with us on Monday, but we had to clear the stage for the next show. People were beginning to drift in and he seemed scared that we might chase some of his clientele away.

We got dressed and sat down with the two starry-eyed couples and I, ever hopeful, suggested a gangbang. The ladies' mouths dropped open in trepidation. I could sense a punch coming from an evilly grinning Voc, so I hastily proposed that we three singles seek out excitement elsewhere.

We left the club and pub-crawled for a few hours until closing time. Still thirsty, we decided to return to our hotel and raid the Sabbath goodies. Each having selected something suitable, we teetered off to the beach front. As we were crossing Marine Parade in front of the funfair, a belligerent security guard insulted us from the entrance, stating that the funfair was closed and we should go somewhere else. We'd had no intention of visiting his stupid funfair; we had only wanted to pass through to the beach. Also, we were not happy about having been spoken to in this manner by a mere security guard. He was definitely in need of an etiquette makeover. Mother and Ryan hurled verbal abuse while I selected an unopened dumpy from my six-pack, aimed and threw with all my might. The missile flew straight but fell just short of target. There was a pop, a tinkle of glass and then a great cloud of foam enveloped the man.

"Got him," I exulted at my accuracy. This initiated a full frontal attack.

Mother and Ryan were now in full charge. Shaking beer and possibly some fragments of glass from his face, the security guard took one look at his would be assailants, and then turned and bolted for the safety of his amusement park. I slowly followed the assault team in. It was dead quiet and there was no sign of any contact with the enemy. Some minutes later, Mother and Ryan returned from the direction of the beach, laughing and describing in great detail what they would have done had they caught up with 'that gook'.

Our bout of excitement over, we ambled over to a park bench on the sidewalk in front of the Wimpy and continued our party. A police van pulled up and a very courteous constable jumped out. He greeted us and we replied with a cautious 'howzhit'. When he discovered that we were foreigners he politely explained that in his country, it was illegal to drink in public and suggested we move a distance out of the direct public eye and continue there.

Graciously we obliged. Our festivity continued for another ten minutes when suddenly, two police vehicles screeched to a halt just behind us. Two large policemen exited from one vehicle and the polite policeman got out of the second, except he had somehow forgotten his manners. We were ordered to drop the bottles in our hands immediately and step into the backs of their vehicles.

No way, mate!

This is our booze, bought and paid for and we are not parting with it for you all to consume. Someone suggested that we pour all the contents out to spite the fuzz. The cops promptly charged, bowled us over, and then locked us in the back of one of the vans. From within the confines of the caged canopy, I spied a man dressed in a uniform. He came close to the wire mesh and grinned at me. I smelled stale beer and recognized him as the security guard who we had attacked earlier on. I think his revenge was sweet to him.

The vehicle started up and jerked forward, throwing our unsteady bodies to the rear. I immediately thought of the *Biltong and Potroast* comedy tapes that we had listened to in the bush canteen (the car pulled up with a jerk, the jerk got out and I got in).

The police drove like ones possessed and I believe they were. We rolled and tumbled around the enclosed back of the vehicle all the while cursing those pigs.

They drove us all the way to Glen Ashley police station and incarcerated us there. We had some fun deriding our attackers and their station bound colleagues while they forced us to empty our pockets of possessions and our shoes of laces. We told them that they were lucky that their cowardly prime minister, John Vorster, had withdrawn the South African Police from service in Rhodesia otherwise we would have beaten the crap outta them. They ignored us for the most part and this was possibly fortunate for us.

In the cell was a fourth man, who greeted us and complimented us on our valour. He told us that he had been arrested for thumping his wife and we flattered him for having taken a stand against women's lib. He then produced three cigarettes and lit them with a match, all cleverly hidden inside his tie. These we shared. When we asked him how he had known where to hide the cigarettes he stated that this was not the first time he had been put into the slammer for cracking his missus. We applauded his stance for justice and liberty, finished the smokes, and drifted off to sleep.

Almost immediately, the cell door clanged open and we were uncouthly ordered to collect our things and bugger off. We stumbled out of the police station totally ignorant of where we were. The dawn was still grey in the virgin sky. Clutched in our hands were our shoes and laces. There was a bus stop nearby and an elderly dear was sitting on the bench. We sat next to her and started to thread the laces into our rather well used shoes. Politely,

I asked her where we were. She just stood up, huffed and walked away, her heels clicking on the pavement. I suppose just having stumbled shoeless out of the lockup stinking of beer did not create a good impression in the old girl's mind.

A bus pulled up with a hiss of compressed air and we clambered on board, not really caring where it was going. A short conversation with the few occupants ensued. One passenger sympathetically informed us that we were headed for the city centre and this made us happy. The bus disgorged us somewhere in the conurbation of Durban, and we dragged our weary feet to the hotel and crashed up the stairs.

Voc and Trevor were there and they asked how our evening had gone. They scoffed at us as we told them about the night's events in great detail. When we asked them how it had gone with the girls, they squirmed a little, trying not to appear embarrassed. The girls had dumped our two friends in favour of more affluent and articulate men. It was now our turn for ridicule and they left for breakfast with our jibes following after. We retired to our beds and a well-earned sleep.

The rest of our stay in Durban was short and uneventful and the drive back to Rhodesia was boring. There was no follow-up score at Mooi Rivier and the journey was long and hot. We retrieved our weapons at Beitbridge and hedge hogged our way back home.

Goodbye Mr Pheasant
Sometime in March 1977, Gary Pheasant took a long period of leave to mooch around in the pleasure spots of Europe. We said our farewells and Gary departed. I did not see him again until the conception of this book. He returned to active duty and was commissioned in July 1977. This was a well-deserved promotion. Gary was also awarded the Bronze Cross of Rhodesia for bravery.

Cross border operation at Nyamapanda
Our new company commander gave us orders to gather intelligence on Frelimo and ZANLA's activities and numbers. This we were to undertake by setting up an observation point close to identified enemy barracks constructed

about two kilometres into Mozambique, opposite the Nyamapanda border post.

If it was possible, we were also to make an attempt to capture, either a member of Frelimo or of ZANLA.

Two sticks were to be deployed by vehicle to a point on the border fence road, 12 kilometres south of Nyamapanda. We arrived at about 16h00, giving us enough time to walk to and cross the fence at dusk, and benefit from the darkness of night as we walked into our position. The vehicles would also have enough daylight to drive back to Kotwa.

When we debussed, our commander noticed that some of his men were apprehensive about the mission, and asked who was willing to go as it would be a dangerous operation. He didn't want any reluctant team mates jeopardizing the safety of the group. I think we feared being captured by the enemy more than anything else.

It should be well noted that we were not Special Forces, trained for this type of operation. The order to observe activity in enemy territory was hard enough for troops of our calibre and the order to capture an enemy soldier was a heavy burden for us to bear. Three men agreed to accompany our commander. The balance of the sticks returned to Kotwa with the vehicles. We had a round 15 kilometre walk to the area we were required to observe. Five kilometres after crossing the border, we intersected the Mudzi River and then continued north along a south flowing tributary. This river was mainly comprised of small pools, replenished by a stream filtered through the sandbanks. Two kilometres from our objective, we cut inland east of the river and progressed through the bush in a dogleg towards our goal. This would position us as though we had been walking inland from Mozambique and hopefully create the impression that our spoor was friendly.

Less than 50 metres from the main road there was a small ridge covered in trees and thick undergrowth. We followed our leader up this rise to a point about 200 metres away from the cluster of buildings that comprised the barracks: some huts, some small brick buildings and a large corrugated iron shed. No fence bordered the complex which straddled both sides of the main road. The thicket of brush was dotted with small piles of shit which stank terribly. There was also no relief as the soft prevailing breeze did not penetrate the undergrowth enough to disperse the smell. To add to our discomfort, fat green flies crawled over the faeces and then buzzed around trying to settle on our faces and lips. We were terrified that that a passer-by would require a bowel movement and enter the undergrowth to discover us hiding there.

Here we lay until afternoon the next day, alternating two men on watch while two rested. We were unable to move by day or night as there was plenty of activity on the road. Frelimo and ZANLA troops constantly walked to and from the border post. One erratic move and we would be running for our lives.

We observed for 36 hours, taking notes of numbers, ordnance, and routines. We left the radio off except for a brief situation report twice a day. When we reported on the morning of the second day, Major Currin gave us an urgent order to withdraw as an SAS operation was to take place the following day.

We could not move across open ground to the border in broad daylight without risk of being spotted. Our leader strategically decided to make an attempt at achieving our second objective, to capture one of the enemy, as we withdrew. This we would do by moving back to Tributary 1 of the Mudzi River and laying up in the thick bush there. When it was dark, we would creep back up to the main road and wait there until opportunity afforded us a capture.

Later that afternoon we left our position on the ridge. As we approached the river we observed a young man. It was quite obviously laundry day and he had stripped to bathe and wash his clothing. We moved into a thick tree line growing on a rocky ridge running parallel to the river and waited to see if he would move, but he had laid his clothes out to dry on the rocks and reclined naked on the sand. He lay on the same bank we were hiding next to with his back towards us.

We heard the sound of women singing upstream. Downstream, the river veered through some open grassland where a number of kraals had been built. Taking this route would put us in danger of being observed. Walking around the women upstream would reveal our presence to anyone on the road. Our only safe route lay past the man sunning himself on the sand and time was running out.

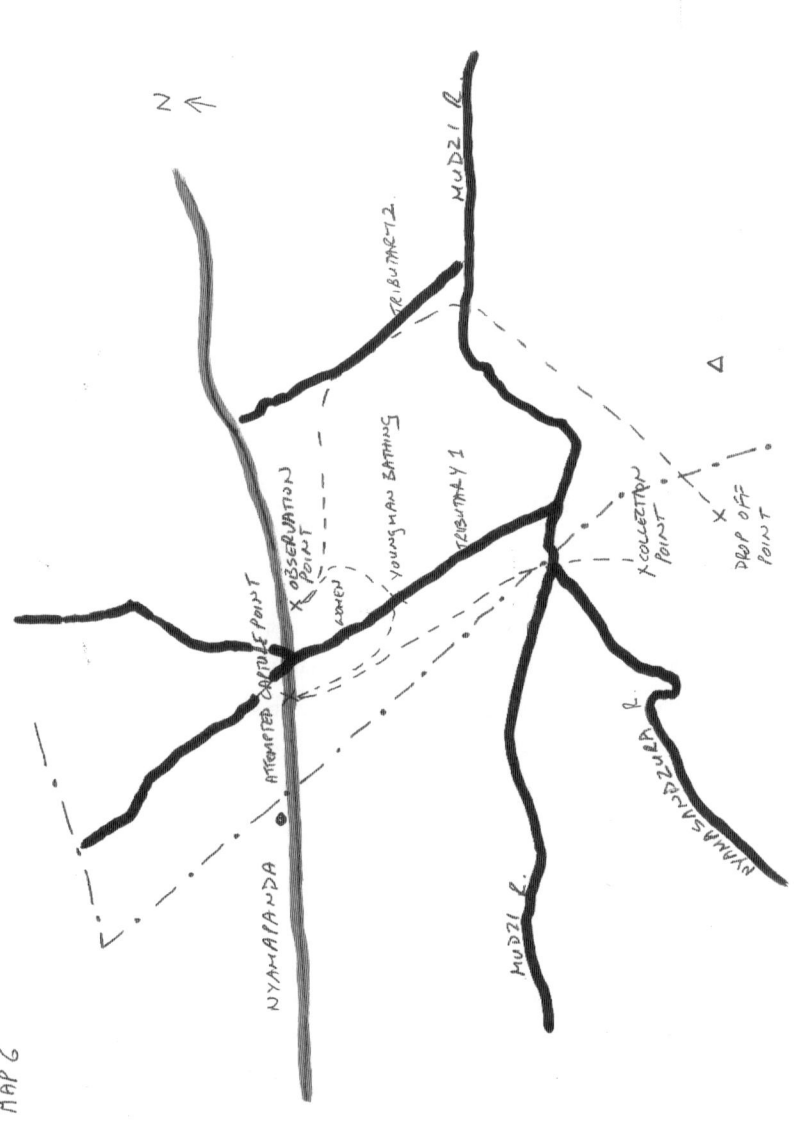

MAP 6

We discussed capturing the resting man but decided against it as he was obviously a civilian who would supply little military information. This implied an unnecessary risk as escorting him to the border would hamper our attempt to capture and escort an enemy soldier. Our stick commander decided that we would have to immobilize him. The plan was to overpower him, gag him, and tie him up. A length of nylon cord and a sock were procured from our packs to enable this operation. If he jeopardized our presence at all we would have to kill him. Of course, we could not shoot him and determined to use knives if necessary. We chose a sheath knife with a three inch long blade and a small Swiss Army knife.

The plan was for all four of us to get closer to the river and then to leave me, being the smallest (it's those skinny arms of mine again) to guard our weapons and keep an eye open. The other three would then sneak up on the unsuspecting sunbather and tackle him.

I kept guard while the others sneaked up and seized the unfortunate nudist. He fought like a trapped buffalo struggling to break free, but he was unable to overcome the three strong and fit men. One soldier tried, unsuccessfully, to smother his shouts using a combat cap stuffed with a camouflage face-veil. The other two were unable to subdue his struggles entirely and panic ensued due to fear that the man would sound an alarm. One man used the sheath knife to stab him in the chest and another cut his neck with the pen knife. This combined hacking and stabbing did not kill the terrified man immediately and only when his jugular had been severed did he weaken and die. They then dragged his body behind some reeds and did the best they could to remove all trace of the struggle by covering the blood-stained sand.

The women upstream had stopped singing.

I was under cover and could not see what was happening. The only indication of any activity was indistinct scuffles and muffled screams as our way forward was cleared. The three assassins then sneaked up through the reeds to where I crouched, waiting. They were all smeared with blood and had a feverish glow in their eyes.

Afterwards, all three agreed that it had not been as easy as it looked in the movies.

We rushed across the river in case the women upstream had heard any sound of the scuffle, and then proceeded up along another rocky ridge on the west of the river to a bushy area near the road where we waited for darkness. While we were waiting, we suddenly heard ululating and wailing and realized that the women had found the body. One of us later revealed that the wailing had made him feel sick. We had most likely heard the dead man's mother lamenting and this had made him reflect on how his own mother would react in a similar situation.

We waited until it was dark and our leader deployed us next to the tarred road. Thick rain clouds had blown up from the coast and the night was pitch-black. Two of us took care of the weapons while the other two prepared to jump any prospective captive. The road was busy and people walked by every few minutes, some of them in small groups.

It was so dark that we could not see our hands in front of our eyes let alone the people on the road, even though some were literally only a metre or two away. It was eerie with the distant wailing of the women and the pedestrians on the road never uttering a sound. All we could hear was their quick and purposeful footsteps and the sound of equipment rubbing or creaking every now and again.

This exercise was fraught with risk and the chances of making a clean grab and getaway seemed limited. The atmosphere was electric and our nerves were stressed past endurance. The final breaking point was attained when one of our men was bitten by an insect as he leaned against a fallen tree trunk. He moved sharply and grunted with pain which made someone on the road shout in fright and run off.

Our cover would be blown when the pedestrian got to the barracks. After hearing the story of the river kill, he would conclude that enemy soldiers were close by and that he had possibly even heard them on the road.

Relieved, we started a night march back to the border. Our leader stuck faithfully to the compass bearing and we hit the border fence a short while before dawn.

The Flying Hunter
Flying in a Rhodesia Airways Viscount from Bulawayo to Fort Victoria one Thursday afternoon, I reflected on how humorous and even ridiculous some

things turned out to be. I was winging my way home after having had a chip of bone removed from my left knee by a certain Mr Robinson, orthopaedic surgeon.

My mother greeted me and drove me home. There I was to recuperate and then present myself to the medical officer at 10RR. On Friday afternoon, Colin Kirkham telephoned and invited me to go hunting with Pales and himself that evening. My mother, who was within earshot, protested hotly but I ignored her advice and agreed to go.

Colin picked me up just before sundown and we drove the 20 kilometres to Pales' father's farm. I took my BSA .22 rifle with me and was planning to shoot a small buck as I had never done this before. Pales was waiting for us with his father's brand new Nissan van which we were going to use for the evening shoot. He had been warned not to damage the vehicle in any way.

We shared some beers from a case and then all climbed aboard the van. Pales was driving and Colin and I sat on the roof of the cab. I threw my crutches in the back. Leisurely, we manoeuvred along a sandy road scanning the bush for any sign of game. A hare jumped out of the grass verge and, mesmerized by the headlights, started to run down one of the road's wheel tracks.

"Get it," Colin shouted.

Pales disregarded any threat from his father concerning the new van and pushed down on the accelerator. The vehicle surged forward and I sat balanced on the cab's roof with my rifle in one hand and a half consumed beer in the other. Thus I rocked back and forth on my bum until the hare realized he was going to lose the race and veered off the road into the bush. Pales swung the steering wheel and his father's brand new van immediately turned sharply to follow the rabbit.

I, however, continued to follow the course of the road and crashed down onto the earth. It was as though I had been sitting in an armchair which had slowly rolled over. My right side hit the ground with my legs still bent in the sitting position. The rifle flew in one direction and the beer bottle emptied itself in tumbling flight. I lay still trying to catch my breath.

Slowly, I felt my diaphragm regain self-control and became aware of two imprudent faces smirking at me. They were checking to see if I was still alive. When my two mates realized that I had not been placed on any terminal list, their bogus concern changed to hilarity. They jested as though it was the funniest incident ever, the jerks. Colin was red faced with laughter and he teased and spurred more laughter out of Pales. And so these two idiots continued to make merry at my expense.

We proceeded with our hunt. Colin and Pales each bagged a small buck and these were loaded onto the vehicle. As we approached a small dam, our headlights revealed a huge kudu bull with a magnificent set of horns. It was my turn to shoot. Pales handed me his .303 rifle and issued instructions on how to drop the animal without damaging the trophy. We drove closer until the horns seemed to fill my vision. The buck just stood there and looked at us. I aimed and squeezed the trigger. There was a mighty bang with a great flash and smoke and the rifle's recoil punched me backwards off the cab into the bin of the vehicle.

And I had missed the best trophy animal I would ever see, at point blank range too. Those buffoons shrieked with laughter at my misfortune. I was starting to get a little irritated but I did see the funny side and smirked at them.

We drove back to the farmhouse to string up the dead buck so that the carcasses could be gutted and skinned. Pales climbed onto the bonnet of his father's, by now, not so brand new van and reached up a gantry for a chain with which to string up the buck. His weight pushed the metal of the bonnet downwards and it made contact with the battery's positive terminal. This caused a red spot to glow on the bonnet which increased in area as the current from the battery flowed through the steel. The shiny enamel paint blackened and peeled back. Finally the steel burned through and the battery boiled and died. I wondered how Pales was going to explain why the van no longer appeared new to his father.

By now we had finished the beer. We were drinking brandy and cola and were ready to skin the buck. As Pales opened the first beast's stomach with his gut hook, the intestines dropped out and splattered on the floor. A fresh stink filled the room. I retched and sniffed and retched again as I hobbled outside in search of clean air. Of course this triggered my retarded friends into more bouts of laughter which I did not share. From then on I sat outside with the brandy and issued instructions on how to prepare my cuts of meat.

"What are you talking about, Toc? You missed yours," they said.

My knee was throbbing a little but I could still walk with the aid of the crutches. There was a bright red mark on the bandage, which grew larger as the evening wore on. When I removed the bandage a few days later, I saw that my crash landing had ripped the stitches apart. This had greatly increased the width of the surgeon's incision. To this day, the scar still reminds me of how humorous and ridiculous some things can turn out to be.

I should also remind you, young man, to listen to the words of your mama. She is much wiser than you.

My Dad, the beekeeper

My mother told me the following story.

My father was enjoying a drink with an old friend who mentioned that he had a beehive he did not want. Dad said that he would like to add to the hive or two that he already had producing honey on his 20 acre smallholding. The friend readily persuaded my Dad that this hive was particularly rampant in the production of a very sweet and nutritious honey. It would complement the small production line that my male parent was enthusiastic to expand, he said. And it was free with delivery included.

My father was fully persuaded.

Sometime later, the friend delivered the hive in a swirl of smoke under a great tarpaulin stretched over the back of his delivery van. My father pointed out, from the safety of his car, where the friend should place the hive. This was done by men clad in heavy denim overalls with mesh stretched over wide brimmed hats amidst the wreath of smelly smoke.

For a year, my father left the hive to settle and peacefully produce honey. Then it was time to harvest. My father dressed in a huge overall and folded the trouser legs into the socks on his feet, which were in turn, pulled into a pair of heavy gumboots. He stretched the gloves on his hands over the long sleeves of his overall and clamped them into place with sturdy rubber bands. He pulled a wide brimmed hat onto his head and tucked the veil that shrouded it, securely into the collar of his overall.

My father, always the intrepid entrepreneur, then wheezed a fog of acrid smoke from a special smoke puffer into the entrance of the hive to dull the senses of the bees. He then bravely lifted the lid from the top of the hive, reached in, and extracted a huge comb dripping rich honey. Smiling, he turned to show this to my anxious mother who was observing the process from the safety of her closed bedroom window.

This was the last vestige of bravado that my fearless old man exhibited that day.

Suddenly he dropped the honeycomb and howled in pressing pain. He started to slap at his head and neck in a fury of spastic blows. Then he made a beeline, absolutely no pun intended, for the front door of the house.

As he hurtled past the bedroom window, he hollered for my mother to unlock the front door. She responded by running to a closed window next to the aforementioned door. She pressed her cheek to the glass and watched as my dad kicked at the base of the door. His hands hung by his sides with swarms of bees hanging off each glove. The bees dangled there like, well, dripping honey. These bees then dropped off onto the floor and surged up into the air to attack my father's upper areas again. No amount of tortured pleading would induce my mother to open the front door.

She sank to her knees praying as she imagined the life ebbing out of her true love. When my dad realized that my mother's concern was orientated only to her own safety he turned and bolted for the safety of the swimming pool.

After a great splash my dad sank to the bottom of the pool and luxuriated in the cooling effect the water had on his bee stings. He hovered there until his breath turned into carbon dioxide. Then he kicked off from the bottom and broke the surface of the pool, simultaneously pulling off the deceptive net that now promised to smother him. The squadrons of bees overhead spotted their opportunity and attacked again. My father gulped a frantic breath and again dived for the sanctuary of the pool bottom.

The four canines that had valiantly guarded my parents and their offspring for many years had listened to enough of the hullabaloo emanating from the front garden. They broke out of their enclosure in the back yard and ran to the pool area baying. The bees stopped attacking the water and concentrated on the dogs. These animals ran and snapped at the aerial offensive and my father took the opportunity to run for the front door again.

Mum had been watching through the huge lounge window and opened the door to admit my dripping wet and frantic father. He is still alive today due to my mother's delayed resourcefulness and the auspicious intervention of our dogs.

Three of the dogs survived the bee offensive due to their thick fur. The fourth survived due to the high pain threshold and thick headedness of the English bullterrier.

The next day my dad called Uncle Eric. Surely he would be interested in a beehive that was very productive with a unique blend of sweet honey. Uncle Eric removed the hive which he enjoyed for a short while before being admitted to the general hospital in Fort Victoria. He was diagnosed as suffering from multiple bee stings.

It transpired that these bees were a special cross-breed of African and vicious South American bees. I have heard that these bees have invaded Africa causing great consternation amongst the fraternity of bee keepers.

I eat honey from the security of a bottle. And only if there is no honeycomb visible in the mélange of bee *vomitus*.

An evening at the Great Zimbabwe Hotel

Dietz and I tailed Lou Boom who was driving his light blue Renault R4 with his mother in the front seat and his little sister in the back. We had shared beers at Lou Boom's lodgings before setting out and we each drove with a dumpy firmly ensconced between our thighs. Arriving together, we entered and sat at the long wooden public bar in the Great Zimbabwe Hotel.

I sat with Blackie, Voc, and Kudu, and we talked a whole heap of nonsense as they were getting fired up with brandy and cane spirits. Laughter and jokes were the order of the day and the atmosphere in the pub was noisy and jovial. It was autumn and very cold outside but the hotel management had ensured our comfort with blazing log fires in every fireplace.

Lynda, Louise, and a girlfriend arrived and the tumult climaxed as small individual groups of men raucously invited the girls to join them. We won and they sat their sexy jeans down on barstools that Blackie and I procured from different positions around the bar. We proceeded to chat these pretty girls up and the atmosphere in our assembly became competitive as the four men vied for the attention of the three women.

Blackie, in a moment of outright fervour pulled an old Webley .455 revolver from his back pocket and put the barrel to his temple. Like this was supposed to impress these ladies. They all voiced concern which increased when he cocked the hammer without removing the barrel from his head. Kudu just swore and hung his head. Voc laughed and said 'go for it,' to Blackie. I shuddered at my vision of Blackie's brains sitting amidst the rows of bottles displayed behind the bar.

Blackie screamed and pulled the trigger. The hammer snapped down on the empty gun with a clack. Blackie roared with laughter, obviously at the look of horror and shock on our faces. The girls screamed and ran out of the pub into the adjoining ladies bar where they fell in with a more passive group of local people. Kudu swore at Blackie and left to sit trembling by himself in a corner of the bar. I riled Blackie with an exasperated explanation of how not to entertain chicks, you idiot. Blackie scowled at me and I realized that his consumption of alcohol had exceeded his limit. I did not relish the thought of being broken by his huge fists so I quickly excused myself and departed for the relative safety of the group in the ladies bar.

It got late and we decided to leave and listen to music at Lou Boom's house. We persuaded the girls that our company was more worthwhile than the group they had acquainted themselves with, loaded our inebriated bodies into our cars, and drove off. The air was crisp and clear and there was a lustrous moon.

Outside, I noticed a young European man sitting in the company of an African man. They sat with their heads bowed together in deep conversation. The young man was a loner and we were all aware of his existence but none of us had ever spoken to him. He lived in a small house in town with his mother and sister. I did not realize it at the time but I was probably the last white man to see Terry Brinson alive!

I drove with Voc, Dietz and Lynda to keep me company. Lou Boom suddenly swerved his vehicle off the road onto the verge. The car quivered to a halt and he leapt out brandishing his FN above his head like a warrior flaunting his spear. With a terrible cry, he charged off into the thick bush.

His mother wailed from within the car as I approached to find out what had happened. Lou Boom's mother simply said that he had complained that he was not going back to the army. He had then slammed on the brakes and hurtled off into the bush as we had just witnessed.

"Please go and find him," chorused Lou Boom's mother and little sister.

I ran off into the bush and immediately stumbled upon a footpath running parallel to the road. Turning left, I ran, hoping that I was going in the same direction as my mad friend. 'What a time to turn bush happy,' I thought. A noise similar to that of a howling dog sounded ahead of me and I knew that I had chosen the correct bearing. Small branches whipped against my raised arms and chest as I ran. Then my feet disappeared from under me and I crashed down into a river bed lined with course sand. I sat up and spat rocks out of my mouth and peeled back my eyelids to remove burning things.

Lou Boom cackled maniacally from where he lay after having crashed into the ground as I had done. He laughed uncontrollably at my endeavours to clean up and grew quiet when I asked him what was wrong and why he had run off. He denied knowing what I was talking about. Then a semblance of sanity returned to his troubled mind and I suggested we return to the road, which we did, and both climbed back into our cars.

As Lou Boom drove off, I could hear his distressed mother berating his unsound mind. On arrival at Lou Booms parents' house, Lou Boom disappeared into his bedroom where he slumbered deeply. We partied until late and then I found a comfortable spot and fell asleep.

The next day was Sunday and word spread that Terry Brinson was missing. His frantic mama had alerted the police. Lou Boom's mother contacted the patrol officer on duty and told him where we had seen Terry late the previous evening.

We returned to our unit some two days later and on our next R & R, Lou Boom's mother mentioned that Terry Brinson had been found a week after his disappearance. An informant had disclosed where he was and the police had found him in a cave close to the hotel that we had all been celebrating in. He had been stripped naked and then stoned to death by the local tribespeople.

Apparently the local ladies had done most of the stoning.

The mango pickers

A number of ZANLA were expected to be meeting at an identified village and we were to surround them in a high-density operation. All three platoons of Charlie Company were walking in from different directions to set up stop groups at various points around the village.

8 Platoon were moving down a slope towards a river through a field of trees when I heard furious slapping sounds combined with stifled whimpers of pain. One of our men had walked into a hornet's nest hanging from a low branch. The angry hornets had dropped into the unfortunate soldier's shirt collar. Trapped here, the insects stung the man mercilessly, leaving him no option other than to try and kill them by slapping at his neck, back and chest. He then threw off his webbing and ripped the shirt off his shoulders. This released the stinging furies and they flew off into the night. I think the most frustrating part of the experience for this poor soldier was that he'd had to maintain a degree of silence to avoid compromising the mission. I admired his fortitude.

We were walking in double file formation. The terrain opened out and we advanced in a north-easterly direction along a small stream. Our platoon commander was leading the file, walking closest to the stream with Blackie behind him. I led the second file as I was to supply firepower to the front with my Bren gun if required. Kudu marched directly behind me with the Bravo stick leader behind him. We thus had an even distribution of firepower and leadership.

There was no moon and this was surely a factor that the enemy had considered when they decided to meet that night. Starlight was sufficient for navigation and we treaded cautiously forward, not wanting to alert any inhabitants of nearby kraals to our presence. The locals had all been subverted by ZANLA and we considered them all to be the enemy as they actively assisted terrorists in any way possible. If we were detected, word would swiftly spread to the ears of those we were now hunting.

Frogs in the pools and reeds were croaking in unqualified nocturnal harmony and they marked our presence by ceasing as we passed by. Thus a band of silence travelled along the stream as we advanced. So much for clandestine movement!

The frogs ahead of us suddenly became silent. All we could hear was the croaking resuming immediately behind us. Then we all saw a flash of white on the other side of the stream, directly opposite our left flank. Reacting immediately, our left flank took cover and laid down fire on the opposite riverbank. Our right flank took cover facing away from the killing area.

I, however, was not going to miss out and dived in between our platoon commander and Blackie and proceeded to empty a magazine at the movement in front of me. There was a blast and a flash of brilliant light and I thought we had fired into explosives carried on one of the enemy. Red tracers flew everywhere in front of us. I saw my own tracer striking the ground and arcing up into the air to dissipate way up in the sky.

"Cease fire," bellowed our commander.

After three or four undisciplined shots, there was absolute silence. Neither the frogs nor any other night life made any sound. There was not even a dog yapping in the kraals on the ridge behind us. The sound of magazines (including my own) being rapidly changed, broke the silence. Blackie turned his head and in a whisper, asked me what the hell I was doing out of position and why I had been firing up into the air. Then he quickly bragged about how well he had targeted with his rifle grenade. Now I knew what had caused the explosion during our contact.

Our right flank was ordered to advance upstream and to cross and sweep the killing area. It was not a normal tactic to sweep an area at night after a fire fight, but we surmised that our targets were either dead, or more probably, civilians, due to the fact that there had been no return fire.

The right flank crossed the stream and swept in extended line towards some motionless shapes on the ground. As we closed in, we made out three people dressed in dirty white robes. There was a fourth dark shape lying between the others. A torch light revealed three men with long beards and shaved heads.

"Mango pickers," someone blurted in disgust.

The area grew a large number of mango trees; in fact, these were the only trees as the indigenous ones had all been chopped down for firewood. Thus, we named the locals mango pickers. These men were actually apostles, members of a religious movement quite popular among the local people.

They must have been caught out by the dusk to dawn curfew enforced at the time while returning home after one of their gatherings. The fourth shape was a green sausage-shaped bag similar to those we had been issued as kit bags.

Since there was no immediate danger, the soldiers across the stream stood up and crossed over. We all stood in a very loose defensive position while our boss established communications with base to report on the latest event. This action would have compromised our assignment as the village we were to investigate was not too far off. The sound of our gunfire and the explosion would have alerted all for miles around.

Suddenly an African voice pleaded with us, "I am not a terrorist, please do not shoot me." This voice belonged to one of the three lying at our feet. One of us asked what we should do.

"Shoot him," the order came.

We hesitated and then one of the rifleman said that he would do it. The combined flash and bang made me jump involuntarily and it was over.

"My second kill," he boasted.

I had not clocked up any confirmed notches on my gun but I thought that if I should have to kill a civilian man in cold blood like that it would surely be a shameful thing. I would have to recall these thoughts a few years later.

We bomb-shelled close by and took turns at guard duty until first light. Walking down to the killing-ground that morning I was amazed to see how much damage we had inflicted. The one survivor had only a hole in his leg, and one in his head from the *coup de grâce*. The next poor fellow had been shot through in the chest, arms, stomach and legs. The state of the third man, however, confirmed Blackie's claim of marksmanship. The rifle grenade had struck the man on the upper thigh, blasting the leg off and doing extensive damage to the other leg and genitals. He had also taken rounds through his body and head. The area surrounding the men was splattered with blood and gore.

Good shooting considering the dark night.

One of us emptied the contents of the green bag onto the ground. There were some religious artefacts, some clothing, and some cloth bank bags containing cash. These disappeared into our kit for later distribution between our platoon members. We left the bodies to be taken care of by the locals and proceeded to march to our rendezvous point, a store some six kilometres away.

After some hours, we approached the store as our vehicles arrived. The vehicle escorts jumped off and ran to the front of the vehicles shouting. Then a single shot rang out. Fanning out into extended line, we rapidly advanced towards our vehicles. There we found that one of the vehicle escorts, Akkie, had fired on a man who had fled from the store when the vehicles arrived. This was the same Akkie I had worked with at Hawker Siddeley Electric some years before.

The man lay on the ground, turned half on his side. He was dressed in blue denim trousers, Super Pro takkies, and a faded drab shirt. He was gasping heavily as Kudu and I advanced on him, ready to fire if he became threatening. His chest was heaving as he drowned in his own blood, which flowed copiously from his mouth and nose and bubbled out of the exit wound in his chest. He breathed his last and stopped moving while we were standing over him.

The round from Akkie's rifle had hit the man under the left shoulder blade and exited above the right breast. This indicated that he had been running in a crouched position which was a good enough reason to shoot him as it implied military training.

We teased Akkie about his remarkable talent as a sniper and recommended that he sign up for the next SAS course. He just grinned, revealing some discoloured teeth, and rubbed his bountiful paunch, stating that he would give it a miss this time, just to give us younger lads a chance, *ek sê*!

There was not much to do and adjourning to the store, we bought lukewarm fizzy drinks to slake our thirst. On returning to base at Kotwa, we showered and lazed around for the rest of the day. The vehicles sent to collect 7 and 9 Platoons returned and our camp was full, a rare occurrence as usually there was only one platoon resting at a time. That evening we let our hair down and had a thirsty party in the canteen to celebrate Akkie's kill.

When we went on leave at the end of our six week stint, our lieutenant gave each of us a share of the booty, some 14 Rhodesian dollars or so. Good money in those days. It ensured that we would have sufficient money to keep us in beer for a while. How much was Lion Lager in those days? About a dollar a six-pack, I guess.

I wondered if receiving this cash pay-out was tantamount to having qualified as a mercenary.

An evening at the bush canteen

The entire company had been called in to base for redeployment the following morning and all of us, moderate drinkers, alcoholics and teetotallers, murderers and drug addicts, big and small, tattooed and clean shaven, friends and enemies, straight and queer, married and single men, met in the canteen at around 17h00 that evening.

The beer and cool drinks were lukewarm but it did not matter. We drank our allotted ration of two beers each. Some bought beer from the non-drinkers, who sold it at inflated prices. Others swapped their beer for cool drinks or cigarettes. Most had stashes of grog that they had brought with them or that kind relatives and friends had sent through the post, bless 'em.

Old Basil Palmer was there. Basil was literally tattooed from head to toe. His one foot stated that it was tired and the other foot tattoo said, 'me too'. I think even his john thomas had been decorated with some expansive statement, if you would pardon the huge pun. Oh, these word games! He had received most of his tattoos in jail.

And Duimpie too! He had, on many occasions, fooled the medic into inspecting a painful toe on his foot. He would take off his footwear and steady himself against the table in the medic's tent. This table contained rows of drugs–the medicines necessary to ensure the wellbeing of 60 odd men. As the medic bent down to examine Duimpie's dirty toe, Duimpie would select a drug, quietly open the container, and pour the contents into his pocket, all the while complaining loudly to distract the gullible medic. On one occasion, Duimpie completed his illicit exercise, returned to his bivouac and revealed his haul–a fist full of Propon capsules–to his friend Chunky.

"Cool," stated Chunky, expecting a portion.

Duimpie just chuckled and threw all the pills into his own mouth and flushed them down with a gulp of beer. Chunky complained bitterly to his treacherous friend but it was too late. No amount of recrimination was going to get Duimpie to 'cough up' his score. Later that evening, Duimpie was seen setting up his machine gun along the perimeter of the camp. When he was asked what he was doing, he calmly slurred that he just wanted to wake the guard up a bit. His friends confiscated his weapon until the next morning!

Duimpie continually grew more aggressive and less tolerant to orders. On one occasion, he was part of an ambush party ordered to attend to duties in Mozambique. Some civilians walked into the killing area and Duimpie stated that he was going to blast them. The lieutenant in charge forbade this action but Duimpie ignored the order and killed all the civilians with his MAG.

Jigger was also present. His nickname explains all and he had a large following of broken hearted girls, none of them virgins!

Lou Laurie also blessed us with his presence and we enjoyed his company as he sat quietly drinking his beer with his friends. The next R & R back home would be Lou's last. He contracted cerebral malaria and died while still on leave.

Everett entertained us with his silly grin while Pally Blue, Willie, and AJ mooched off for a smoke on their own. They came back red eyed and smiling and when a joke was cracked they appreciated it the most.

Our commanding officer would leave us to it as long as there was no trouble and we could perform properly when required. On the odd occasion, someone transgressed and paid the price in detention barracks. This meant that the transgressor did not go home when R & R was due, as he was required to give six weeks active service per call-up.

One morning, AJ got fired up on liquor and drugs and started putting pressure on Everett. Everett warned AJ to stop but he persisted and fists started to swing. All who were present in camp that day gathered around to watch the two heavyweights having a go at each other. Everett knocked AJ into the middle of the next week. AJ was then placed under arrest to await orders when he was sober. The following day he was sent to the box for two weeks. Everett won his case by claiming self-defence.

Mike Hayward was there too, the very same Hayward who had cracked under pressure during our first ambush at Wankie. There had been repeats of this incident with other units and he had been deemed unfit for patrol, after which he had trained as a caterer and been promoted to camp cook. Now he was a sergeant and in charge of all the goodies. We had remained friends which meant that I could request additional rations when needed.

"Sheesh, Toc!" Mike would exclaim, "You're so thin that you are in danger of falling out of your own backside." Or he would tease: "You're so thin I can smell the shit through your ribs." I would rag back saying that he was three meals ahead and two shits behind which was why he was so chubby. Nevertheless I always had fresh onions and tomatoes to supplement my patrol rations.

The Grundy was again boring us with the details of how he had tried to terminate his girlfriend's pregnancy by sitting her down in a vinegar bath. The same story every time he got inebriated, but we still laughed and encouraged him, which he enjoyed. One day I suggested that he would make a good father. The stories stopped from then on.

Allan and Koos were brothers in law and spent their time chatting to each other about their wonderful families.

Dick Tibbits mooched in and out of the canteen with a garland of beads swishing around his neck and a bowler hat balanced on his head.

Lou Boom listened more than he spoke and he would sit and smile away the evenings sipping on his beer. Lou Boom started smoking cigarettes in the army to disguise his liking for marijuana.

Dietz was present as well. He was a sex maniac with a sharp mind. During one high-density operation, a female soldier from the Intelligence Corp was stationed at our base for a short period. She was billeted in a tent in the centre of the camp. Her job was to conduct body searches of female suspects for any intelligence or arms. Though she was not attractive, Dietz roamed the perimeter of her tent for hours every night, trying to make her conduct a body search on his own person. She complained to our commanding officer who threatened to clamp Dietz in irons if he persisted with his nocturnal exploits.

I once attended a party with Dietz, at which we were accosted by a certain Miss Nicholson who was a prim and proper snob. When introduced to Dietz, she immediately stated that he looked like a small dwarf.

"Small dwarfs got big cocks!" he blurted out.

Miss Nicholson hastily departed, red faced, into the laughing crowd.

On one of his passes, Dietz had a relationship with a divorcee who had no front teeth. This caused him much ribbing from all of us, especially when we asked what it had been like to receive fellatio with gums. I laughed out loudly at the thought. Dietz just stared at me in a surly manner which should have warned me that I was pushing some of his buttons.

Another welcome person was Sergeant George Carew. I could easily see the scars caused by the gas cooker that had malfunctioned and burned his legs during a patrol. He had then led his stick to the pickup point at a fast rate as the swift walk caused cooling air to assuage the agony. Later George was diagnosed with cancer and he married Dawn. Sad to say, he passed away shortly after the wedding. He was a good man!

Digger was our signaller who hailed from Wankie. He was a cool, quiet redhead who occasionally had a drink with us and infrequently took a puff of grass, just to make that day seem right. Digger had repeatedly asked the army to transfer him to another battalion closer to Wankie. This was because he lost at least two days of each R & R driving from Wankie to Gwelo. In the end this contributed to the failure of his marriage.

Mother ranted on about finding and killing Madega. Madega was the commander of a section of insurgents who had made contact with Mother's stick. In the ensuing melee, Martin van Rooyen had been killed by a shot through the head. As the evenings wore on, Mother would get aggressively drunk and argue with his companions who would try to calm him down.

Morgie the Raider was always present, chuckling away at things amusing and others not quite so amusing. He was just a happy fellow.

Our second platoon driver, Smith-Rainsford had a habit of peeing into his truck's exhaust pipe prior to deployment. When the truck was started, the exhaust would cough a smelly spray of urine and soot onto any one unlucky enough to be standing in the way. Big joke and he roared with laughter each time he caught an unfortunate. Sometimes this would result in nasty exchanges but he continued with his prank regardless. He would also depress the exhaust brake of his truck when coasting down a hill. This gave off a loud sound like machinegun fire, which resounded over the rear of the vehicle as the exhaust pipe terminated just above the drivers cab. Smith-Rainsford thought this extremely funny as it had terrified many a troopie. One day Koos thrust his rifle through Smith-Rainsford's open window and threatened to kill him. The jokes from Smith-Rainsford slowed down somewhat after that incident.

Blackie and Kudu would sit by themselves in a corner and converse quietly in Afrikaans. If I joined them they would politely switch to English. I was quite fond of these two and I spent a lot of time with them.

Voc, Phil, Huku (chicken in Shona, so called because his surname was Henwood) and I would often hang out together drinking whatever was available and smoking rolls of weed confiscated from locals. Huku did not smoke at all and would castigate us for wasting away our lives.

I sort of miss all those buggers!

Chapter 6
Eastern Highlands. Continuous call-up

Fight with Dietz

Our unit, in transit from Kotwa to the eastern border, stopped at Mtoko base for the night. That afternoon, a number of us became moderately inebriated and I decided to phone Clair, a pretty young lady that I fancied at the time. There was a public callbox close by and a queue of men stood there, each waiting his turn. I fumbled through my pockets and scraped enough coins together to ensure a reasonably long call.

When my turn came I plied the instrument with money but when Clair answered, I became tongue tied. This was because the men behind me were now intent on listening to my conversation. I pretended that I could not hear Clair and said, "Hello, hello?" when she answered. After a minute I replaced the receiver and ambled off feeling embarrassed. This was exacerbated by the teasing of the men, who said that they had been able to hear Claire and asked why I had not.

I got angry and threatened to shoot them. This stimulated more teasing and laughter. I cocked the Bren, raised it into the air pointing over their heads, and then dropped the barrel to line up with their chests, all the while breathing out venomous threats. The queue dissolved as men yelled in apprehension and scrambled to get out of my line of fire. Some just stood dumbly. As the barrel levelled off I was halted by a sharp command.

"Walsh, lower that weapon and make safe."

Thankfully CSM Spud had been standing off to one side while I teetered on the edge. His voice returned some sanity to my clouded mind and I dropped the Bren onto its bipod and made the gun safe. He ordered me back to my tent and I shouldered the Bren and left. The men who were queuing for the phone returned to their respective positions and eyed me with trepidation. As I stumbled by, I ranted threats to return and destroy the whole lot of them. I meant it too! Fortunately, I crawled into my sleeping bag and fell sound asleep.

I woke up at 21h00 when my colleagues returned from the canteen. Dietz fired up his gas cooker to make coffee. During the process he spilled hot water on his finger and squeaked in pain which started me laughing. I had not realized that thoughts of malevolent intent had been brewing in Dietz's mind. These malicious thoughts had gestated when I had laughed about his toothless girlfriend. Dietz flew into a rage and attacked me while I lay wrapped in my sleeping bag. He threw punches at my defenceless head and I bawled in anger and called him a coward. This further incensed Dietz and he roared and continued punching my head and face.

Lou Boom and Huku grabbed Dietz, held his arms to his sides, and pulled him away from me. I ripped the sleeping bag open and launched myself at the restrained Dietz. In a mad fury I threw as many punches at his face as I could. Lou Boom and Huku released Dietz who charged me like an injured buffalo. His shoulder struck me on the chest and we rolled out of the tent onto the gravel outside. I was on top and punched Dietz again. He skilfully flicked me off and punched me hard in the left eye.

Recovering consciousness, I was aware of Dietz holding me by the collar and threatening me with all sorts of terribles if I laughed at him again. There was no more fight in me but I managed a feeble laugh and told him he looked like an arsehole. He released me in amazement.

We made coffee and sat chatting like old friends, which we were. My left eye had swollen closed and he sat facing me with a fat lip. Others gathered, drawn by the noise, and laughed with us. What a mad bunch we were.

The following morning I woke, packed my kit and then searched for a pair of sunglasses to hide my black eye. A new member had recently joined C Company and he lent me a pair of prescription sunglasses. These, he explained, were very expensive and I was to look after them well or it would surely cost me.

As my luck would have it, I lost the sunglasses a day later and I had to spend half of my army pay on a new pair to replace them.

The breakout

C Company was based at the Nyanyadzi police station, 15 kilometres south of Hot Springs. The prosperous Cashel Valley farming region lay just 60 kilometres to our south-east. For insurgents, this was an easy route in from Mozambique. Our objective was to patrol the Chimanimani Mountains between Cashel Valley and Chipinga to impede these incursions.

The police camp had a swimming pool and our R & R days became luxurious as we were able to cool off in the murky green water. The police gave up hope of maintaining the pool a week after our arrival.

The evening found soldiers gathered in small groups. Some just talked or prepared for patrol, while the rest of us made the most of an opportunity to get high. I sat in a group with, amongst others, Smith and Pally Blue. The canteen was dry, courtesy of our new commander, Major Newton, so we sat drinking whatever the guys had in their possession.

A few joints were passed around as marijuana was freely available in the district. Many of us were despondent, mainly due to the continuous call-up system having run for so long and Newton's pathetic leadership. Smith and Pally Blue were expressing a need to be back on civvie street. I innocently suggested that it would be fairly easy to steal one of the unimogs and make a break for Gwelo which was a three hour drive away.

It was getting late and I was in no mood for any more complaining from those two so I excused myself and made for bed. My toiletries were in order and my kit was ready if I needed it urgently. I busied myself unlacing and removing my footwear in preparation for sleep.

Some shouting and the echo of a vehicle starting in the night alerted me. This shouting came from CSM Spud and rang with urgency. I ran barefoot to see what was happening. One of the unimogs had been reversed out of its parking area and was facing the security gates. Smith was driving the vehicle and Pally Blue sat in the passenger seat with his MAG pointing out of the open window. The double gates, which opened out onto the main tarred road from Umtali to Birchenough Bridge by day, were now chained closed.

Aglow in the beam from the vehicle's headlights, Spud was standing in front of the gates preventing any forward movement. The driver and passenger were shouting and waving at Spud to move out of the way.

Smith jogged the vehicle forward and Spud jumped up onto the front bumper. The vehicle idled for a short period and Spud was urged to step off. He interjected with an order to switch the engine off and fall in.

Smith then accelerated again and charged the vehicle at the gate. Spud niftily sidestepped on the bumper and then dived for the grass verge as the vehicle crashed through the gate, ripping it off its hinges. The gate fell flat on the ground and Smith drove right over it. Ever the impeccable driver, he indicated a left turn and headed south down the main road, the indicator light winking as the vehicle drove away.

Spud picked himself up off the ground and headed in the direction of our operations room to report the incident. The vehicle's drone faded to silence down the road. There were a few shots and then a long burst of automatic fire. They were making the most of their freedom, were those two.

With no further action I made my way back to bed. In the morning, we heard through the grapevine, that the military police had stopped the vehicle at a roadblock outside Fort Victoria and arrested the pair who had surrendered without a struggle. Presumably, they'd had enough time to sober up during the drive.

They were sentenced to detention at Brady Barracks. I never saw Smith or Pally Blue again. On completion of the operational tour I was transferred to a different unit

Morgie the Raider exacts revenge

Mucuna Pruriens, commonly known as the buffalo bean, is infamous for the extreme itch it produces on contact with skin. The severe itching is caused by the hairs that line the seed pod and scratching the affected area transfers these fibres to other areas of the body.

Our platoon had just arrived back at base camp. Having had a long and dreary patrol we were in no mood for any bull, but Major Newton declared that our platoon's discipline was at an all-time low and that everything should be brought to order, quick time. CSM Greenway, who had recently replaced Spud, took it upon himself to ensure that his master's wishes were more than realized, and set out to make our lives truly difficult, over and above the call of duty.

They lined us up for inspection and we were all derided for being in general poor order, which included weapons in need of cleaning. Some of us were charged with having hair too long and ordered to present ourselves to a barber in Chipinga for a haircut. Transport for this would be arranged the next day. We were ordered to fill sandbags for the rest of the day. Boozing was banned and the canteen was off limits to our platoon. Furthermore, everyone was to present himself clean shaven by morning.

We were aggrieved but, undeterred, polished off our tasks in short time and then skived off out of everyone's sight. When it grew dark, we gathered in small circles and busied ourselves with our own stashes of grog.

To hell with Newton and his orders specific.

Morgie the Raider disappeared from our small group and we just assumed that he had gone to answer a call of nature. When he returned, he cautioned us to be aware that there may just be some fun to be had after all, that night. No more questions would Morgie answer.

"Just wait and see," he said.

We all crashed at around 21h00 and were immediately aroused by wild yelling and loud cursing. There in the moonlight, we observed a prancing Mr Greenway dressed only in a pair of baggy army issue underpants and his gold rimmed spectacles. He was bellowing at the top of his voice, ordering the whole company to fall in while he danced in the moonlight like an enchanted goblin.

Most of us thought that we were under imminent threat of attack and hurriedly fell in to await orders. Greenway uttered many impolite words and threatened us with all sorts of awful things.

He wanted to know which of us *%#@ bastards had thrown *%#@ buffalo beans into his *%#@ sleeping bag, you *%#@ shits. He was wriggling and writhing on his feet, all the while scratching himself all over his body and head. Visible welts had appeared all over his skin as he desperately tried to relieve his prickling anguish.

Naturally we all started laughing at him and this infuriated him all the more. This in turn aggravated our humour and soon all were baying with laughter. He was seething and foaming with rage. Spit flew from his lips as he shouted and his speech was incoherent and slurred, such was his anger and discomfort.

Newton tried to bring his troops under control but was duly ignored, which was about time. He dragged Greenway off to the company medic for treatment and we left the parade area laughing boisterously.

Greenway was not present at muster parade the next morning. We were told that he was in his tent lying on a spare stretcher as his own sleeping gear was unusable. He had been sedated and covered in cream from head to toe. When we saw him after our next patrol, he was a changed man, having become a true gentleman.

Morgie the Raider, one of our platoon drivers, had endured Greenways despotic nonsense for many weeks. When he discovered the buffalo beans, he had filled a plastic bank packet with them and bided his time. Choosing the right moment, he had entered Greenway's tent at dinner time and emptied the contents of the buffalo bean packet into Greenway's sleeping bag.

I was called up into a different unit in which Greenway was the CSM, sometime later. He repeatedly ordered me to shave off my beard for the full six weeks of the camp. I ignored him and he took no action against me.

I think he secretly feared further reprisals.

Rifleman E. Bento

Bento joined our platoon in October 1977. He was a quiet fellow with black hair and eyes; a thoroughbred Porra. His smooth, pale skin immediately fell foul of mosquitoes and the sun, and I surmised that his future in the Territorial Army would be a bleak one. His English was slow as he translated to his mother tongue, and during my one conversation with him, I realized that any message in English would have to be repeated. But a good man with a gentle heart was he.

Bento had endured his basic training as an S-CAT. This was a special category unit comprising men who had health issues and could not endure the rigors of combat training. During national service, they were utilized as clerks, administrators, and regimental police.

On completion of his national service, the military had left him alone until the manpower shortage had forced his call-up. Some arsehole officer had deployed Bento as an operational soldier. After a short period of retraining in which he had only practiced firing and cleaning his weapon, he was hastily dispatched to our company on operational duty.

On arrival, Bento joined our platoon as we were being re-deployed. Each section had been allocated a certain site to ambush and all successfully entered their positions without being compromised. During the night, while on guard duty, Bento left his position to relieve himself in cover close by. On his return, the section leader stirred, and seeing an armed man walking straight towards him, surmised that he was a terrorist.

Bento was shot dead on the spot.

Bang goes the relay station

Once again the responsibilities of relay station duties fell upon my undernourished shoulders. This particular outpost was located at the top of a hill. It was of a permanent nature with a fortified building located inside a deep dugout surrounded by sandbagged walls, complete with firing positions in the parapets. The summit of the hill was surrounded by an arrangement of claymore mines. These were aimed to face perimeter positions likely to be used as cover by the enemy. The system was designed for detonation from inside the reinforcements. Due to the wide expanse of bushveld that could be seen, the relay station doubled as an observation point.

On the third day, bored with the tedium of relay station and observation duties, I sat daydreaming under a tree on our boundary. I was supposed to be observing the area for any signs of insurgents. Instead, I was busy looking at a convoy of two of our trucks through the old binoculars we had been issued. The trucks were manoeuvring along a rough dirt track. As I sat watching them languuorously, the lead vehicle suddenly jumped into the air and was immediately engulfed in a cloud of dust. It crashed down onto the trail and the troops on the back of the vehicle unstrapped themselves, threw themselves over the sides, and scrambled for cover in the grassy verges of the track. The dust cloud was quickly dispersed by the strong wind.

The dull thud of the exploding landmine reached my ears followed by the muted popping of gunfire as the troops cleared the surrounding area. My lethargy was instantly dispelled and I charged off to where the rest of the relay team had gathered. Excitedly we discussed the incident. Naturally I was the lead orator as I had been the only eye witness to the event. Looking down towards the scene, we all saw the unmistakable smoke and flames of a bushfire ignited by the discharge of ordnance. We watched the flames racing towards the east in a direction which would ensure that we were safe from engulfment.

With the excitement over we returned to whatever pastimes we had been busy with prior to the landmine episode. Handing observation duty over to one of my comrades, I picked up a dog-eared *Scope* magazine and leered at ladies clad in nipple stars, so far from our reality.

A whiff of smoke alerted me and I looked up to see flames curling up the hill towards our position. The wind had changed direction and danger was now rampantly climbing the hill towards our station. Somebody cried an alarm and our signaller voiced concern about the fire setting off the claymore mines. He ordered us to remove the detonators from the mines and retrieve as many as possible before the fire made them explode.

I ran down the hill in the direction of the approaching fire but it was too late. The blaze swiftly snarled up the hillside and the heat became intense. I shouted a warning to the others to take cover and bolted over our stockade just before the first mine exploded.

Blam!

The shockwave seemed to rock the bunker up through its foundations.

The other two soldiers then tumbled into the bunker and we all hooted with laughter. The next mine went off with another huge bang and we sat in hilarious trepidation, waiting for more explosions.

No more bangs transpired and we huddled in the bunker for a full hour until we were sure it was safe to exit. On leaving the bunker, we saw three mines that had been scorched by the flames but had not exploded. One of the two plastic legs on one of these mines had melted, and the device had drooped slightly and swivelled to face our stockade. It stood there and leered at us. We radioed this information to our commander, who instructed us not to interfere with the mines in any way, and told us that he would order engineers to remedy the situation the following day. It was past 16h00 and too late for engineers to travel safely to the relay station.

The fire had rolled down the opposite side of our mount and sizzled off into the distance. Half of the southern side of the hill had not been burned. Later that night, the fire flared and the untouched southern section of our rise burned fiercely. The heat at our post was so intense that it exploded the mine that had been pointing towards us. Some of the steel balls in the apparatus thudded into the sandbags and gum poles from which our shelter had been constructed. It was due to good foresight that we had decided to stay under cover till morning.

At 07h00 the engineers arrived to explode the remaining mines and set up a new installation. With our relay station restored to full protection, it was back to normal, bar the acrid scent of freshly burned grass.

A soldier takes a fall

Our trenches were constructed with overhead cover comprising four thick gum poles planted at each corner of the dugout. Bolted onto these was a lattice made of thinner gum poles, on top of which were a number of sandbags and a section of conveyor belting which protected the trench's occupants from mortar fire.

Vinnie had made a hammock from a length of canvas and hemp rope which he had secured to two of the main gum poles. Here he reclined every afternoon while the others burned up energy playing volleyball.

Late one afternoon I approached Vinnie for a chat. He was antagonistic and indicated that I should leave with a huge gnarled hand. Unfazed, I mimicked a fake apology for having disturbed him. As I stood up to leave, I wedged my half smoked cigarette into the knot above his head where the hammock rope was tied to the support poles.

I sauntered over to the volleyball field and endured some teasing as both teams refused me admission to the match. Instead, I ran a derogatory commentary on the players until the long awaited call came from the canteen.

Deserting the volleyball field we converged on the canteen as one.

That is, all of us except Vinnie, who now lay unconscious at the bottom of his trench. My elementary fuse had, within minutes, burned the rope enough to weaken the strands to breaking point. Vinnie had crashed down into the bottom of the six foot hole, landing on his head and shoulders. The impact had knocked him out and he lay oblivious to the banter coming from the canteen.

Vinnie awoke when we were well into our second beer and crawled out of the trench with murder in his heart. I was his prime target as he had correctly surmised that I was guilty of having caused his fall. He rushed into the canteen area shouldering past the hessian wall, and strode up to where I stood talking.

I had forgotten all about my transgression and was thus unprepared with no opportunity to escape. He cursed, grabbed the front of my T-shirt, and raised an enormous first as he pushed me backwards.

The company in the canteen moved out of the way and gathered around to watch the fight. I was bailed out by Greenway who barked an order for Vinnie to stand down. Vinnie did this and then stood looking at me with a nasty grimace. I mistook it for a smile of forgiveness so I relaxed and smiled back, even though he still had me in his vice-like grip. Then he threw a hard punch at my chest. I winced and fell to the canteen floor gasping for breath.

Just goes to show, payback just cannot be resisted.

Trevor's last ride

One Saturday night I was attending a charity disco at the sports club in Fort Victoria, and bumped into Trevor. He was one of our local motor mechanics and an amiable person. His girlfriend was accompanying him but he was far more interested in his new car. I have no idea what type of car it was, but he told me that it had been souped up and could pop a wheel spin like no other.

Trevor and his good lady disappeared into the crowd and mingled with their other friends. I popped outside with some of my friends to suck on a *zol*. When I returned to the bar, I saw that the majority of people had drifted outside. I bought a beer and strolled to the main entrance where most of the patrons were congregating.

The centre of attraction was Trevor's new car. It was lined up to the entrance of the sports club with its engine idling. The street light reflected off shiny chrome bumpers and the machine gleamed from much waxing and polishing. Trevor had collected his car from the parking area and driven it to the club's entrance to pick up his girlfriend who was not feeling too well.

Trevor was the star attraction. He opened the passenger door to permit his lady to enter, sauntered around to his side of the car, climbed in, and flicked his foot over the accelerator. The engine growled and the chassis swayed with the motor torque. He then put the car into gear, revved the engine, and dropped the clutch. The rear tyres spun wildly throwing up a great cloud of dust and stones. This enveloped all the onlookers, most of whom started coughing and cursing.

We heard the car racing towards the street with engine revving and gravel flying. Then there was an almighty bang followed by a crashing sound and all the lights in the area went out. Silence reigned for a moment and then Trevor's girlfriend start to curse. She raised her voice and called Trevor names that ladies do not utter. As the dust cleared, we could make out Trevor's parking lights across the street. There was an eerie glow coming from under the car. We all surged forward to help as Trevor fumbled out of his car swearing passionately.

Then a man started to laugh.

I walked forward and worked out in my mind what had happened. When the car had surged forward, Trevor had lost control and streaked across the street instead of turning into it. The car had pitched over the road and crashed into a wooden electrical pole. The pole had snapped at ground level and fallen into a yard located behind it. This had caused the overhead wires to short and trip the main circuit breaker in the local substation. The headlights of Trevor's car had popped out on impact, and they now hung by their electrical connections, facing down and casting a morbid glow on the ground beneath them.

The laughing man said that it looked like a Pekinese that had been hung by the tail causing its eyes to pop out. The crowd started to laugh in unison but an upset Trevor did not join in. He locked his broken car and we all walked back to the club. The club manager had already phoned for a repairman to attend to the electricity supply. We used the club's phone to call a breakdown truck to tow Trevor's car away. While we waited, we drank some more beer in the candle lit pub. Poor Trevor! He was mercilessly mocked by many. He sat there holding his girlfriend's icy hand as she glared at the floor.

A small swelling on her forehead was turning blue to match her disenchanted mood.

Chapter 7
Apprentice call-up system

In January 1978 I was called up for six months, as were all apprentices at that time. This was a wise strategy devised by the government to allow trainees to spend some undisrupted time learning their trades while still serving the military effectively. At that time, the Territorial Army was called up each year for six weeks in and six weeks out, which was certainly better than continuous call-up.

The demise of the anglebox

Friday night again and I was preparing to enjoy my last weekend at home before presenting myself at the drill hall for call-up over the next six months. I was not looking forward to the time ahead and proceeded to drain the contents of a bottle of gin. At around midnight I told Lynda to find her own way home and pointed the bonnet of my old anglebox somewhere towards where I thought I lived.

I fondly referred to my Ford Anglia as the old anglebox.

The road was long and winding and there is a blank space in the journey. I came to my senses as the old anglebox was leaping summersaults through the air. Then there was a deafening crash and everything went black.

I recovered, lying on the right hand side of the roof inside my upturned car. Laying in the moonlit dimness, I tried to work out what had happened. My senses returned slowly and I realized that I had crashed my car and needed to get out and find help. There was a lot of pain in my chest, back and other parts below my back.

The left side of the car's roof had landed on the corner of a concrete structure used to house equipment for the water pipeline from Lake Kyle to Fort Victoria, and was crumpled down onto the front passenger seat.

I vaguely remember thinking how fortunate it was that I had not driven with Lynda or I might then have been looking at her crushed body.

Jerking slowly like a cautious chameleon, I pushed my way out of the driver's window and steadied myself on my feet. My parents' house was about three kilometres away on a plot surrounded by other smallholdings. I cut across country and arrived at home in the wee hours of the morning. My dad was not impressed when I woke him up but when he saw me covered in blood, his face registered mild panic. He stated that I needed medical attention at once.

He drove me to hospital and I was admitted by a very grumpy duty sister who said that she did not have time for persons who involved themselves in the evils of drunken revelry. The next day Dr Warne ordered x-rays of my back and chest and declared that aside from a lot of bruising, I would be fine. He removed a number of glass shards from my back and buttocks and stitched the cuts closed. All the while I vomited a steady stream of rancid gin into a kidney bowl and he teased me about having overdone the party bit. My vexed mother collected my jacket, shirt, and jeans, which she threw away as they had been cut up beyond sensible repair. I spent the next night in hospital and was discharged a healthy fellow the following morning.

I was not sure which I had bruised more; my body or my ego!

First call-up under the apprentice system
I reported for duty the next Friday. My first call was to the company medic as I had started coughing blood and required reassurance that I was not about to die. The medic referred me to a doctor who sent me to the hospital for x-rays and then affirmed that there was nothing wrong in his professional opinion. All I required was the removal of stitches in a week. He then dismissed me, told me not to be such a malingerer, and said that I should be proud to serve my country as a soldier of the Rhodesia Regiment.

"Yes sir," I replied.

I stood up, coughed heavily, and hawked a huge red globule out of my chest, which I spat into the basin in his examination room before walking out of his surgery. He shouted after me and ordered me back. He seemed furious that I had proved his prognosis incorrect but grudgingly admitted me to hospital for observation. The bleeding was the result of some internal bruising and it was not serious. I protested that it was painful to cough or move but the medical staff ignored me. In their defence, they did give me a nice sleeping pill each night.

After three days, a letter stating that I was to be on light duties was given to me for my commanding officer. I was discharged and transported to my unit which was based on a farm in the Selukwe area.

Here I met my old friend, CSM Greenway, to whom I handed my sick note. He told me to assist in the kitchen and ordered me to shave. I next visited the company medic and complained about the pains in my chest. He prescribed an extensive course of Valium tablets. I immediately drank one of these in his presence and then had another once he was out of sight. Why he prescribed Valium I have no idea but I loved him for it. I was to take one twice daily, but I shortened the course by taking one whenever I felt the effects of the previous pill wearing off. Man, I hovered around that campsite like a happy balloon and I was in love with everyone.

Grinning like a Cheshire cat, I asked Greenway where he wanted me to doss down. Pointing towards the camp's perimeter, he instructed me to find a bivouac there and settle in. He stated that I would be patrolling as soon as my sick note had expired and told me that I had better have shaved by then.

No worries mate.

Floating in the direction that Greenway had indicated, I saw a huge fat man sitting outside his tent like a Buddha. I rushed over, jumped onto his back and kissed the top of his head. In an instant he hiccupped with momentary panic, farted involuntarily and thrust me off with a shrug of his mighty shoulders. Tripping over my pack I sprawled on the grass where I lay helpless with laughter at his fright. An angry Blackie stood up to kill me. Fortunately he recognized my pretty face and calmed down before destroying it. He scolded me for having given him such a fright as he had recently been diagnosed with a serious heart condition and could have keeled over at any moment. When I asked him what he was doing in the bush with a bad heart he just shrugged and said he was working on it.

He suggested that I bivouac with him and I agreed. I was a most agreeable person. Then the clever bugger announced that we had to dig a defensive trench before nightfall. Or rather, as he put it, I would have to dig or the exertion would cause his heart to attack him. The scheming fat man bartered his share of the work for half a bottle of Scotch he had stashed in his kit.

He also hinted that there would be some terrible bodily damage to my person should I shirk this duty.

The soil was not hard or rocky and I completed the trench with some hours to spare (if I ever own a construction company I will supply my workers with Valium). Blackie saw that I had not overly exerted myself and tried to trade a good portion of his whiskey back, but my period of agreeing with everyone had just expired (I must surely have been due for another Valium by then).

'Aye, me laddie, and tanight ye'll be a sharin' Haig afore ye slumberrr.'

Now whiskey and Valium mix really well. Blackie and I missed muster parade the next morning. Greenway half-heartedly scolded us while we beamed inanely at him. After his experience with the buffalo beans he was not about to take a chance with any of the old Charlie Company *okes*.

With a shake of his head he, once more, ordered me to shave.

A curfew breaker takes a bullet

On the expiration of my sick note (and unfortunately, the exhaustion of my Valium) Mr Greenway allocated me to a stick commanded by Corporal Herb. He was ex RLI and a bit of a ruffian who I grew quite fond of.

Greenway again ordered me to shave.

That night, we were to patrol a short distance from our drop off point to a feature from which we were to set up an observation point. Our stick consisted of Corporal Herb, an MAG gunner, a rifleman called Gant, and me. We debussed on the move, the drivers slowing down to a crawl as we jumped off. Slowly, we made our way down a shallow slope leading from the road to a small river just over two kilometres away. We gradually negotiated the incline, trying not to leave any sign that would betray our passing. As we neared the river, a figure emerged from the opaque soup of darkness in front of us.

Herb halted as the man walked in front of us and then turned in our direction. I was walking directly behind Herb and stepped sideways, intent on shooting this curfew breaker but I was too slow as Herb fired his G3 from the hip. There was a loud bang and a long pencil of flame lashed out from the muzzle of the rifle towards the man's abdomen.

The bullet hit the man in his stomach and punched straight out through his spine. The velocity of the round threw him backwards onto the ground. He lay there swearing at us in English, calling us every foul name we had ever heard, this interspersed with dreadful screams of pain and terror.

I could not bear to listen to it. I knew that no commander in the field would authorise a casualty evacuation for a curfew breaker at night and told Herb that I was going to end his suffering. Gant said that I should not, as he was enjoying every scream that came from the man's mouth. I told Gant to go take a jump and walked forward to the figure lying on the ground in front of me. His screaming had now abated and his low painful moans sounded like mournful singing.

Kneeling down, I positioned my rifle parallel to the ground with the barrel close to his skull and pulled the trigger. I did not want the flash hider to touch his head (it is really strange how a mind can think while under duress). The round passed through behind his cheek bones. He let out a single piercing scream and then fell silent. I felt terrible about the whole affair and turned to walk away. Gant asked why I had not placed the muzzle of the rifle on his head and told him he was about to die, just for the fun of it. I quelled a terrible and unreasonable urge to smash Gant's face with my rifle butt.

We lay up for the night just over the river and at first light, retraced our steps back to where we had left the dead man. A small group of men were gathered around the body and they had already lifted him onto a flintstone vehicle. The keening and wailing of women could be heard from a group of huts a distance away. It seemed the man had been walking from one group of huts back to his own when we intercepted him. One man from the group introduced himself as the dead man's brother. He stared at us dispassionately but hatred smouldered deep in his smoky eyes. I wanted to apologize but realized that this would be fruitless and stood back while Herb questioned the group.

The deceased man was elderly and well dressed. Gant asked the brother if he would like a new pair of shoes. The brother answered indifferently, saying that he wouldn't mind a new pair. Gant pointed at the dead man's feet and told him to help himself. Gant laughed and the hatred in the African man's eyes flared. I feared for a second that he might react but he just bowed his head passively as tears gushed down his cheeks onto his dry, dusty shirt. I silently cursed Gant for his inappropriate comment and cast my eyes down in shame. I saw two vertebrae lying in the dirt next to a black mass of congealed blood.

It was strange to note that the bits of bone were pink, even though they didn't have a shred of flesh or blood on them.

I called to Herb asking if we could leave and he complied. We walked back up the incline to the road where we awaited pickup as our mission had been compromised. Avoiding the company of my stick, especially that of the callous Gant, I got miserably drunk that night. I pondered the thoughts I'd had when the mango pickers were killed a few years earlier at Kotwa. I wondered how much I had changed, or if I'd changed at all?

I was not completely successful in avoiding my comrades. When Gant commented on some trivial issue, I screamed my pent up rage at him and attacked his shocked face with my fists. Corporal Herb put his thick arms around me, pinning my elbows to my sides, and turned me around. He then led me off to my bivouac, all the while softly crooning words of comfort into my ear.

Greenway made no more comments about his requirement for me to shave. I think he was slightly alarmed at the aggression that his skinniest rifleman had displayed that evening. Some weeks later at the end of our stint in the bush, we were transported to the drill hall to demobilize for leave.

When I arrived back home my girlfriend giggled at me and said that there was no way she was going to go out with me until I had shaved. I looked in a mirror for the first time in six weeks. Patches of hair hung on my boyish face like bird's nests.

Now where the hell had I packed my shaving gear?

Toc Walsh does it again
Friday night was set to be an explosive adventure with the re-opening of an old resort located on the bank of Kyle Dam. I drove out early on Friday morning to reconnoitre, and took the right fork of a junction I encountered on the dirt road. Less than 100 metres farther I had to brake for a tree trunk that had been placed across the road to warn motorists about the dam having burst its banks due to an excellent rainy season. I reversed and took the left fork to the venue.

That evening, I accompanied the twins, Pales and Bill, and we drove to our watering hole at a reckless pace. As we came to the fork in the road,

Pales steered right and I immediately warned him about the tree in the road. The twins misinterpreted my warning and burst into laughter at the thought of a tree growing in the road. Then there was a resounding thump as the car ramped over the fallen trunk and surged forward to sink into the muddy bank of the dam. There we remained stuck until TJ appeared with his father. They had also taken the wrong turn. They laughed at our muddy situation but helped by fastening a towrope to the car and extracting it from the mud.

The twins and I arrived at the scene and strode into the entertainment area with muddied trousers and shoes. The bar, which could be accessed by a narrow stairway, was situated on a raised section under the thatched roof. Once on top, we pushed our way to the bar counter through the small crowd of revellers. There, TJ and his father had taken over as barmen. We ordered a round of drinks and TJ charged us an amount somewhat more than usual. When we queried this he stated that it was for the TJ benevolent fund and we should not argue or we would not be served.

The evening grew hazy and I was explaining to a friend how, two years previously, I had kicked Audie Murphy. I demonstrated by letting loose with an enthusiastic right boot complete with the victory shout and clicking of fingers like a Spanish dancer.

Olé!

A lightweight barstool rose into the air, folded over the balcony wall and fell into the entertainment area below. There was a horrendous crash and the music fell silent. Some girls screamed and took flight outside. I looked over the balcony to see pieces of broken barstool surrounding a very smashed hi-fi set.

An angry manager looked up at me. I limped down the stairs with my right foot throbbing to see how I could recompense. The miserable bugger did not want to hear my story or my apologies and ordered me off the premises. Most of the crowd agreed with him as I had destroyed the only source of music for the evening. I limped out of the building like a disgraced muddy puppy.

However once outside I cheered up when I saw the van Helsdingen sisters. I walked behind them chatting, completely unconcerned about where we were going. We walked between some caravans and tents and I naively followed them into the side tent of a caravan. A burly frame filled the tent's entrance and old man van Helsdingen stepped out, took three steps towards me, and slapped the beer bottle out of my hand. This went flying I know not where.

I explained that I had merely been chatting to his two pretty daughters without any intent (really, I was just chatting).

"If that is true then why is the zip of your pants open?" he shouted in his guttural Afrikaans accent.

I looked down and attempted to close the culpable mechanism, all the while explaining that it had nothing to do with my intentions towards his daughters. The fly catch had stripped and it slid down whenever I moved. His two daughters giggled at me from the confines of the caravan doorway. He pushed me back and told me to leave as I had done enough damage for the night. A condescending group of campers had gathered around to add to my embarrassment.

Talk about grumpy people. I sat on a small stone wall and sulked until I was able to bum a lift home.

My girlfriend and the policeman

I picked her up at around 19h00 and we drove straight to a house party in an upper-class suburb of Rhodean. We walked, hand in hand, to the house from which thundered heavy music with loud shouting and laughing. As we entered the dimly lit lounge I collided with a tall, good looking man. I muttered an apology but he ignored me. Instead he turned to my girlfriend and greeted her. She responded enthusiastically, clutching him around his neck and kissing him on the cheek.

She introduced him to me as a policeman, stationed at Ngundu Halt.

I left to deposit my cooler bag in the kitchen where I bumped into some friends. We chatted for a few minutes and then I made my way back to the lounge in search of my girlfriend who had disappeared. Worried, I traipsed back to the kitchen and asked my friends if they had seen her. She had disappeared into thin air, it seemed.

I decided to drive to her house to see if she had maybe gotten angry with me for spending too much time chatting to my mates in the kitchen, and caught a lift home. As I climbed into my car, she ran up and climbed into the passenger seat. She was breathless and perspiration lined her top lip.

"Where the hell have you been?" I asked, exasperated.

"Just hanging around," she panted.

We had a minor argument and I took her home. I left her crying at her front door and drove away in an ugly mood.

Three weeks later while I was at home one Friday evening, my father received a telephone call from the police. One of his crews had been ambushed while driving home from contract work in Chiredzi. It was dangerous to drive at night so my father planned for us to leave at first light. I was to go along as I would have to drive the crew's vehicle home.

We left home as the sun was creeping over the skyline, drove for an hour and then arrived at the ambush site. The vehicle had been pushed onto the verge of the road. I saw bullet holes in the driver's door and through the rear bin. There was thick blood on the driver's seat and tools and materials lay strewn about the rear bin.

A police Land Rover drove up, its tyres humming on the tar road. Out climbed a stick of policemen. Their leader was the handsome policeman my girlfriend had introduced me to. He greeted my father and me and explained what had happened.

At about 17h00 the previous afternoon, a group of terrorists had fired at the vehicle from a rocky ridge. He indicated the location of the ridge with a sweep of his forearm. Only four rounds had hit the vehicle and one of these had injured the driver. The men had all escaped. The police had given the injured man first aid and transported him to hospital.

"That RPD gunner must have been a shit shot," concluded the handsome policeman, pointing at the van's undamaged windscreen.

My father then followed the Land Rover to the police station to collect his other employees. I stayed behind with the fetching policeman. As the vehicles drove away, he turned to me and said, "Sorry about what happened the other night. It's just that she digs my bod!"

He smiled cunningly at me and winked.

At first I was puzzled and told him that I didn't know what he was talking about. He laughed and told me not to worry about it. Although we chatted awhile, I had an uneasy feeling that I had missed something important.

My father returned and handed me a piece of cardboard to use as a barrier between the driver's blood and my backside. As I followed my father home, I thought about the handsome policeman's comment.

It suddenly dawned on me that he had hived off to some secluded place and had sex with my girlfriend at the party. My heart thumped horribly at this revelation and I drove on licking dry lips and trembling with shock and anger. The ride home seemed to go on forever. Blood seeped through the cardboard, soaked my shorts, and dripped slowly down my leg. I did not notice.

I did not follow my father home.

Instead I drove directly to my girlfriend's house. She was surprised to see me as I was only due to pick her up that evening. One look at my face and bloodied leg led her to conclude that I had been involved in an accident. When I angrily refused her invitation to enter and be cleaned up, she stared at me perplexed. I told her that I had chatted to her handsome policeman and knew what had happened at the party. She burst into a flood of tears, stating that it had been a mistake and that she was very sorry. Me too, I thought. Then I chucked her and drove away leaving her on the threshold crying. I only spoke to her once after that. It was at another house party and she sat crying alone on the veranda. When I asked her what was wrong, she hesitated and then explained that the handsome policeman had been killed in a contact with terrorists. I muttered some condolences but my heart was rock hard. I felt nothing for her or for him.

Sometimes payback is like an uncontrolled explosion. It can hurt everyone!

Business with Bravo Company, Gokwe

Our second call-up as apprentices was with B Company, 10th Battalion and we were based at a farmhouse in the Gokwe area under the command of Major Wolmarens. This was comfortable as the troops were housed in the old barns and workshops that had been deserted by the farmer.

The troop carriers we used were protected by curved armour plating on the sides and there was an armoured gun turret, fitted with an MAG, behind the drivers cab. The turret rattled and clanged the journey long but when the vehicles were ambushed it was the best place to be. Inevitably, an apprentice would be ordered to man the turret as it was an unpleasant task.

I experienced this one afternoon while motoring back to base. A soldier behind me warned that there were troops in a disused village we were passing. Glancing in the direction of the ramshackle huts, I made out the shapes of armed men carrying AKs. They were running away from our vehicle at an angle and started to fire shots in our direction, some of which clanged into our armour plating. I struggled to turn the turret, shouting for assistance as my thin legs strained against the inertia of the heavy steel. No one assisted but I finally brought the gun to bear.

Pulling the butt of the machine gun into my shoulder instead of leaning into the gun, I fired. The gun and the turret shook as though I was in a huge stone crusher. Correcting my stance, I leaned into the weapon as we had been trained to do, and continued firing. The gun was now easy to control. I fired long bursts into a field of dry, stunted maize through which the gooks had fled, and glimpsed cobs, stalks and leaves disintegrating under the scathing hail of bullets. The bullets generated an enormous dust cloud as they struck the dry earth. I saw a figure running along the horizon some 400 metres distant and loosed off rounds in his direction for some three seconds until he disappeared over the rise. I had forgotten to adjust elevation to compensate for the long distance.

Idiot!

I fired at random objects in that abandoned clump of huts, which shook as ragged thatch flew and mud walls collapsed. Satisfied that I had penetrated any position in which the enemy was likely to have been hiding, I ceased fire and grabbed my rifle.

Debussing the vehicles and leaving only the drivers as guards, we four escorts charged through the area looking for any enemy soldiers to kill. There were none lying in wait and we found no evidence of anyone having been shot. I could not believe that our rate of fire had gone so unrewarded.

On our return to base, the headquarter staff jeered and told us that we were useless shots. This we accepted and hung about waiting for the canteen to open, quite despondent. Later that evening, Major Wolmarens informed us that dead people had, in fact, been found in the village. Police had investigated and found the corpses of two females and a middle aged man. The women had been hiding in a grain bin and the man had fallen in the middle of the maize field.

What amazed me about Gokwe was the number of incidents that were reported by the residents. This was because ZANLA and ZIPRA were both operating in the area and hunting each other down. The majority of residents were Shona, and thus supported ZANLA. They were very keen to report any ZIPRA presence to the Rhodesian security forces. Thus we were able to notch up a few easy kills.

An informer told us that a group of ZIPRA soldiers was due to visit his kraal that evening. The kraal was located close to a small store from where the ZIPRA element was going to approach. We were instructed to set up an ambush with the store entrance as the focal point in the killing-ground. Two other sticks were to act as stop groups covering each side of a track that passed the store front.

At 16h00 we left by vehicle and motored to a point some four kilometres from the store. We debussed while the vehicles were on the move and the vehicles continued for some distance away from the vicinity of the ambush area and deployed a stick. This was a deception tactic to promote the misconception that we were interested in activities other than the planned visit by ZIPRA.

We ambushed fruitlessly the first night. Withdrawing at 04h00 after removing any conspicuous signs of our ambush, we holed up in a thicket of trees some three kilometres away. That evening, we returned to the store at 20h00 and started to walk to a suitable spot adjacent to the previous night's ambush position. The waxing moon was dim but shed enough light to see clearly some short distance ahead.

We approached the store through the shadows of a thin tree line and our stick leader saw movement in front of the store. He indicated that we should take cover and each soldier silently slid down to ground and lay still. As we watched, we could see more figures looming out of cover east of the store. I counted six enemy soldiers gathered in various positions around the building. I wondered what they were doing here as we had assumed they would just walk past the building and continue to the kraals they intended to visit.

There was a muted whistle from the low lying ground to our right, answered by a man standing on the store porch. Quietly, one man stood up out of dead ground to our right and we watched his head bobbing against the horizon as he walked cautiously by. He approached the store and conversed with his companion for a few minutes. Our stick leader indicated that the gunner should remain where he was and signalled us riflemen to crawl into position adjacent to him. As we moved forward, the two terrorists bolted. One disappeared into the shadows of the store and the other hightailed down the road joined by two others who appeared from nowhere. We opened fire on this group. I was aware of muzzle flashes in the store area to my left. Rounds popped close overhead and hit the ground all around us, spraying sand and grass into my open mouth and nose. I spat, blew out snotty grit and switched fire. My nose carried on running and I tasted blood. Our gunner traversed his weapon and sent a scathing burst of fire towards the store. Rolling onto my back, I pulled an antitank rifle grenade from my webbing and loaded it onto my rifle. Kneeling hurriedly, I pushed the butt of my rifle into my shoulder just like Blackie did (normal firing drill for this weapon was to tuck the butt in under your arm) but Blackie was a lot heavier than I was. I aimed towards the corner of the store where it seemed an RPD gunner had taken cover, and squeezed the trigger.

Jeezlike!

What a kick. I picked my rattled body up off the ground some metres from my pack. I had lost my rifle and crawled around scratching in the dirt in a desperate attempt to find it before some armed bandit found me. This was absolute terror, far worse than *The Exorcist* or the shadowy hand from my youth. My missile had destroyed a standard that had been supporting the porch roof. A section of the roof had collapsed and the RPD gun had fallen silent. The contact lasted for about five minutes. These ZIPRA certainly had more balls than the cowardly ZANLA.

After the fire-fight the silence was broken by some low moaning from the vicinity of the store. There was some fumbling in this direction which triggered us and we opened fire again. On the order to cease fire we lay waiting, ready to discharge our weapons if need be.

A loud bang, immediately followed by the popping of rifles some 500 metres distant, indicated that the stop group there had initiated contact. I hoped they would be more successful than my stick had been. Well, at least we had plugged one man as was evident from the sounds of distress we had just heard. The moaning stopped and we withdrew from our position and slid into the ditch nearby. My nose did not bleed for long but it felt numb for a while. Some grit had nicked the membrane inside one nostril but it healed fast. The dried blood caking my face and arms did make an impression the next morning!

The night was long. Sleep came slowly and then I was being shaken awake for guard duty. When my two hours were over, I surrendered the watch to the next man and fell asleep instantly. It was a short lived moment of bliss and I was roughly woken by my stick leader. We prepared to sweep the area in search of any dead or injured terrs. A vehicle was on the way with trackers.

We swept the area in a circular fashion around the store prior to sweeping through positions likely to contain any dead or injured enemy. As we started down the track, we came across one man, dead from multiple gunshot wounds to his back and legs. The clearance patrol continued and we arrived back at our starting point. Now we were to sweep through the contact area to the left of the store. Here I knew that we would find a man, either dead or severely injured. We walked through and found no one. Not even a discarded weapon or gear.

There was a blood trail though and we marked it for the trackers. As the support trucks sounded in the distance, a native man walked up to us and politely indicated his need to talk. He explained that some time after the shooting the previous night, a group of men had invaded his village. They had ripped a door off its hinges so that they could use it to transport an injured person. Our stoolpigeon sported a very swollen face and broken skin as a testimony to the passage of these thugs.

A convoy of two vehicles arrived with police and trackers. Four trackers approached our stick, two of whom departed to assist the stop group with their follow-up operation. This stick had also killed a terrorist. We relayed the native's message to the trackers and set off for the village.

When we arrived at the assaulted man's kraal, the villagers all gathered round and urged us to hurry up and find these *gandangas* and kill them. I had never experienced this obvious enthusiasm about seeing their own kind destroyed from them before.

Tribalism!

The trackers found spoor and we immediately followed up. Flight seemed to have been in the general direction of the Gwehava mission just south of Gokwe Township. This information was radioed to base and Major Wolmarens prepared a stick as a stop group to attempt to intercept their line of flight.

As we tracked, villagers came and spoke to our black trackers and passed on information about the group we were following. There were three of them on foot and they were carrying a fourth injured man. The villagers explained that the seriously wounded man was expected to die soon.

A woman then appeared out of the bush and asked us to follow her as she would show us where the injured terrorist lay. He had been abandoned by his comrades in a small thicket and there the locals had found him. They had proceeded to torture the injured man by hitting him with sticks cut from the surrounding trees. He had been beaten to death. As we arrived, the triumphant assailants burst into song and danced around the mutilated body.

The three surviving men had stolen a car and escaped. The stop group at Gwehava mission was uplifted and vehicles arrived to transport us back to base.

A few days off in Bulawayo

The weekend started in Gwelo after we were demobbed after our six month tour and due to return to work for our civilian employers. I joined my new buddies Pete Donaldson and Lurch who decided to drive through to Bulawayo where Pete had a girlfriend. Lurch and I were in no hurry to leave but we had both underestimated how crazy Pete was about that girlfriend of his.

"Let's go," ordered Pete.

But Lurch and I first wanted to stock up with snacks for the drive. We stopped at a supermarket to buy biltong and crisps and then went to a bottle store to ensure that we would have enough refreshment for the two hour trip. We also helped an under aged girl to purchase some grog. The annoyed bottle store owner refused to serve her, stating that he would lose his license. No worries to us. We took her money, paid the angry bottle store owner, walked out, and gave her the booze. She smiled rebelliously and left with a flounce of her hips. Before we could follow to introduce ourselves, Pete's irate voice grated, "C'mon guys, let's go. It's getting late and my date's waiting."

He had a Morris 1100 and we threw our groceries into the small boot which was also accessible from the back seat. As we negotiated the roads of Gwelo, a bracket holding up the exhaust pipe was somehow damaged by a large speed hump. The exhaust fell to the tarmac and dragged along the road. Lurch tried to persuade Pete to stop so that we could tie the exhaust back up with a piece of wire. Pete set his face like flint and stated that we had wasted enough time. We were now on our way and we weren't going to stop for anything, not even beer. Lurch and I both praised ourselves for having at least stocked up on enough grog to tide us over until Bulawayo.

The exhaust pipe scraped loudly on the tarred road and we soon became used to this new noise. As the journey progressed, the car engine's muffled drone grew louder until it was a loud roar. The sun set in a crimson inferno ahead of us. When it was dark, Pete exclaimed and told us to look out of the rear windscreen. There we saw a blaze of sparks arcing up into the sky. When we arrived in Bulawayo, Pete dropped us off in front of Talkies. We inspected the exhaust pipe and discovered that it had been ground down to a long, fine point. This included the actual exhaust muffler box which was why the sound of the engine had become so loud.

Pete bade Lurch and me farewell and drove off with a trail of fire curving up into the air behind him.

Lurch and I strutted into Talkies and were nearly bowled over by the blaring music. We handed our weapons and kit in at reception and joined the party. After a much enjoyed evening, we both left for a communal flat that Lurch used from time to time.

The apartment lay just a few blocks away and we were within a few minutes of it. The lights were all on and there was no need for Lurch to use his key as the door was unlocked. On opening the door we were greeted with a rowdy welcome from Ray, Robbie, and Shears. This was excellent cause for celebration and we dumped our kit and joined the boys on the balcony just in time to puff on some weed.

Ah, what a relaxing feeling. We stood on the balcony riling all and sundry that passed by. Shears was a little spooked as he had recently been busted for possession of marijuana and there was a lot of police activity that night with sirens sounding from all over the city. Suddenly a police car swerved under our balcony and a policeman switched on the siren as the car drove by.

Shears shrieked, "It's a raid," and bolted.

He ran straight into Ray and knocked him flat onto the floor. Shears shouted at Ray to get out of the way, you useless old goat. Ray was about three years older than us which qualified him as a geriatric.

Shears ran into the flat shouting as Ray picked himself up off the floor, all the while cursing Shears. The rest of us burst into laughter at these two. Ray hovered, perplexed, and then snarled at us and limped to the kitchen to fetch another beer. Ray had contracted polio when he was a kid. We calmed our humorous spirits down and went to find Shears who had flushed all our *zol* down the toilet. He was sitting on the edge of the bath shaking. We were not impressed at the loss of our herbs but there was more in Robbie's car.

Robbie was a wild young man who lived on his parents' farm just outside the mining town of Shabani. His hair was long and unkempt, normally with a gook combat cap balanced on top. Lurch and I often visited him at home where we could unwind and listen to rock and roll on Robbie's powerful hi-fi. He had acquired the use of a cottage on his parents' farm and we could blast away all day without the noise being a nuisance to anyone. I am under the impression that Robbie's parents were very relieved when Robbie moved into the cottage.

Whatever Robbie could consume to make himself high was fair game. One afternoon Robbie was without any drugs or alcohol and he climbed up onto the diesel tank which stood in the farmyard. Opening the filler cap, he cupped his hands around the open hole and breathed in deeply.

It was late afternoon and the sun was setting when Robbie regained consciousness. He lay on his back on the earth where he had fallen after having been anaesthetized by the strong fumes coming out of the tank. His head throbbed with the after effects of the fumes, not unlike a hangover he told us.

Robbie made use of the flat in Bulawayo when he had to attend the technical college. He met a pretty young girl who he became quite fond of. One weekend she committed suicide and left Robbie devastated. The girl's father blamed Robbie for the death of his child. It was a terrible tragedy filled with bitterness and I hope that forgiveness overcame their hurt.

I last saw Robbie in the early 90's. He told me that he was working at Daggafontein in Springs, near Johannesburg. Where else?

Ray recovered from the embarrassment of his incident with Shears and chatted to me about the acquisition of his new toy, a .308 rifle with a classy sight. He was very impressed with this brand new plaything. Ray lived on his parents' farm north of Bulawayo. He told me that he had shot a stray male dog off the back of one of his prize bitches who had just come into season.

Coitus interruptus taken to the extreme, for sure!

Then, in a conspirational whisper, he told me that he had fired the rifle from that very balcony the previous weekend. After drinking far too much, he had been inspired to test his marksmanship, loaded the rifle, and aimed at a distant streetlight during the early hours of Saturday morning. Gently squeezing the trigger, he had sent a bullet speeding down one of Bulawayo's main streets. The streetlight had just winked and gone out. The shot and recoil had sobered him sufficiently to quickly run back into the flat, switch off all the lights and hide the rifle in a cupboard.

The next morning we rose before noon and made our way to a popular watering hole in Bulawayo. Hung-over, we sat in the beer garden and ordered a round of cold beers which we chewed through slowly. When sufficient alcohol had permeated our bloodstreams, the effects of substance abuse were sufficiently countered for us to be able to enjoy the taste of beer again. The proverbial hair of the dog caught in our throats had successfully been coughed up and spat out. The obligatory need to chew the brewed liquid turned into enthusiastic quaffing.

Our moods altered from condemnation by terminal disease to just recently experienced reprieve akin to a miraculous cure. We proclaimed our good health to all present. The good mood at our table was infectious and influenced the other patrons. They rejoiced with us and we swapped witty absurdities.

Then I saw one figure that did not seem to be enjoying his day. There in the middle of the beer garden sat a solitary man hunched over one of the tables. Billy Botha sat all by himself and scowled at his glass. He drank one beer after another, ordering from the waitresses rudely. Everyone seemed to be avoiding him.

Corporal Billy Botha was the most evil man I met at Llewellin barracks. As our instructor, he trained us in the art of war but also relished any amount of pain he could inflict on his recruits. This fetish became more pronounced late in the evenings. The NCOs would harass us by rushing into our barrack rooms screaming and shouting different orders to cause confusion and alarm after bouts of boozing in their mess.

Some of the tortures they imposed upon us involved excessive physical training by means of pointless tasks like running double time to fetch a certain leaf (inevitably the wrong one) off a distant tree. 'The leaf next to it, you shithead!'

And there were also change parades.

Change parades were designed for a number of reasons, among others, to disrupt our free time. The objective was to induce sleep deprivation and then train us to follow orders without question even though we were half dead. We used most of our free time preparing for morning inspections. Carefully prepared kit would be soiled in the evenings and we would have to sacrifice sleep to return it back to good order for inspection.

Billy loved the inconvenience of change parades. First drill kit, and then a change for PT, followed by combat kit. He particularly relished making us leopard crawl in our drill kit. This crawling scratched the shiny boned toecaps of our drill boots, which had been polished until they could reflect an observer's image. Sometimes he forced us to carry our carefully prepared beds out and then trash them in the dirt. He even ordered us to present ourselves naked one evening. Those were certainly terrible days.

He was also ugly first thing in the morning while struggling to clear his head from the night before. Botha's favourite torture was to jab his victim repeatedly on the sternum with his knuckles while tracing the poor man's lineage back through history with his sour breath. And a sordid picture of low life did he paint for you. He left the beer garden by himself, his face flushed and angry, a lonely man, scorned by all.

The law of payback clearly states that if you treat people with disdain, your beer will eventually despise you.

Home on the range

Lurch and I hung out at my parents' house during one pass. One day we arranged to go to the rifle range just outside Fort Victoria armed with over 200 rounds of ammunition each. We had not had an opportunity to zero our weapons during our last call-up, so we decided to do this in our own time and we intended to have a blast. My father dropped us off on his way to work as both Lurch and I were without transport that day.

We checked out the butts as we did not want to shoot anyone hiding there accidentally. With the area clear, we placed some old tins and boxes on the parapets above the butts. On our way to the 100 metre firing position, we noticed some old falling plates in the grass next to the range. These are steel plates which are used as targets and designed to fall over if struck by a bullet. We placed these next to the boxes and tins and then proceeded to our intended firing position.

"In your own time, carry on," we ordered each other and sensibly started shooting at our targets.

This was to zero our rifles and we did quite well. There was no need for any adjustment and we continued shooting from prone, sitting and standing positions for fun. We blasted away until each target had disintegrated or been shot down behind the parapet. We saved the falling plates for the most exciting event of the shoot, firing our weapons from the hip on automatic. When all the plates had been knocked over, we fired indiscriminately into the butts until all our rounds had been expended. There were plenty more at home.

It was now just on 10h30 and we congratulated each other on a worthwhile shoot and excellent timing as the public bar at the Flamboyant Motel was just opening. This motel was located just across the main Fort Victoria/Beitbridge road and it took us less than five minutes of cross country walking to get there. Our rounds may very well have been expended but we had plenty of money in our wallets and we intended to make good use of our fortune.

Beers first of course! A half dozen or so. Then juicy steaks and fries ordered at the bar. Then onto shorts, mixed with cola or lemonade.

We also played a hilarious game called 7-14-21. This is a dice game played by any number of people at any public bar, preferably one where they don't call the police when their patrons get sloshed. The dice are thrown until someone throws a seven. This person then nominates a drink. After a couple of rounds these drinks can be quite diverse. A whole beer glass gets filled with a variety of spirits and a devious selection of liqueurs. We would even get the barman to fetch chillies from the kitchen to spice up the drinks and any insects or frogs that were unfortunate enough to be caught would also be used to increase the appeal of the concoctions. These drinks were the most disgusting and powerful that I have ever experienced.

The players continue to throw dice until a 14 is thrown. Whoever throws the 14 has to pay and tip the barman based on the latter's efforts to acquire the ingredients for the blend. The players throw the dice some more and the poor unfortunate who rolls 21 gets to down the drink.

Lurch and I struggled through three or four rounds of this dumb game before we decided we'd had enough.

"No, no! It doesn't count if the dice roll onto the floor."

"Lurch, I have picked up the dice. C'mon, let's get on with the game. What are you doing with your head wedged under the foot rail? Are you sleeping?"

So we decided to play ants. This is an easy but painful game. You just sit on your barstool until anyone, even you, shouts, 'Ants!' Then everyone has to throw themselves off their barstools onto the floor. It is a sane precaution to ensure that no one has left an anvil behind your barstool. The last one onto the floor has to purchase the next round. When I say that this is a painful game you have to believe me. It is not, in essence, immediately painful but the pain grows on you unless you play ants fast and drink heaps. Then the game only pains you the next morning, hopefully not from a hospital bed.

We played these games for an eternity until the barman announced that it was closing time. I am not sure whether this was a license requirement or if he just wanted to get rid of us. I suspect we were becoming unruly, though very amusing in our own eyes.

Collecting our rifles from the motel reception, we lurched out into a very hot day. Town was two kilometres away and we had no intention of walking there. The obvious solution was to mount a roadblock and hijack a lift to town at gunpoint. A dilapidated truck coughed its way towards us as we staggered out onto the highway. Standing as straight and as steady as we could, we signalled the driver to stop. Lurch asked the driver where he was going but told him to shut up when he answered as it did not matter anyway. We then ordered him to give us a lift to the Chevron Hotel in town.

The truck's cargo area was clean and empty except for a group of 20 odd farm workers. We ordered them to the front of the vehicle and they huddled together behind the cab. I covered Lurch as he climbed up, slipped and nearly broke his teeth on the tailgate. He then covered me while I skirmished over the rail and together we aimed our empty weapons at our prisoners. I am forever grateful that those workers never realized that our weapons were empty or they might have overpowered us. Considering the state we were in, that would have been easier than giving a hungry dog a bone.

It took ten minutes to drive the two kilometres and Lurch and I nearly fell asleep. Fortunately the truck creaked and clanged to a halt and we both debussed, issuing the occupants a dire warning that if we ever met again it would surely be the worse for them.

The ladies bar at the hotel was deserted but for the barman who we greeted with a 'howzhit'. We then promptly lay on the couches and fell asleep, spooning our rifles.

Some hours later, we woke up to the noise of a bar full of people who had gathered to quench their after work thirst. When we sat up they all cheered and we were invited to join the crowd. Here we drank and socialized with the other patrons, somewhat slurring and with terribly disjointed eyes.

The long-legged sergeant
Patrolling with Sergeant Rob was a strenuous affair. He was the original Kalahari kid; miles and miles of bugger all. His legs were so long and lanky that his waist was level with my chest. Lurch and I struggled to keep up with him as we patrolled one night, since Sergeant Rob appeared to be pacing himself by trying to step over the moon. We both complained that we were having great difficulty keeping up with him. He told us to shut up before we compromised our assignment. I argued that the speed at which he was walking was noisy enough for all the gooks in Zambia to hear but he carried on at his usual pace. We continued on our way and my thoughts wandered

to the new Eric Clapton record I had at home: 'Dear Lord, give me strength to carry on, oh I've done so much wrong,' the melancholic words droned through my mind.

My song was interrupted when unexpectedly, the sergeant disappeared from the skyline in front of me. There was a splash combined with a dull thud and a groan of pain. Lurch and I took cover, thinking that was what our leader had done. There was the sound of a struggle up ahead and also some stifled cursing. We thought Sergeant Rob had been tackled by some adversary so we moved forward to help him.

There in the moonlight we saw Sergeant Rob with his left leg buried up to the hip in an abandoned aardvark hole. The hole had been full of rainwater and the hydraulic action of his leg plunging in had forced litres of dirty water up the leg of his shorts and soaked our sergeant up to and beyond his left armpit. His other leg was stretched out at a right angle behind him. He was stuck and struggling to extract his leg from the hole.

When Lurch and I had determined that he was in no danger, humour began to bubble up inside our chests and we started to chuckle. This giggling became laughter when he stated that, not only was he stuck, but his balls had been squashed against the side of the hole. They were still squashed and painful and it was not funny and if we didn't stop laughing...

Lurch stepped forward to pull our unfortunate superior out of the hole. He attempted to negotiate assistance in return for a slower pace but was told that guard duties awaited him back at camp if he hesitated any longer. I tried to help but was markedly weakened by amusement. Lurch was also so convulsed with merriment that we were unable to extricate the unfortunate man. Sergeant Rob lost his cool, forgot all about our serious mission, and swore at us using deeply descriptive words. We pulled on his webbing and laughed uncontrollably at the absurdity of the situation. Finally sanity prevailed and Rob's shoeless foot emerged from the hole with a soggy pop. Sergeant Rob ordered us to reach down into the hole and retrieve his boot while he nursed the pain out of his crushed testicles. We refused so Sergeant Rob reached down as soon the pain had dispelled enough for him to bend his waist. He could not reach deep enough and we continued marching with a sergeant who now wore only one boot and had his left side muddied up to his ear.

The area was strewn with devil thorns, each with two sharp spikes about two millimetres long and our pace dropped dramatically. Lurch and I both teased that he should up the pace a little as we would not reach our objective in time. We laughed at him when he sat down to strap his combat cap onto his foot.

Payback sanctioned by divine intervention is surely the most satisfying of all.

Putting for golf

Friends Mike, Harry and FL had rented a farmhouse near Salisbury which they messed in whenever they were on leave from the RLI. They had converted the shed into a pub, complete with bar counter and foot rail. One Friday during Rhodes and Founders weekend I arrived for a visit. I had driven up with the twins Pales and Bill. We parked the car, threw our bags into a bedroom, and then adjourned to the pub where everyone had congregated. With cold frosties in our hands, we reacquainted ourselves with old friends. Dan from special branch was there sitting with Judy. Tony, ex intake 138, was sitting in a wheelchair. During a fireforce operation he had parachuted in high winds and damaged his back. His brother Murray was also there. Phillip and Lulu sat holding hands at the bar next to Mike and Jean amid a herd of strange new faces.

Music blared from wall-mounted speakers surrounded by a world of military souvenirs. Mounted on the wall behind the bar was an old musket. Mike was busy telling the crowd how he had taken the musket from a dead terrorist who had actually fired it at him. I popped his bubble by stating that the musket was actually my fathers, and that it had mysteriously disappeared from our house some months earlier.

Mike actually blushed!

He was healing from injuries that he had sustained in a contact. A bullet had broken his left humerus and another had ripped a hole through his upper thigh, narrowly missing the bone. Jean turned and thumped him on his left shoulder calling him a bullshitter. Mike turned from red to white like a strange chameleon, and a hiss of pain escaped his drawn lips. He turned to Jean and warned her to stop hitting him every time he said something she did not like.

Ah, the joys of relationships!

Murray was packing back the drinks and when I turned to him an hour later, he was standing next to the bar naked. Nobody seemed to mind and I was told that this was Murray's normal weekend procedure.

Murray was recounting an incident from earlier in the week. He had wanted to tow an old car frame to a panel beater and instructed a farm labourer to steer while he towed in his land cruiser.

"If there are any problems just hoot," Murray cautioned the man.

Off Murray drove down farm roads towards town. Halfway there he forgot that he was towing another car and sped up. The frantic labourer pressed down on the horn which did not work as the battery had been removed. Murray eventually looked in the rear view mirror to observe his car being dragged down the road on its roof while the screaming farm hand clutched at the steering wheel.

Murray thumped him for rolling the car.

Night fell and the pub became noisy. The twins disappeared into the house and returned dressed to the nines. They had ransacked the cupboards in the bedrooms and chosen random items of clothing to wear. One twin was decked out in a satin dressing gown, gum boots, and a top hat, and the other wore a Scottish kilt and nothing else.

They then proceeded to trash the joint with much raucous laughter. When asked why they were acting in this manner they appeared astonished. Pales replied that they had been promised that this was the only pub in the country where they could do as they liked without the police arresting them. That was why they had come to visit.

And no one was going to stop them now!

"So stand aside," yelled Bill, and threw a glass against the rear wall.

Pales roared, picked up empty beer bottles, and threw them as well.

Most of the people in the bar hurriedly snatched their drinks and disappeared into the main house. I sat behind the bar counter with FL and Harry and we handed either twin whatever he demanded. Soon every item in the bar was broken, torn or bent, including my father's old musket. Only a few unopened beers remained intact.

"So what we gonna do now?" one twin asked the other.

"This place is boring, there's nothing else to do here," replied the other.

So the twins left the pub to create havoc in the main house. FL and Harry sat motionless as though they had just witnessed a major crime.

"I hope they enjoyed themselves," groaned FL as he surveyed the havoc. I sat sipping my beer and grinned.

That was a good start to the weekend, I thought.

That night, beds creaked and horny groans echoed through the old house. I was in no mood to listen to anyone getting what I was not, so I stole a pillow and a blanket from one unconscious twin and went to the pub where I slept on the floor.

The following morning, I was horribly roused by a gunshot being fired against the outer wall of the building. The walls shook and debris floated down from the open rafters. This was followed by manic laughter and another shot was fired. This time buckshot obliterated the window above my head. Shards of glass sprayed all over my blanket and the charge ripped into the opposite wall, blasting out a section of plaster.

"Hey, what the hell do you think you are doing?" I shouted, "I'm trying to sleep in here!"

There was a momentary hush followed by more fanatical laughter. Obviously the fools had not realized that I had decided to sleep in the pub. Another shot crashed into the wall. By now I was a little wary of the mental condition of the shooters and crawled to the open door. I peeped around the door jamb and watched FL popping two more cartridges into a smoking double-barrel shotgun.

"Hey," I said, "stop this. Someone is going to get hurt."

"C'mon Toc, we are just practising for a game of golf!" smiled FL.

Now I was really worried.

One of the twins lifted the shotgun he was handling and aimed down the barrel with red eyes. The tremulous barrel swung in my direction.

Boom!

Pellets tore splinters out of the door frame but I was nowhere near it as I had already charged to safety behind the bar counter.

"C'mon guys, someone is going to get hurt just now." I pleaded, "And that someone will most probably be me!"

I managed to talk my way out of the Lone Star Saloon and make my way safely into the house, all the while being observed by intimidating men with quivering hands holding deadly guns. The toilet beckoned me and I sat on the pot. Something on the floor caught my eye and I picked it up. It was an oversized playing card with a picture of naked people doing weird things to each other printed on it. This was the first time I had ever been exposed to pornography. I felt strangely disgusted but fascinated at the same time.

Back to the previously mentioned game of golf. FL gathered everyone and we all drove off to Darwendale Sports Club. When we arrived, we gathered under a huge tree off the fairway. We joined up with Eric and Nonno, Phillip Nel's older sister, and FL pulled out the hugest *zol* I have ever seen. He lit up and puffed away merrily. When it was my turn, I dragged the smoke into my lungs gratefully and exhaled.

"Aaaaah! Nice."

I puffed some more and then passed it on to Murray. My brain was buzzing by the time we walked to the first tee.

Now we were going to play golf but I saw no golf bags or caddies. FL was carrying a putter. He placed a stained golf ball on the grass, sighted down the putter dramatically, and took a wild swing at the ball.

"Four!" he hollered.

The ball shot up into the air and dropped down five odd metres from the tee.

"Beautiful," exalted FL.

The crowd clapped unconvincingly.

"Next!" he shouted.

And so the gang took turns to hit the ball in short lengths down the fairway. Now the cannabis had started to take effect and I was giggling at nothing in particular which became infectious. Dan started giggling as well and the others followed. Soon we were all laughing and stumbling over the grass. None of us knew what was funny or what we were all laughing at. This seemed to make the humour funnier and we couldn't stop laughing.

Other golfers whacked balls past us as we sat or lay on the grass howling with laughter. They cast looks of contempt and muttered about reporting us to the club manager.

Now it was my turn to play. Someone thrust the putter into my sweaty hand and pointed at the ball. Standing above the ball, I realized the group had grown strangely silent. They were all looking at me intently, as though I was about to hit a record hole in one. I smiled bashfully and they all stared back, stone faced.

"Come on, guys, cut it out," I muttered.

They stared even harder. I tried giggling again but they didn't take the bait. They were just standing there staring at me like zombies. I decided to ignore the imbeciles and looked down at the golf ball nestled between my ankles. I took a few seconds to realize that I would have to step back to be able to hit it. I did this and refocused on the ball which was now positioned near my bare toes. Someone in the crowd got impatient and told me to hurry up. I looked up and noticed that the crowd had grown. It seemed that I had backed up some other golfers.

Jeez, now I felt the pressure.

I positioned the putter next to the ball which seemed very distant, like a tiny planet glowing gloomily, far away in the depths of the earth. I lifted the club over my shoulder, swung with all my might, and then looked up over the fairway to see where the ball had gone. Some low giggling started in the crowd and I looked back to see what was so amusing. FL looked at me cross-eyed and pointed at my feet. There lay the ball, unmoved, next to a ditch excavated by my putter. Perplexed, I repositioned myself for a second shot which produced the same result. Frustrated at my inability I start swinging wildly at that *%#@ useless ball with the *%#@ useless putter. Clods of earth flew until the now bent putter thumped down and destroyed my big toe. I howled in pain and dropped to the grass to nurse the crippled digit.

Through misty pain I saw my *%#@ useless friends and the other *%#@ useless golfer's mouths wide open in thrown back heads as they laughed at my *%#@ useless dexterity. I swore at FL and threw him the *%#@ dumb club cursing the *%#@ stupid game of golf. FL was now annoyed with me for having damaged his putter. He tried to hit the ball but the putter was beyond any normal use. We retired to the clubhouse for breakfast. While we were gathered around the pub, FL exacted revenge for his broken putter.

"Barman," he shouted, "a round of drinks for the clubhouse to celebrate this man's hole in one!"

He pointed at me.

Everybody at the bar yowled with laughter and immediately ordered expensive drinks. When the barman had served all he presented me with a bill I could not have hoped to pay in a thousand years. I have never swung a golf club since!

Another boring weekend at home

My new girlfriend, Patricia was a girl who had developed very interesting talents. A good time was what she lived for. One Saturday afternoon I picked her up in town and we drove to Morgie the Raider's home to attend one of his famous weekend parties. Afternoon became evening and we had both had our fill of smoking hemp, drinking, and dancing to wild music. Patricia and I decided to adjourn to the bathroom to rinse our sweaty bodies but as nature would have it, the atmosphere in the bathroom became rather steamy. I was vaguely aware of squealing, grunting, and waves of water slopping over the side of the tub onto the floor. This inevitably attracted the attention of the Raider who rudely banged on the door with his knuckles.

"Hoi, what's going on in there?" he enquired loudly, and followed up with some vulgar advice on how to do the job properly. He said that Patricia was making a big mistake cavorting with me and suggested that she allow him to take over as he was certain to be better at it than I was. All the while I urged him to bugger off and find alternate amusement. Spilled water flowing out from under the bathroom door encouraged him to make further observations about my shoddy love-making.

By now the incessant commentary was impeding my style and I extracted my burning body from Patricia's generous grasp, hopped out of the tub, and skidded my way to the door which I unlocked and opened. Pointing down I indicated Mr Willy, glowing pink and arcing down in a short parabola of disinterest. He was sulking with a bowed head, despondently dripping water onto the floor tiles.

"Now look what you've done," I angrily accused him.

Morgie the Raider swayed backwards, slipped, and collapsed onto the wet floor with a howl of wild laughter. This revealed most of the other party goers standing behind him. They all shrieked in simultaneous mockery, guffawing at my predicament. Morgie's wife pointed at me and clutched her ample stomach. Then she leaned on the wall, slid to the floor, and sat there quivering with laughter like a plate of jelly placed on the top of a running tractor engine.

Lou Boom and Voc each chortled and ridiculed my embarrassed member. Sue, Susan and Phillippa screamed with outraged glee and ran to the lounge where they collapsed onto the furniture and discussed my manhood between bouts of hysteria. I beat a hasty, red-faced retreat back into the bathroom. Patricia was laughing with tears running down her rosy cheeks, her breasts wobbling with irrepressible mirth.

"Not you too," I cried, as I ran and promptly lost my footing on the wet tiles.

I back-pedalled while skidding forward like a skilled ice skater until my toes banged up against the base of the bathtub. My feet lurched back and I crashed, head first, into the bathwater. Pivoting on the side of the bath with my backside in the air gave my disorderly audience full view of never before exposed bits. I breathed bathwater deep into my lungs. Coughing and spluttering, I thrust Patricia's lame legs out of the way and managed to manoeuvre my mortified body into a more dignified position in the bath. My spastic coughing caused gas to escape and boom off the bottom of the enamelled bathtub destroying any vestige of dignity I had left. This created a strange submarine sound which caused further convulsions from the crowd of morons who were all trying to squeeze their heads through the bathroom door at once. Once again I climbed out of the bathtub and pitched my way to the door which I slammed closed and locked before a foot could jam it open.

Between bouts of uncontrolled giggling, Patricia slowly enticed me back into the water, saying that I should do this without hurting myself so we could make more whoopee. With an injured expression, I said that we needed to wait for Mr Willy to recover from his ordeal.

"Don't wait too long, my love," she teased sweetly, "or I may take Morgie up on his offer..."

We climbed out of the bath, dried and dressed. I followed Patricia out of the bathroom with as much dignity as I could muster.

Music rattled the windows as Meatloaf sang like a bat out of hell.

We stepped onto the porch where our friends had all gathered. As one, they broke out into an inebriated cheer and started singing, 'For they are jolly good fellows, and so say all of us.' This initiated another bout of laughter.

Hip hip hoorah to you too!

I was now past embarrassment. I superciliously sauntered over to the cooler box and extracted a beer each for Patricia and me. Voc busied himself making a fire for a braai.

Someone suggested a game of bezant and I promptly supported the proposal with the prime objective of removing attention from my recent escapade. Now this is a cool game in which a tin is placed on the ground and a participant blindfolded. This person is given a hockey or similar type of stick and spun around with one end of the vertical stick on his forehead until he is truly dizzy. Then he is pointed at the can and he has to evaluate where the target is and run and hit it.

The fun starts as soon as the participant reels around trying to judge where the tin is. This usually results in observers running, screaming and laughing, away from where the frenzied blind man is about to strike. On the rare occasion on which the participant actually hits the tin, great aerobics are performed by persons trying to dodge the flying missile.

It is even more fun if you fill the tin with stones or cooking oil.

Morgie the Raider emerged from his garden shed carrying a pick handle. The only tin available was a five litre oil can that had been used to contain petrol for Glyness' clapped out old car. It was nearly empty but there was an inch or so of the flammable liquid sloshing around the bottom.

Tim volunteered to be the first participant and we spun him around until we were sure that he was truly dizzy. After facing him in the direction of the tin, we loosed him enthusiastically, shouting expressions of encouragement. He hurtled forward and with a great swipe, hit the tin can amidships, promptly spun in a circle, tripped, and crashed onto the lawn. The pick handle bounced up off the grass and cracked him on the forehead. There he lay clutching at his forehead and groaning in pain.

The tin, however, curved up into the air trailing a fine mist of petrol from a slit caused by Tim's crushing blow. It crashed solidly into the side of the braai, burst into a ball of flame, and cartwheeled over to the veranda. With wild shrieks, the girls charged off into the night. All of us boys, who were assembled in a half circle playing the game, turned in alarm. We then stumbled backwards to our haunches, weak kneed with amusement at the girls' fright.

All except for Morgie the Raider who immediately charged off for the garden hose. He was obviously concerned that his house was about to be engulfed in flames. The Raider reached the hose, which was neatly coiled, and turned on the tap. Latching his greasy hand onto the nozzle of the hose which he then curled around his wrist, the Raider ran towards the fire like an Olympic athlete. The fire was now burning ferociously and flames were gushing onto the cement floor next to the now rapidly melting cooler box. Following him was the hose in a series of coils, which snagged on an old stump in the garden. The hose stretched taut and the Raider's legs continued to run and climb. He fell on his back and air exploded out of his mouth. There he lay gasping for breath while a sniggering Voc unsnagged the hose and extinguished the fire.

The girls had escaped injury except for some singed hair. Tim sported a shiny blue bump on his forehead which made us compliment him on his great shot.

Payback is wonderful and I began to slate the Raider on his excellent performance as a fireman. He sat on the lawn breathing gratefully. The crowd now turned their attention to the Raider and supported my rhetoric. He stood up and pulled an ugly sign with his fingers, which he enforced with some of his RLI slang.

Truly untranslatable it was.

I suggested that we continue with the game as the tin was now purged of any flammables but the ladies, as one, threatened that there would be consequences if any of us so much as touched the tin.

"OK girls, keep yer hair on," I commented. This brought on further irritated commentary as each of them had had their hair singed to some degree.

The party continued into the night and the barbeque was great with the meat cooked juicy and tender. As the night drifted on and dawn broke, we all found ourselves cooking breakfast on the fire and one by one, each person found a spot to sleep.

Thus we fared sumptuously that weekend.

We awoke later on in the day and continued with our merriment until late on Sunday evening. I dropped Patricia off a block away from her parents' house. This was because she had self-righteously informed me that her father wished to talk to me about my bad influence on his daughter's decadent lifestyle.

I drove to my parents' house in my car, acquired second hand some months previously. It was a nineteen sixty something Simca 1501 and it had replaced the old anglebox quite comfortably. Nice and speedy it was and I usually parked it under a huge peppercorn tree at home. Our dirt driveway was covered in a layer of granite chips and I used to roar in at speed, slam on brakes, and skid to rest under the tree in a cloud of dust.

On this day though, the hinge that kept my accelerator pedal in place broke where it had been fastened to the floor. As I raced into the driveway, the accelerator slipped out of the hinge assembly and fell under the brake lever. As I pressed the brake, the accelerator was activated and the vehicle shot forward, crashing through the hanging branches on the far side of the peppercorn tree and snapping the stay wires that supported my father's television aerial. The 70 foot television aerial came twanging down to earth, bending over any obstacle in its path like an ostrich laying its neck down on bumpy ground. This included a small chicken run and it roused much squawking and clucking.

My father was away on police reserve call-up and mother lay sleeping in bed. Having been woken by the noise, she surmised that the house was under attack by terrorists. She fell out of bed and, fervently praying many Hail Mary's, crawled to the gun safe where my father stored his shotgun.

I was a little under the weather and swore a tirade at my useless car. She heard me, realized that I had crashed into something, and climbed back into bed hugging the shotgun. My ferocious language had assured her that there was no terrorist attack taking place. I may also add that my course language surely saved me from a charge of buckshot.

The next morning she strongly voiced her opinion of my giddy lifestyle and I wondered if it would have been better to face Patricia's father!

Durban with Dietz

Dietz and I had planned a quick trip. We were to visit one of his cousins in Messina and stay with another in Durban. Dietz and I had both been neglected by the opposite sex for a while. As we crossed the Limpopo River, I quietly told Dietz that he was next on my to-do list if I did not get friendly with a girl before we returned. This, I assured him, would take place in the car right in the centre of the very bridge we were now crossing.

Dietz eyed me quizzically to see if I was joking but he could discern no humour in my expression.

Once we had crossed the border, we turned off the main road, drove through Messina, and sought out Dietz's cousin. He was much older than Dietz, and married with a pretty daughter who was due to matriculate that year. Her name was Petro and she turned out to be rather timid, especially around any boy whose mind was wholly occupied with her fudd. She teased instead. I responded with a request that she ask some of her more boisterous friends to date us on our return. She faithfully promised to introduce us to two of her good friends.

We left Messina and drove to Durban. There we found accommodation with cousin number two. This man was our age and stayed in a one bedroom flat in central Durban. Dietz and I shared the lounge, Dietz on the couch and me on the carpet. No worries for either of us as we did not plan to spend too much time in these digs. It was a sleeping place only.

Together, we went to see *Grease,* starring John Travolta and Olivia Newton-John. Ensconcing ourselves in the small ladies bar located on the cinema premises, we consumed a number of miniature whiskeys prior to the film and bought more to take into the cinema with us. There was a smoking ban in the cinema but we ignored this and puffed away merrily. No one objected to our blatant disregard of the no smoking signs and some other viewers lit up with us. When the movie was over, we left a pile of empty miniature spirit bottles filled with cigarette butts and spent matches. We had fallen in love with the music and bought the cassette tape for our homeward trip.

The next night, we visited a nightclub and watched some girls stripping off their clothing. The morality law enforced in South Africa at the time limited fleshy exposure to nipple caps and some kind of covering below the navel, such as a flap of cloth or a thong.

A cute girl rocked onto the stage in time to a bawdy tune. She saw my innocent face in the audience and bounced over to sit on my knee. Looking impertinently into my eyes she pointed at her thighs. This stirred Mr Willy who promptly stood to attention. He tried to peep out of my jeans to see what was happening and I struggled to clamp him down clandestinely. She instructed me to undo her suspenders which were holding up a pair of tatty net stockings. I fumbled at the unfamiliar clips with a stupid look on my face and appealed to Dietz for assistance. He helped by squeezing the cute bum hanging over my leg, pointing invitingly at him. The girl squealed and a bouncer stepped up to Dietz and warned him that behaviour like that was not welcome in their establishment. The stripper strutted back onto the stage haughtily while the rest of the audience laughed riotously. I pretended that Mr Willy belonged elsewhere.

But that sexy chick was not finished with me yet.

A slow number came up to which the woman gyrated very seductively. Swivelling expertly off the stage she flounced down on me again and clutched at the surreptitious swelling in the front of my jeans. Using this as a lever, she pulled me, red faced, up out of my chair and dragged me, protesting feebly and feeling even more stupid, onto the stage. The audience went wild with laughter at this cocky scene. Ah, these puns! Once on the stage she let go of my manhood and grabbed my crimson ears with both of her hands. I immediately covered the modest bump in my jeans with my hands as I no longer trusted her. I was conscious of very loud laughter from the crowd of people watching the show.

She pulled my head down and forced me onto my knees. Then this vivacious vixen attempted to grind my face into the front of her suede bikini bottom–the bit that is shaped like the bonnet of an original Volkswagen beetle. She took me by surprise and I caught a whiff of something rather sweaty. I jerked my head back quickly. With a thrust of her hips she forced my face into her pelvis again. Then I opened my mouth and bit her steamy meat pie.

Yes, a trifle salty.

But not a hard bite, mind you, just hard enough to register mild protest at this treatment. The stripper screeched in indignation which initiated another din of laughter from the audience. The bouncer jumped up onto the stage, grabbed me by my shirt collar, and started dragging me towards the entrance of the joint. I am certain that he intended to thump me outside. Mr Willy lost interest in the whole affair and went back to sleep again. I twisted while still in the bouncer's grip, grinned at the stripper and gave her the thumbs up. She smiled and then turned and wiggled a well rounded bum at me.

If only we had met under different circumstances, I would surely have enjoyed her fusty fudd.

Dietz saved me by pulling the bouncer's tie and the three of us performed some mad alpha-male ritual that had the audience and the stripper laughing and applauding us. The exasperated bouncer let me go and then Dietz let the bouncer go. Ever the opportunists, Dietz and I fled that fateful establishment, found my car and cautiously drove for the sanctuary of his cousin's apartment.

The next evening, Dietz felt the well overdue need for sexual fulfilment. He persuaded me to drive down Point Road where prostitutes plied their trade on street corners. We saw one lonely lady in a mini skirt with low hung top.

'A window of promiscuity,' I thought.

I stopped the car and as one we opened the car doors and approached her. She was a young, pretty girl who claimed to be a student, hooking to pay her way through university.

Yeah, sure!

But she promised us both (with the help of a friend) a full house treatment for a hefty cash price. We did not have the correct amount of hefty available so we asked her if she would accept a traveller's cheque.

"No cheques of any kind accepted here, boys," she laughed.

So we beetled off to the nearest hotel. Sorry, we were told, they wouldn't cash traveller's cheques unless we were hotel residents. This statement was repeated at every hotel we visited that night. The banks and money changers were all closed as it was well on the way to midnight. What a bummer. We returned to the lady in a vain attempt to beg for a free service. It was our last evening on holiday and we were due to return to Messina the next day.

"You'd better hope Petro has organized us a couple of likely chicks for tomorrow night," I joked as we climbed into my car, "cause yer backside is on the line here, my mate."

Dietz giggled and sucked his cigarette nervously. He then grew very quiet and sat still in the passenger seat of my Simca. When we reached his cousin's house, he ran upstairs without speaking and crawled quietly into his sleeping bag. I somehow think that he had taken me seriously! I giggled myself to sleep imagining Dietz somehow acquiring a champagne cork to push up his bum for security...hehehe.

The following day we drove up to Messina uneventfully to be met by a triumphant Petro who had organized us each a blind date for the evening. Petro directed us to one of the girls' houses. We knocked and the door was opened by a pretty brunette. A lovely blond gaped at us over her shoulder.

We took the girls to the Messina Mine club. Hey, this was the only place that was open in the thriving metropolis of Messina. We treated them to a few drinks and a tasty meal. Dietz then borrowed my car and took off with Blondie. I escorted my date to the swimming pool around the back of the club. It was getting late and, as it was a weekday, there was no one around.

A speedy discussion left us both in agreement that skinny dipping was the order of the day. Throwing off our clothes, we both dived into the tepid water.

The next morning we left for the border in a jovial mood, feeling refreshed. Dietz told me how his evening had gone with the pretty blonde and then anxiously asked me how my evening had gone.

"Don't worry Dietz, you are off the hook," was all I said.

Dietz sighed with relief! I imagined him throwing the champagne cork out of the window.

We went through customs formalities at the border post and retrieved our weapons and webbing from the police station. Driving at full speed, we crossed from European farming land into Mtetengwe Tribal Trust Land.

Some 20 kilometres after crossing into this tribal area, we tore past a car parked on the side of the road. A black man was helping a white woman to change a tyre. I pressed on the brake pedal as hard as I could and the Simca screeched to a halt some distance past the couple. Dietz and I both knew that this area was dangerous as there were terrorist gangs operating in almost every portion of the country. I reversed and offered to assist. The woman strode towards us and shouted at us in a Scandinavian accent, saying that she did not want any help from the racist white people of this country. We warned her that both she and her helper were in great danger. She smelled beer on my breath and emphasized that she would in no way accept help from us drunken racists.

She further stated that the black man was not her helper but in fact, her husband.

We grabbed our webbing and a fresh beer and moved off into the bush to sit under the cover of a huge mimosa tree. Knowing that they could be brutalized or even killed if terrorists discovered their presence, we sacrificed a little of our time to guard them. Angry at the woman's attitude we discussed shooting her and blaming it on terrorists but we both knew that our hearts had not yet grown that hard.

We had just come face to face with the attitude of a lot of people living in the rest of the world; hostile and unwilling to hear or understand the Rhodesian side of the story.

Ignorance is bliss they say. I don't know, this poor lady seemed pretty worked up.

The correct method of applying payback
Between call-ups, I was granted an apprenticeship transfer to Gaths mine in Mashaba so that I could obtain some experience in heavy industry. My journeyman was an ex-Zambian by the name of George. I enjoyed working with George as he was knowledgeable in his trade and patient enough to teach me his different skills.

He also possessed an excellent sense of humour.

George went hunting one weekend and stumbled upon a group of terrorists. He was driving his Toyota Stout van and the terrorists fired an RPG rocket which slammed into the ground in front of the vehicle. The explosion damaged the vehicle badly. George and his companion received some minor shrapnel injuries and were shell-shocked from the explosion, but were able to escape.

After being discharged from hospital, George returned to work. During one shift underground, he went into the toilet, closed the door, and sat down. Percy, who had seen him going in, waited a minute and then hurled a brick against the steel door with all his might. This resulted in a horrific bang. Percy howled with laughter as George, who was still a little shell-shocked, screamed in fright. George then cursed Percy and warned him that payback was now due.

Our crew stored tea goodies in a cupboard located in an underground substation. It was common to find that a night shift worker had broken into the substation and stolen all our tea and sugar.

We needed to discourage the thief.

We experimented with bombs made from a mixture of oxy-acetylene gas compressed into plastic packets and tins. A fuse was introduced into the gas mixture and connected to an electrical circuit. The container was then effectively sealed to prevent the gas from escaping. After many lunchtimes spent experimenting, we had developed a powerful device which we placed in the cupboard and wired to blow when the door was opened.

On arrival every morning, we would set this off to test its effectiveness and enjoy the explosion which was normally followed with laughter and expressive comments about how loud the bang had been. The wooden cupboard slowly expanded as the explosions stressed the sides and screws started to strip out of the wood. The door grew quite rickety too.

One morning we arrived at the substation to find that the lock on the gate had been broken off. As we entered the enclosure, we saw great skid marks on the floor, caused by gumboots. The cupboard door had swung open and fallen to the floor as the top hinge had ripped apart. We had obviously achieved our goal and scared off the thief.

As stated previously, George was a patient man. He waited for months to get even with Percy. I was mobilized on call-up but when I returned to work, George presented me with a hilarious tale of vengeance.

George had been wiring the lighting circuits for a new underground winch station. Percy joined him every lunchtime and they would talk and eat together as they were good friends. Percy also developed a habit of always sitting on the same bench. With revenge still bright in his heart, George wired an electrical circuit as a surprise for the unsuspecting Percy.

When Percy arrived for lunch and sat himself down that ill-fated day, George excused himself, stating that he had to complete a certain task before his shift ended. Percy sat chatting as George continued working. George then made his way to the electrical distribution board on pretext of testing a circuit. Percy was quite unaware that George had wired the circuit to simultaneously trip all the lights in the section, set off a siren just behind Percy's head, and detonate a homemade bomb inconspicuously placed as an old paint tin under Percy's seat.

As Percy raised his mug of tea to his lips, George hit the fateful switch. The underground section instantly fell pitch dark. The bomb exploded with a tremendous bang behind Percy's feet and the siren screeched like a cat with a stomped on tail. The siren harmonized well with Percy's terrified screams. George switched the lights back on and saw Percy lying on his back with his legs over the upended bench. Tea had splashed all over Percy's face and overall and he lay there on the ground with an open mouthed expression of pure dread. He later stated that he had wanted to run but could not. He thought there had been a rock fall and that he was dead.

George of course laughed until his ribs were about to break. He sat with tears running down his cheeks as he revelled in Percy's discomfort.

The bemused and trembling Percy struggled to his feet and then smiled crookedly at George. He called him some names, said that he had forgotten about George's threat and told George that he had done a bloody fine job.

That's my boy!

Girls understand payback too!
Lou Boom and I worked together at Gaths Mine as apprentices, but for some reason we were not privileged to attend the same call-ups. Thus we did not frequently cross each other's paths at work. However, when we were at work together, we would drive home to Fort Victoria after work each day instead of retiring to our single quarters. There we would stay at Lou Boom's family home. Lou Boom's parents also did not mind if we partied, drank excessively and played loud music. At least his mother did not. She joined in!

Lou Boom was also not very polite to his little sister. One evening as we were on our way out, he interrupted the aforesaid sister while she was busy with her homework. He threw a blank TDK cassette tape on her bed and instructed her to tape his new long playing record.

She glared at him without saying a word.

When Lou Boom returned home later that evening, the cassette tape lay on his pillow with 'KISS - LOVE GUN' printed neatly onto the label. The next morning, he deposited the cassette into the rack in his car.

After work the following day, we lifted two other colleagues to Fort Victoria. Rough and tough mining types they were with tattoos and broken teeth. On the way, we popped into Temeraire Club and purchased a bottle of cane spirits and some cola. There was a collection of dirty glasses in Lou Boom's car and we charged four of these up for the journey home.

Lou Boom thrust his newly taped KISS cassette into the tape deck and turned up the volume. Gene Simmons and his cronies battered our ears with Christine sixteen and Got love for sale.

Lou Boom's little Renault R4 coasted merrily down the road with four happy persons drinking happy mix and listening to happy music. The music thundered to quietness and we waited for the next track. Then the giggling voice of one little sister announced that she would now play her senile older brother's most favourite song. We then listened to the voice of Tweety Bird singing, 'I taut I taw a puddy tat a cweepin' up on me

I did! I taw a puddy tat…'

Lou Boom snapped his hand down and shut off the music, muttering a threat that sounded a lot like, 'I'm going to kill that little bitch'. The silence lasted for another millisecond before Lou Boom's three passengers burst into a cacophony of strident laughter. Lou Boom's thick beard bristled but it did not hide his glowing cheeks as he blushed like a hairy little girl. Naturally this spurred us to more laughter and great mockery. Lou Boom turned his head and laughed with us. He knew he had been well caught out by someone he considered his inferior.

And his little little sister at that.

Of lions and braai hawks

I loaded Lurch, Lynda, and Louise into my Simca and we drove to Kyle Dam for the day. We were en route to the Kyle Boat Club where we were to meet some other friends for a braai. I mentioned that we were going to arrive at the boat club early and suggested that we detour through the Bristow Lion Park.

All agreed so I turned onto a dusty road and drove through a huge gate made of thatch and gum poles. Here we paid the entrance fee and drove into the park. After half an hour of slow driving we coasted into the midst of a pride of lionesses. They had been lying low in the tall grass in the shade of some msasa trees. I stopped the vehicle and we sat and looked at the lions.

Well, this was what we had come to do, wasn't it?

A curious lioness raised herself onto her haunches and gazed at us with a quizzical expression. Lazily she stretched and yawned and then stood up and slowly padded over to the car. Some nervous twittering stemmed from the ladies on the back seat as the huge cat strolled up to the car. She sniffed at our closed windows and eyed the girls through the glass. Their nervousness mutated into terror and Louise screeched in horror. The lioness jumped back, growling at this new sound. She then peeped at Lurch, sitting on the front passenger seat. I told him he had nothing to fear as the lion was more scared of his ugly face than he was of her. Ever the gentleman and not wanting to offend the ladies in the back, he mimed a loutish word at me.

By now Louise was getting a little upset and kicked the back of my seat, urging me to drive off. I told her not to be silly as I could not; the lioness was now walking in front of the car.

Lynda told me to run the lioness over!

The predator nonchalantly strolled over to my window. I turned and reached for the cooler bag on the floor behind Lurch's seat. Before anyone in the car realized my intent, I pulled a piece of boerewors out of the bag. I then swivelled the triangular side window open and pushed out the tube of spicy meat. The lioness smelled the sausage and pulled at it with her small front teeth. The wors disappeared into her mouth and was swallowed whole. There was a smear of meat on the window and she tried to lick this up. Then the cat opened her mouth and grunted and bit at the window. Her one bottom canine tooth scratched the paintwork of my car door with a chilling sound of agonized metal.

This sound mixed well with the orchestra of panic coming from the back seat and the noisy hole in Lurch's troubled face. I quickly started the engine and drove off in a cloud of dust, spinning the wheels.

After leaving the lion park we drove to the boat club where we sat at the bar waiting for the others to arrive. We drank a few beers and when all of our friends were present and accounted for, we moved outside to where the boat club attendant had lit a row of fires in half drums. These fires had burned down to hot coals. We placed wire mesh over the coals and started to barbeque our meat. The ladies pottered around making salads and buttering buns.

In general, life was great.

Lurch and I occupied one of the braais at the end of the row and Voc warned us not to leave our meat unattended or a hawk might pinch it.

"Ha," I retorted, "a hawk just like you."

Voc sneered at me and called me a wise guy. Lurch walked off to the bar and I strolled over to where the girls were dressing salads and chatted for a minute. Then there was an urgent shout and I turned to see a yellow-billed kite swoop over my braai grid and fly away holding my sizzling roll of boerewors in its talons. As the bird flew, he alternated his grip from one foot to the other. I was astonished that he had figured out how to prevent the hot meat from burning his feet.

And so we sat without any boerewors and a lofty Voc needled me incessantly. Voc then asked me to keep an eye on his meat and left to purchase some drinks from the bar. I lifted the wors off his grid and dropped it onto mine. When he returned I said that he would be wise to heed his own words and never turn his back on a braai hawk. Voc stabbed me in the left buttock with his braai fork.

It took over a month for the greasy wound to heal.

Cast your vote

During April 1979, Rhodesia held its first one-man-one-vote elections to determine who the country's next leader would be. Mugabe's thugs were roaming the country in full force, disrupting the process as much as possible as his party was not to be represented at the elections. The polling stations had to be guarded to ensure a free and fair election. Already on call-up, Lurch and I were convoyed to the show grounds at Fort Victoria with the rest of our unit.

As we milled about, I saw a soldier who made me smile. He could have been a Selous Scout for he had very long hair. Perfectly arranged waves of curls flowed out from under his pure white Stetson. His jowls were covered in a huge, immaculately combed beard that rested on the front of his starched camouflage smock. The beard was coppery in colour and gleamed in the sun. Around his waist, he had strapped a brace of bone handled revolvers. These stainless steel masterpieces were fitted into worked leather holsters which were tied down onto his thighs with red string. His camouflage trouser ends were tucked into a pair of shiny cowboy boots with a set of spurs protruding from their heels. When I saw these I thought he must be a Grey Scout– mounted infantry.

I pointed him out to Lurch who burst into breathless laughter. As we laughed, the cowboy turned and looked at us. I saw that he was an officer but Lurch and I could not suppress our humour. He scowled, turned on his shiny heel and walked away. I have no doubt many a soldier laughed at him that day.

What a conceited turd!

We were assigned to a mission station in the Matibi area. Our unit arrived some days prior to the elections and we busied ourselves constructing trenches and filling sandbags. When this job had been completed, I roamed over to the mission library for a book. *Sand in the Wind* was written by Robert Roth and is unarguably the most interesting novel I have ever read. I spent the next three days skiving off to a quiet spot to read.

On the day the polls opened, the local populace came in their hoards to cast their votes. We did not feel like voting but were encouraged to do so as the number of people who voted was somehow important. We were told to vote for any party we liked and to spoil the papers if we genuinely did not want to vote. I pushed my spoiled paper into the ballot box and left the voting booth, feeling that this was the beginning of unwelcome change.

That evening, I left my tent barefoot and banged my foot on the mushroomed dome of one of the tent pegs. The cut was deep and blood flowed. The medic inserted some stitches and applied a small bandage. The next day we helped the internal affairs department to dismantle the polling station. As we stripped down a corrugated iron roof, the wind gusted and a sheet of metal banged against my right wrist. I felt no pain but found my hand numb and unable to operate as I willed it to. Then I saw a deep, copiously bleeding cut on the side of my wrist. I went back to the medic who asked if I was accident prone. He stitched and bandaged the cut but could not help with the loss of feeling. The resourceful man promptly arranged a trip to a doctor in an internal affairs aircraft.

The flight was destined for Fort Victoria. What a genuine stroke of good fortune, I rejoiced. Teasing all my mates and especially Lurch, I packed my gear and left for the dusty airfield. The flight was awesome if scary. The small single engine two-seater airplane was tossed and buffeted by air currents and it was far more exciting than any helicopter ride I had experienced. The pilot said not a word to me at all. Not even a greeting. He communicated by pointing with his hand. He did not answer a single question of the many I asked. Maybe I needed a new toothbrush, or something.

The aircraft did not crash but landed safely on the tarmac at Fort Victoria aerodrome. Transport awaited me and I was ferried to the hospital at the local joint operational command for the Operation Repulse area. There I waited until a disinterested doctor examined my hand and stated that I should wait for the injury to heal and then assess what to do. In the meantime I should go home and return to him a week later. A quick phone call and my mother collected me at the 4 Brigade Headquarters gate. I enjoyed an extra week's paid leave which I spent lounging around and benefiting from a well-deserved rest.

Sensation slowly returned to my hand. When I returned to the army doctor, he pronounced me quite well and I returned to the drill hall in Gwelo, where I spent a day, and then demobilized with my unit as it was time for our R & R.

The blue-jobs visit my home
While I was away guarding the voting station, an Alouette crew literally dropped in to visit my two sisters. The two girls had met the seven squadron crew at a party in town. They were based in Fort Victoria for a time, helping to prepare for elections. During conversation with the aircrew, my sisters mentioned where they stayed and described the premises in detail. The pilot stated that he knew the house from having flown over the area many times and declared that they would drop in for tea that Sunday afternoon.

After Sunday lunch, my sisters were relaxing with two of their friends when they heard the distinct whine of a helicopter. They rushed outside to see a helicopter circling the smallholding. The pilot hovered over a patch of open ground below the lawn in front of the house and then set the machine onto the ground. The screeching abated slowly as the pilot shut down the engine.

My older sister ran towards the helicopter to greet the crew. She loped to the edge of the lawn and it appeared to my younger sister and my father that she was going to walk into the still spinning rotors. My father shouted a warning which went unheard as the engine noise was still very loud. My younger sister screamed as she thought she was going to see her sister decapitated by the blades. Her fright was serious; the type that ages you in an instant, but there was no danger as the helicopter was parked a distance from the edge of the lawn.

The crew deplaned and chatted to their astounded hosts. They kitted the girls with a combat jacket each and invited them on board for a quick flight. The helicopter took off and thrilled the girls with an exciting roller coaster excursion over Lake Kyle. This was their first experience of flight and they were both exhilarated. Half an hour later the helicopter returned and landed on the same spot.

The crew were invited inside for tea. Some neighbours had arrived, curious about why a helicopter had landed at our house and they joined in the fun. I do believe that the tea party evolved into a bit of a booze up and the crew left a while later to the exaggerated waving of a rather boisterous crowd.

Chapter 8
Incidents experienced while working in essential services

I completed my apprenticeship as an electrician in August 1979 and was employed by the Electricity Supply Commission of Zimbabwe-Rhodesia. Initially, I was based in Fort Victoria but secured a transfer with promotion to Chiredzi in early 1980. As it was essential to maintain the supply of electrical power to the country I was exempt from call-up. During the bush war, the operational staff always went on repair callouts in the bush in pairs. We would also be accompanied by a police guard detail. Although not on active service anymore, I did experience some incidents which I feel are worth mentioning.

A tribesman finds a grenade

In early October 1979 I was driving at the head of a small convoy consisting of two Electricity Supply Commission Land Rovers and a truck loaded with gum poles. We were being escorted by a police vehicle en route to replace some power line poles that had burned down in a bush fire. I had been driving along the Fort Victoria/Salisbury road for 30 minutes when a local man ran out of the bush to flag us down. I paid no attention and bypassed him, continuing on our way. Three hundred metres farther, I saw a figure lying on the side of the tarred road. I signalled the convoy, pulled over, and ran over. It was a young man in dire need of help.

I immediately saw that both his hands were missing from just above the wrist. He was on his stomach attempting to crawl. The bones poking out of his arms made a crunching sound on the tarmac. He then collapsed and rolled onto his back. What a mess. There were two gaping and bloody sockets where his eyes had once looked out of his face. Part of his mouth had been smashed inward and an internal organ was squeezing out of a gash in his abdomen through the tatters of a dirty blood soaked shirt. He was not bleeding much from the injuries to his face or arms, only from his abdominal wound.

The man who had attempted to flag me down arrived and asked if we could help his friend. I sent someone to fetch the first aid kit and asked what had happened. The friend said that they had found something in the bush and it had exploded while they were trying to dismantle it. He showed me an object and I recognized the fragmentation spring from a 42Z rifle grenade. Had they not stripped this off, they would both have been very dead.

The first aid kit was devoid of anything I could use to assist the man. I found some rags in our equipment boxes and used these to bandage what wounds I could—his wrists and some other minor cuts on his arms and legs. I also draped a loose bandage over his eyes. Not sure what to do about the abdominal injury, I left it. I tried to keep the man on his back to stop him from incurring further injuries by scraping his protruding bones and internal organ on the tar.

Porkyfisher, the electrician accompanying me, radioed our depot for help and they contacted the joint operational command at Fort Victoria airport. An Alouette helicopter was dispatched with a doctor on board. After landing he quickly stabilized the man and applied a drip. He castigated me for having left the abdominal injury unattended and said that I should have placed a wet cloth over it to prevent the liver from drying out. The doctor supervised some of our men as they loaded his patient onto the helicopter and they took off for the government hospital in Fort Victoria.

We continued on our way to conduct line repairs and the next day my foreman informed me that the injured man had died during the night.

Johan

Johan was a crafty middle aged man who had just been released from jail after having served time on a charge of fraud. The commission employed him because there was a great shortage of qualified artisans in the country. He lived in one of the company houses in Fort Victoria with his very pretty lady and had managed to furnish this accommodation lavishly. How he had managed to acquire funds for this opulence was a mystery to us all.

On a hot day in early December, we were changing a pole mounted transformer in the Chatsworth area. The task required an electrician to disconnect all the wiring from the transformer. Then an experienced but lazy line gang would unbolt and rig the unit down onto the back of a truck and then lift and secure a new transformer to the structure. The electrician would then reconnect the wiring and re-commission the sub-station. It was a simple but time consuming task.

Johan said that he needed to be back in town before the close of day as he had some business to attend to. I warned that we would only be back in town after sundown as the line gang was not renowned for speedy work. It would take around two hours before we could start reconnecting the wiring. This seemed unacceptable to Johan and he wagered me a case of beers that he could get them to complete the task in less than an hour. I laughed and accepted.

Oh, the gullibility of youth!

Johan had a word with the line gang leader who spoke to his team in Shona. Suddenly there was a flurry of activity and the men doubled their rigging efforts. Johan said that I should quickly go to the bottle store and buy beers. I could see that I was going to lose the bet so I drove into Chatsworth and purchased a crate of lager.

When I returned to site, the transformer was rigged and Johan was busy connecting the wiring. Within the hour we had commissioned the sub-station and were ready to leave. I acknowledged defeat, pointed to the case of beer, and asked how he had managed to motivate the men. He simply took six beers out of the crate, turned to the line gang and told them to help themselves to the remaining 18 beers.

I was flabbergasted!

The men all helped themselves to a beer and the African line gang leader raised his bottle to me in a mock toast. Johan beamed and laughed derisively. I was not amused but he opened two beers and gave me one. After a few sips of the cool beer I regained my sense of humour, joined in the merriment, and conceded that I had been fairly caught.

Christmas day arrived and Johan and I were both on standby. We received a call to attend to a power supply problem at a remote pump station on a farm. On the way, Johan told me that he was anxious to be home in time for Christmas dinner.

We arrived at the pump station, tested the equipment, and concluded that the fault lay on the power line. This meant that we would have to call the line gang out to walk the line which implied that we would be out fault-finding all day. Johan argued not a word. Instead, he offered to start walking the line with his assistant and told me to stay with the vehicle and police escort. When the line gang arrived I was to deploy them from the other end of the line.

This sounded like a sensible idea and Johan started walking. Less than five minutes after he had left, I heard several shots coming from the direction in which he had gone. I grabbed my rifle and webbing and charged off to help him. I met him running in my direction with his wide eyed helper hard on his heels.

The police escort stayed with the relative security of the vehicles!

"Run," shouted Johan, "gooks, and plenty of them. I fired some shots at them and they ran off."

We all doubled back to the vehicle and drove off in great haste. I radioed our depot and reported the incident and our controller said that we should leave and return to the depot immediately; he would report the incident to the police. Johan sat in the passenger seat and smiled at me contently when he heard this transmission.

On the way home I thought about the incident and asked Johan why he thought the gooks had not returned fire. Johan did not answer and I did not press him. I thought he may have been a little traumatized. We arrived back home in good time for Johan's Christmas dinner with his family and friends.

The next day we were interviewed by the police who stated that they could find no evidence of the group of terrorists that Johan had fired on. To this day I am convinced that the devious Johan pulled the wool over all our eyes and concocted the scene so that he could leave early.

I wonder if he ever found his way back into jail!

George gets more payback
I was transferred to work in Chiredzi in April 1980, the day Robert Mugabe came into power. My old journeyman, George, applied for a job with the commission and was posted to our depot in Chiredzi in May 1980. He loaded his now repaired Toyota Stout and a homemade trailer with treasured possessions—tools and stuff—and drove down to his new company house in Chiredzi to offload. He was to then return and collect less important things like his wife and children.

George had just turned off the main road from Fort Victoria to Beitbridge at Ngundu Halt. He was accelerating to his cruising speed of 100 kilometres per hour when an intoxicated ZANLA war veteran slouched onto the road in front of him. To denote his important status, the war veteran was dressed in the fashion of the day: a wide brimmed felt hat with a leopard skin band and a shirt half tucked into jeans which hung halfway down his buttocks. This was complemented by a pair of boots with protruding tongues from which the laces had been removed. The man motioned for George to stop with a lazy hand. George held his course and his left rear view mirror missed the man by an inch.

The homemade trailer had been constructed from the bin of a pickup truck with a longer axle than George's Stout. George glanced at his left rear view mirror as he passed the man and saw the mudguard of the trailer catch him at knee level. The man was lifted off his feet and somersaulted before hitting the tar. There he spun a few circles and then lay still.

George continued on his way without stopping, satisfied that chance had allowed him to exact some small revenge for the damage the RPG rocket had caused him a year earlier.

An episode at the assembly points

In April that year during the election period, all the ZANLA cadres gathered at certain assembly points around the country. Located in the midst of Hotel camp were three pumps that supplied irrigation water to extensive agricultural systems in the region. The meters for these pumps had not been read for many years. In June I was tasked with driving to these installations to read the meters and perform some necessary maintenance.

George and I drove our respective cruisers to the pumps. The drive over unmaintained roads which, for many years had only been used by military vehicles, was laborious. We drove as fast as we could and suddenly found ourselves in the centre of an assembly point.

Hundreds of scary guerrillas immediately appeared out of an array of tents, all fully armed. We had startled them and they appeared quite aggressive. I stopped my vehicle and left my hands on the steering wheel. Many ferocious looking black men surrounded us. One man with a hairy face and mucus in the corners of his eyes placed the muzzle of his RPD machine gun under my nose and grinned at me. I sat still and saw a dirty hand reach in and steal a packet of cigarettes from the dashboard.

An important looking man marched up to the crowd and barked an order. All the men stepped back and made way for him to approach. He stepped up to the vehicle and questioned our presence at length. I explained the work we needed to do but he told us to leave or he would order his men to shoot us. My two assistants, Peter and Benson, were feeling uncomfortable and urged me to hurry up. The terror leader told them to shut up or die with the *murungu* (white man). I requested permission to radio George and relay this information to him. The leader raged at me and threatened me with death if I touched the radio.

"Go," he shouted, "before my men shoot you!"

I reversed quickly and drove out of the assembly area with George close on my rear bumper as we made our way back to the depot in Chiredzi. The meters were read months later, after ZANLA had been dispersed from the assembly points.

The Grundy interrogated

The Grundy was busy with a construction job opposite the CID offices in Fort Victoria. The foundations for the building under construction were being excavated. Due to the presence of solid rock, explosives were being used to loosen the band of granite. The Grundy was supervising the drilling of charge holes into the stone.

It was a hot day and he felt the need to cool his tongue so he handed the operation of charging to his foreman. The Grundy then visited the sports club for a few beers. On his return, he confirmed with the foreman that the charging was complete. Whistles blew and men waved flags to evacuate the blast area. Slightly pickled, the Grundy pressed the red button on his exploder.

BOOM!

Only the boom was much louder than it should have been. It transpired that the foreman had pushed much more explosives than required into the holes, thinking that this would speed up the job. The blast threw tons of rock into the air, most of which landed on the police building next door. Rocks crashed onto the roof and flew through windows. The foundation of the building was shaken and every window was blown inward.

The police were convinced that they were under attack. When they were informed that the explosion had been caused by the construction team across the road, they arrested the Grundy on a charge of terrorism and interrogated him for hours in an attempt to make him confess. When they finally released the Grundy, he drove home to his irrevocably pregnant wife and instructed her to prepare to leave the country.

The Grundy and his family went on holiday and never returned to Zimbabwe.

Epilogue

In July 1981 I immigrated to South Africa. Sitting comfortably in a South African Airways Boeing 727 in flight from Harare to Johannesburg International Airport, I looked down out of the square window with rounded corners. Through gaps in the sparse clouds I could see my old home town of Fort Victoria floating slowly by. When I next visited it would be called Masvingo. Kyle Dam glinted at me as the sun reflected off the distant surface of the water and nostalgia tugged my heart.

I reflected back to the day on which I had grieved for my uncle Delville Vincent, slain by terrorists some seven years previously. I had not exacted revenge for his murder as I had imagined I would. However, I now felt in my heart that Del would not have required me to blaze a trail of death and destruction on his account.

War has a detrimental effect on the way some people choose to interact with others. By necessity, these people are pulled out of their daily lives and forced to perform military duties. For some, their normal way of life is replaced (or enhanced) with a propensity to reject acceptable social protocol. This could be similar to young children who are brought up by indifferent parents and are unable, or unwilling, to conform to society's acceptable standards.

The disgruntled soldier may then rebel within a lattice he designs to protect himself from the wrath of his superiors who are mostly indifferent to his needs. This framework is constructed around his need to remain anonymous, to avert discipline and punishment, and yet take care of certain physical and mental requirements. Thus, when unrestrained, he may resort to mayhem to counter his feeling of helplessness within the confines of the military organization. This can result in many antisocial tendencies such as excessive consumption of alcohol, drug abuse, rebellion, violence, and other ills.

My account includes atrocities committed by Rhodesian soldiers and insurgents alike. Although these actions are in no way condoned or acceptable, they did happen. And I understand why they happened. I am aware of the pain experienced by people who lost dignity or family and despaired when innocent lives were taken unnecessarily. Nevertheless, I also feel for the perpetrators of these crimes and realize that their actions may have altered their own lives terribly. Some may live miserably, trying to void their condemning conscience by way of excessive lifestyle, which can snowball and hurt those who are close to them.

My lifestyle has been influenced by the gracious intervention of Jesus Christ, who I now aspire to follow as well as He enables me. For anyone who has suffered at the hands of another, I urge you to forgive as you pray the words of our Lord Jesus who said:

"Give us each day the food we need, *and forgive us our sins, as we forgive those who sin against us.*"
– Luke 11:2-4, New Living Translation

And for those who are haunted by demons afflicting their conscience, again the Lord Jesus urges:

"Come to me, all of you who are weary and carry heavy burdens, and I will give you rest. Take my yoke upon you. Let me teach you, because I am humble and gentle at heart, *and you will find rest for your souls.* For my yoke is easy to bear, and the burden I give you is light."
– Matthew 11:28-30, New Living Translation

Roll of Honour

I include this list out of respect for my friends and colleagues who were killed in the bush war.

Field reservist Del Vincent
British South Africa Police Anti-Terrorist Unit
Killed in action by a gunshot wound while on follow-up operation
3 April 1973

Trooper Rocky Walton
Special Air Service
Killed in action by a gunshot wound
14 March 1975

Rifleman Steve Byrne
Charlie Company, Tenth Battalion, Rhodesia Regiment
Killed on active service in a shooting accident at Kotwa base camp
25 July 1976

Rifleman Alistair Wilson (Mowser)
Engineer
Shot when he responded to an ambush by charging the enemy position. A real unsung hero.
June 1977

Rifleman Martin Kaschula
Second Battalion, Rhodesia Regiment
Killed in action
15 September 1976

Rifleman Deon White BCR (posthumous)
Charlie Company, Tenth Battalion, Rhodesia Regiment
Died from a gunshot wound received in action. He killed six of the enemy in this contact while drawing enemy fire away from the rest of his section.
30 October 1976

Rifleman Freddie Koen
Three Independent Company, Rhodesia Regiment
Killed in a contact in the Tanda TTL, Makoni district
25 November 1976

Rifleman Andre Lotz
Two Independent Company, Rhodesia Regiment
Killed in action in a contact
16 December 1976

Rifleman Joey van der Horn
Second Battalion, Rhodesia Regiment
Killed in action
26 February 1977

Patrol Officer David Ralston, (Sadza)
British South Africa Police
Killed in a landmine explosion in the Lupane district
13 September 1977

Trooper Mark Harris
Grey Scouts
Killed in action
11 October 1977

Rifleman E Bento
Charlie Company, Tenth Battalion, Rhodesia Regiment
Killed in a shooting incident when he was mistaken for one of the enemy
during an ambush
November 1977

Lieutenant John Pritchard
Charlie Company, Tenth Battalion, Rhodesia Regiment
Killed in action
16 August 1978

District Officer Robbie Carruthers MCM (Posthumous)
Internal Affairs
Killed in a vehicle ambush in the Chiswiti area. Return fire from the vehicle
resulted in two terrorists being killed
28 November 1978

Captain Doug Havanar
Support Company, Tenth Battalion, Rhodesia Regiment
Killed in a mid-air collision between two helicopters while manoeuvring for
an open line of fire into a cave harbouring terrorists
2 January 1979

Second Lieutenant Bruce Burns
One Squadron, Rhodesian Corps of Engineers
Killed in action when shot down by an RPG7 rocket while flying in a
helicopter over Mozambique
6 September 1979

Major Bruce Snelgar
First Battalion, RLI
Killed on active service in an air accident when the helicopter he was flying
in crashed into overhead power lines
26 September 1979

Rifleman Frank Wiggell
Charlie Company, Tenth Battalion, Rhodesia Regiment
Killed in action by an enemy mortar bomb
30 October 1979

You all paid the ultimate cost for your country and your loved ones.
You are all remembered!

Obituary

Shears was killed a year after I last saw him. He drove a vehicle over a command detonated landmine on the way to Buchwa Mine. RIP Shears. It was good to know you!

Dale Venters, an old school friend, was killed when the Posts and Telecommunications vehicle in which he was travelling, was struck by an RPG7 rocket.

Acknowledgements

To Gary Pheasant for contributing successfully where my memory failed dismally. Thank you for being an excellent soldier and leader.

To Elsie for her much needed encouragement, patience and understanding throughout the project.

To Dr Richard Wood for giving me permission to extract information from Rhodesia: Roll of Honour on his website, www.jrtwood.com

The lyrics from Wrex Tarr's song, *The Terrorist's Lament*, were used with kind permission from Roan Antelope Music on behalf of Mrs M. Tarr.

Many thanks to the following for allowing the use of photographs: Gary Pheasant, Norman Surgeon, Jackie Williams, Marlene Thomas, Alan Dongworth and Mike Armstrong.